Cavorting
on the Devil's Fork

The Pete Whetstone Letters of
C. F. M. NOLAND

Edited, with introduction, by
Leonard Williams

Cavorting on

BRUIN AT BAY.

the Devil's Fork

Memphis State University Press

**Library of Congress Cataloging
In Publication Data**

Noland, C   F   M   1810-1858.
   Cavorting on the Devil's Fork.

   Bibliography: p. 268
   Includes index.
   1. American wit and humor. I. Williams,
Leonard, 1941-   II. Title.
PN6158.N6   818'.3'07   79-10302
ISBN 0-87870-047-1

ACKNOWLEDGMENTS

My thanks are due many people who helped me in bringing this volume to completion. The directors of the following libraries either gave me access to their collections or sent materials . for my use: The University of Louisville Library, the Phillips County Community College Library, the Louisville Free Public Library, the Phillips County Public Library, Brister Library of Memphis State University, the Mississippi University for Women Library, the University of Arkansas Library, the Little Rock Public Library, the University of Texas Library, the Indiana University Library, the University of Mississippi Library, Perkins Library of Duke University, the University of Illinois Library, the Yale University Library, the Tulane University Library, Alderman Library of the University of Virginia, and Hillman Library of the University of Pittsburgh. Additionally, materials came from the Arkansas History Commission, the Arkansas State Archives, the Independence County Historical Society, and the United States Military Academy.

A number of people helped locate materials for use in the annotations: Wilbur E. Meneray of Tulane University; Terry Wooten of the Alexandria, Virginia, *Gazette*; John L. Ferguson of the Arkansas History Commission; Bill Worthen of the Arkansas Territorial Restoration; Clyde McGinnis and Wilson Powell of Batesville, Arkansas; Richard Boyd Hauck of the University of Washington; Duane Huddleston of North Little Rock, Arkansas; Kenneth W. Rapp of the United States Military Academy; John Q. Anderson of the University of Houston; Carl Parmenter of the University of Illinois; Harold Blythe of Eastern Kentucky

University; Janene Williams, Maxine Franklin, and Anne Hoagland of Helena, Arkansas.

I am also grateful to Francis L. Berkeley and Edmund Berkeley, Jr., of the University of Virginia, for permission to quote from the Berkeley and Noland papers. Connie Dunlap of Perkins Library, Duke University, kindly granted permission to quote from the Turner manuscripts. Mary Bleecker Noland of Richmond, Virginia, graciously sent information copied from the Noland family Bible.

I am indebted to several of my colleagues at Phillips College. Jean Knowlton, Eloise Kalb, and Louis Ruman supplied me with books and searched out information for annotations. Dean Gene Weber and President John Easley freed me from many time-consuming duties and granted brief leaves of absence so that I might work on the manuscript. Maurine Anderson, Leda Bloesch, Margaret Howard, and Joe Forte of the college library cheerfully ordered materials and helped search out answers to difficult questions.

Librarians at the University of Louisville were always ready to assist me with whatever materials I might need. Wayne Yenawine, Louise Galloway, and Martha Gregory were especially helpful.

Leon V. Driskell, H. Edward Richardson, and Leonard Curry of the University of Louisville carefully read the manuscript and offered valuable suggestions for its improvement. J. A. Leo Lemay of the University of California at Los Angeles gave suggestions concerning the text. Douglas E. Wilson, of Anniston, Alabama, thoroughly inspected the text and read the entire manuscript on behalf of the Modern Language Association Committee on Scholarly Editions. His suggestions considerably improved the textual accuracy.

Assistance and encouragement came from several close friends, including Robbin Cummings, Phil Young, Stephen Brill, Christine Hoehne, Cindy Hoagland, Mark Hoagland, who also made the photographs, and Morse Gist, who also patiently and carefully proofread the manuscript several times. My children,

Chris, Marc, and Anna, were helpful and understanding while Daddy was working.

My greatest debts, however, are to E. R. Hagemann of the University of Louisville and to my wife Rose Marie. Each contributed a great deal and might well be listed as coauthor. Without their aid and encouragement, this project could not have been completed.

For
Rose Marie Williams
and
E. R. Hagemann

TABLE OF CONTENTS

INTRODUCTION
C. F. M. NOLAND AND THE ROOTS
OF SOUTHWESTERN HUMOR

During the period from about 1830 to the outbreak of the Civil War, a body of robust literature, now known as the humor of the Old Southwest, developed and flourished upon the American frontier—an area roughly comprising the states of Arkansas, Louisiana, Mississippi, Alabama, Tennessee, and Georgia.[1] Perhaps the high point in its development was the publication in 1845 of *The Big Bear of Arkansas, and Other Sketches, Illustrative of Characters and Incidents in the South and Southwest* (Philadelphia: T. B. Peterson). This collection of tales was edited by William T. Porter, the editor of the *Spirit of the Times,* a weekly journal published in New York and devoted to a wide range of interests but appealing especially to sportsmen.[2] Most of these

---

1. The geographical definitions of Southwestern humor were first indicated by Franklin J. Meine, *Tall Tales of the Southwest: An Anthology of Southern and Southwestern Humor, 1830-1860* (New York: Alfred A. Knopf, 1930); and Walter Blair, *Native American Humor (1800-1900)* (New York: American Book Company, 1937; rpt. San Francisco: Chandler, 1960). Outstanding studies of the American frontier include Frederick Jackson Turner, *The Frontier in American History* (New York: Holt, Rinehart and Winston, 1920); Thomas D. Clark, *The Rampaging Frontier: Manners and Humors of Pioneer Days in the South and the Middle West* (Indianapolis: Bobbs-Merrill, 1939; rpt. Bloomington: Indiana Univ. Press, 1964); and Clark, *Frontier America: The Story of the Westward Movement* (New York: Scribner's, 1959).

2. (1831-1861); hereafter cited as *Spirit.* One valuable biography is by Porter's nephew, Francis Brinley, *Life of William T. Porter* (New York: D. Appleton, 1860). Excellent studies of the *Spirit* are Norris W. Yates, *William T. Porter and the Spirit of the Times: A Study of the Big Bear School of Humor* (Baton Rouge: Louisiana State Univ. Press, 1957); and Richard Boyd Hauck, "The Literary Content of the New York *Spirit of the Times,* 1831-1856," Diss., Univ. of Illinois, 1965.

1

tales first saw print in the pages of the *Spirit*. In his preface to *The Big Bear*, Porter speaks of the rise of this humorous literature in a manner suggesting his realization that something new and important was happening: "A new vein of literature, as original as it is inexhaustible in its source, has been opened in this country within a very few years, with the most marked success" (p. vii).

After tracing the earlier publication of these tales, Porter claims that the *Spirit* "became the nucleus of a new order of literary talent:"

> In addition to correspondents who described with equal felicity and power the stirring incidents of the chase and the turf, it [the *Spirit*] enlisted another and still more numerous class, who furnished most valuable and interesting reminiscences of the pioneers of the far West—sketches of thrilling scenes and adventures in that then comparatively unknown region, and the extraordinary characters occasionally met with—their strange language and habitudes, and the peculiar and sometimes fearful characteristics of the "Squatters" and early settlers. Many of these descriptions were wrought up in a masterly style; and in the course of a few years a generous feeling of emulation sprung up in the south and south-west, prompted by the same impulses, until at length the correspondents of the "Spirit of the Times" comprised a large majority of those who have subsequently distinguished themselves in this novel and original walk of literature. (pp. vii-viii.)

Porter's boasting aside, the *Spirit* did virtually discover an extremely popular literature. He is, however, doing much more here than merely indulging his pride; he is defining, fairly accurately, Southwestern humor. This huge assortment of tales *was* remarkably consistent. "Thrilling scenes and adventures" filled them; the language, habits and activities of characters unique to the frontier made up the nucleus of each. And, as Porter says, many were "wrought up in a masterly style."

But dynamic and vital as it was, Southwestern humor was a casualty of the Civil War. Most of the writers hailed from states which became part of the Confederacy; most of the publishers and many of the readers resided in states which remained in the Union. The breach was deeper and wider than the tales could span. Then, too, the postwar years in the South were not conducive to laughter, and the few efforts at humorous literature largely fizzled. The robustness was gone, and the humor of the Old Southwest—Big Bear Humor—died and was nearly forgotten.[3]

Not until the 1930s was attention, in the form of scholarship and criticism, once again paid to Southwestern humor.[4] But however late, it provoked interest and respect, if only among the cognoscenti, when it suggested that these writers were not only forerunners of Mark Twain and William Faulkner but also artists in their own right. In so many words, challenge was being given to "Official American Literature," though many years passed before this challenge was taken seriously.

Of the several treatments of Southwestern humor, beginning with Franklin Meine in 1930, only Norris Yates hints at the significance of C. F. M. Noland in the rise and development of Southwestern humor. None of the others does more than name him. While each study contributes to scholarship in Southwestern humor, each is inadequate in its treatment of Noland, one of the earliest, most prolific, most popular, and most influential of these humorists.

Biographical information on Charles Fenton Mercer Noland is both spotty and contradictory. No full-length treatment has appeared. The few short examinations are limited to brief periods of his life; are largely undocumented or based upon questionable evidence and are, therefore, untrustworthy; or, on occasion, are blatantly fictional.

A most unusual thumbnail biography was written by Alfred W. Arrington. It is, as James R. Masterson points out, "probably the most remarkable character sketch ever composed about any

---

3. One of the few exceptions was Henry Watterson, ed., *Oddities in Southern Life and Character* (Boston: Houghton Mifflin, 1882). Although several other studies and collections of American humor appeared after the Civil War, few included works by the Southwestern humorists, and almost none offered serious discussion of their works.

4. The most significant studies are examined in the "Note on Sources," following. For an excellent discussion, see John Q. Anderson, "Scholarship in Southwestern Humor—Past and Present," *Mississippi Quarterly*, 17 (1963), 67-86.

Arkansan." [5] Although no evidence exists to suggest that Arrington, who wrote under the pseudonym of Charles Summerfield, ever met Noland, that fact seems to have had little dampening effect upon his enthusiasm. This sketch, at once outrageous and delightful, is itself a piece of Southwestern humor:

Such is the versatility of his [Noland's] genius, that he seems equally adapted to every species of effort, intellectual or physical. With a like unerring aim, he shoots a bullet, or a bon-mot; and wields the pen or the bowie knife with the same thought-swift rapidity of motion and energetic fury of manner. Sunday, he will write an eloquent dissertation on religion; Monday, he raw-hides a rogue; Tuesday, he composes a sonnet, set in silver stars, and breathing perfume of roses to some fair maid's eyebrows; Wednesday, he fights a duel, and sends a bit of lead whizzing through the head or heart of some luckless desperadoe; Thursday, he does up brown the personal character and political conduct of senators Sevier and Ashley; Friday, he goes to the ball, dressed in the most finical superfluity of the fashion, and shines the soul of wit, and the sun of merry badinage, among all the gay gentlemen, and the king supreme of all tender hearts among the ladies. And, to close the triumphs of the week, on Saturday night, he is off thirty miles to a country dance, in the Ozark Mountains, where they "trip it on the light fantastic toe," in the famous jig of "double shuffle," around a roaring log-heap fire in the woods, all night long, to the tune of "The Buffalo Bull came down the Mountains—long time ago," or the glorious air of "Old Dan Tucker;" while between each dance Fent Noland sings some beautiful wild song, such as "Lucy Neal," or "Julianna Johnson," or that melody most serene, "Such a gitten up stairs!" And thus is glorious Fent entitled to the praise of universal versatility—a myriad-minded Proteus of contradictory characters, many-hued as a chameleon, fed on dews, and suckled at the breast of a rainbow.

We have had our doubts and hesitation about admitting him to a

---

5. *Tall Tales of Arkansaw* (Boston: Chapman and Grimes, 1942), p. 32. Masterson also reproduces this sketch. A facsimile reprint of Masterson's heretofore rare volume has recently been published under the title of *Arkansas Folklore: The Arkansas Traveler, Davey Crockett, and Other Legends* (Little Rock: Rose, 1974). For an account of Arrington's career, see Ted R. Worley, "The Story of Alfred W. Arrington," *Arkansas Historical Quarterly,* 14 (1955), 315-319.

niche in the glorious temple of desperadoeism. Indeed, there is a quality in his nature that defies precise classification. In genteel society, a more polished gentleman never moved on the earth. To see him in the libraries of the learned, or in the caucus among the politicians, in the courts before the judge, or in the salon with the ladies, we would swear that he had studied nothing all his life but the science of refined courtesy, and the art of saying the most beautiful things. But this view presents only one half of the man.

Observe him in a circle of Desperadoes—listen to the roars of laughter aroused by his wild anecdotes—hear him sing his favorite, "Such a gittin up stairs," or "The Hudson was a Bully Boat;" look at the hilt of the long knife in his bosom, or the half dozen pistols that swing around his beaded Indian belt; or see him practising at ten paces, driving out the centre every shot, or bringing down the sparrow on the wing;—and you would reverse your former judgment of the man . . . and set him down for the beau-ideal of duelists, the Corypheus of all irredeemable desperadoes.

His personal appearance is somewhat singular, and contrasts rather strangely with his intellectual and social character. He is of the ordinary height, very slender-shaped, with light blue eyes, fair hair, and save when unusually excited, has a very pale, melancholy countenance, as if afflicted at the same time with some serious bodily disease, and some deep-sealed sorrow of the soul.

His health is indeed extremely delicate; and I have been told by his intimate friends that he is subject to long fits of the saddest gloom, when he longs to die, since life is then an intolerable burden.[6]

So much for fiction; the truth is more interesting.

The Noland family appears in Virginia records as early as 1724, when Philip Noland, the great-grandfather of Fenton, registered a land grant in Stafford County.[7] Philip's will, dated 15

---

6. *The Lives and Adventures of the Desperadoes of the South-West: Containing an account of the Duelists and Dueling; Together with the Lives of Several of the Most Notorious Regulators and Moderators of that Region* (New York: William H. Graham, 1849), pp. 73-74. Interestingly enough, Arrington also used his own version of Pete Whetstone is his novel, *The Rangers and Regulators of the Tanaha: or, Life among the Lawless. A Tale of the Republic of Texas* (New York: R. M. DeWitt, 1856). This book, which was not originally announced as a novel, gave rise to the mistaken idea that Pete had migrated to Texas. Arrington's character, however, is similar to Noland's only in name.

7. Information concerning Noland's ancestry and birth is from the Noland family Bible, now owned by Mrs. William C. Noland of Richmond, Virginia.

Figure 1: Noland's tombstone in Mount Holly Cemetery, Little Rock.

photo by Mark Hoagland

March 1794, names his son Thomas. Thomas, whose will is dated 14 May 1811, married Eleanor Luckett and fathered seven children: William, Dade, Samuel, Thomas, Lloyd, Elizabeth, and Jane. William, who was born on 14 February 1775, married Catharine Callender of Carlisle, Pennsylvania, on 12 April 1796. Catharine died in Aldie, Loudon County, Virginia, on 26 April 1849. The date of William's death is uncertain; he did, however, survive his wife. To William and Catharine were born five children: Frances Callender, born 19 April 1797, who married Lewis Berkeley; Thomas J., born 22 February 1799; William Henry, born 7 April 1808; Charles Fenton Mercer, born 23 August 1810; and Callender St. George, born 6 March 1816.[8]

Considerable disagreement surrounds the date of Fenton's birth. Both James R. Masterson and Noland's official alphabetical card, United States Military Academy, West Point, date his birth as October 1808. Noland's tombstone in Mount Holly Cemetery, Little Rock, erroneously places his age at death in 1858 at fifty-two years; this would fix the year of his birth at 1806. There is no explanation for an incorrect date of birth being given upon admission to West Point; however, the accurate date would have revealed Fenton to have been just under thirteen years old. Neither is it clear who authorized Noland's headstone or why the age was recorded incorrectly. In any case, however, the family Bible, with its date of 1810, appears the most authoritative.

A military career must have been planned for young Fenton, for he was admitted to the United States Military Academy at West Point on 1 July 1823. There he listed his age as 14 years, 9 months, rather than the actual 12 years, 11 months.[9] His prog-

---

8. Some confusion exists concerning the number of children. Ted R. Worley and Eugene A. Nolte, eds., *Pete Whetstone of Devil's Fork: Letters to the Editor of the Spirit of the Times by Charles F. M. Noland* (Van Buren, Arkansas: The Press-Argus, 1957), p. iii, place the number at eight, naming, in addition to those listed here, Robert Callender, Mary Eleanor, and (again) Robert Callender. Neither an explanation of the double listing nor a source of information is provided.

9. Letters from Kenneth H. Rapp, Assistant Archivist, USMA, 1 April 1969 and 26 November 1969. A member of the USMA class of 1828 (one year behind Noland) was Jefferson Davis. It is possible that the long friendship between the two men began at the Point.

ress at West Point was anything but distinguished. At the end of his first year of study, he "stood number 53 out of 85 (Nos. 59 to 85, inclusive, failed.)" [10]

Referring to his stay at the Academy, one of Noland's obituaries, though florid and affected, does perhaps grasp the truth:

> With all the frolic and heedlessness of boyhood, he did not attach the importance to graduation at that national school which more mature age would have brought, but thought more of amusement than study; and his slender frame being unequal to the fatigues of military exercise (for he fainted once on drill, and was bourne into the superintendent's house, where he remained several days), he left the institution in about two years. [11]

Actually he flunked out. At the end of his second year he stood 52 out of 61, was deficient in both mathematics and drawing, and was discharged on 21 September 1825. [12]

In 1826, young Fenton arrived in Batesville, Arkansas. [13] His father, Major William Noland, had been sent there by President Monroe as receiver of the Arkansas Territory's land office. [14] Possibly Major Noland, disappointed with his son's failure at West Point, viewed bringing him to Batesville as punishment—life on the frontier was certainly not as leisurely as in Virginia. And, too, family embarrassment over Fenton's failure might well have hastened the removal of the boy from the company of gossipy neighbors. Regardless of what motives may have influ-

---

10. Letter from Col. R. S. Nourse, Adjutant General, USMA, to Mrs. Jerre B. Noland, 15 January 1948.

11. "Metarie," "Death of Charles Fenton Mercer Noland," *Spirit*, 28 (31 July 1858), 291.

12. Letter, Rapp, 26 November 1969.

13. Sworn deposition, C. F. M. Noland to Jesse Searcy, County Clerk, Independence County, Arkansas, 7 September 1850. Noland also wrote in 1850, "It is now four-and-twenty years, man and boy, that I have been in this neck of the timber." See *Spirit*, 20 (9 November 1850). 450.

14. The office registered homesteads. The term "Major" was evidently honorary. No record of his earning the rank exists. Similarly, Fenton was, in later years, addressed as "Colonel" Noland.

enced Major Noland, Arkansas Territory won the youth, and, except for brief visits and one extended absence of five years, he remained there throughout his life.

In Batesville the two men roomed with Judge James Woodson Bates, and by January 1827 young Fenton had begun studying for another career. The Major writes, "Fenton is reading law with [Judge Bates]. The Judge has an excellent library and is a fine classical and belle lettres scholar." [15] In the same letter, the Major also speaks of two features of young Fenton's life which were to become characteristic: on the one hand, his health, which was delicate even during his youth, and, on the other hand, his love of sport and the outdoors; he and a friend had, a few days previously, gigged a salmon weighing fifteen pounds. In a letter to his sister Frances, written scarcely a month later on 28 February, Fenton does not express quite the same enthusiasm as his father had. "Oh how happy would I be (I often think) if I could spend but one sweet hour amongst you—but hope still buoys my mind and bids me look far ahead to that lovd delegated hour when I shall be calmly seated in the midst of my friends." But he also speaks of his studying law and of his apparent intent to remain in Batesville:

> I . . . have become much more attached to the study of law than I was when I first commenced—and I think that I have a very fine prospect in this country—by pursuing the profession which I have chosen or rather has been chosen for me by a kind and affectionate father.

When the Major lost his appointment and returned to Virginia in 1827, he instructed Fenton to watch over his property holdings in Batesville. By 4 November 1827, the date of the first surviving letter following the Major's departure, young Fenton, at seventeen, had become keenly interested in territorial politics.

---

15. HLS [holograph letter signed], William Noland to Catharine Noland, 22 January 1827. Univ. of Virginia, Alderman Library, Berkeley Papers, 38-113-32. Wherever possible, documentation for the Noland family correspondence has been incorporated into the text. Each of those letters (HLS), unless otherwise noted, is housed with the Berkeley Papers, 38-113-32 through 38-113-34.

His letter related the partisan circumstances leading to a duel between two acquaintances of Major Noland, Henry W. Conway and Robert Crittenden.[16] This interest in politics, which brought Noland considerable influence and pleasure in later years, also drew him into a situation which caused him much grief.

Young Fenton had hoped that in 1829 his father would be appointed governor of Arkansas Territory, but the office went to John Pope of Kentucky.[17] Possibly the disappointment he felt contributed toward his viewing Pope with disfavor. His criticism became public in a pseudonymous newspaper article:

> Plainness and simplicity are the characteristic traits of republican government; ostentation and pride bespeak aristocracy. In a free country like ours, the latter is hated—the former admired. But however much we may dislike ostentation and show, yet we are bound to admire them when placed by the side of meanness, narrow-heartedness, and that worst of all human passions, avarice. You may ask the most genuine republican, him who would cavil on the sixteenth part of a hair, for plainness and simplicity, and he will say give me any thing in preference to avarice. A state of things exists in Arkansas that is a perfect anomaly; the office of the Governor of Arkansas has dwindled down from its former respectability into a complete catch-penny business. The Governor, not content with retiring to a hovel where it is impossible that he can have the comforts, to say nothing of the enjoyments of this life—has stooped to the pitiful (in his case) office of retailing liquor. If Governor Pope was poor and involved, and wished by such a course to free himself from debt, it might then in some measure palliate the offence. But so far as the writer of this can learn, he is wealthy and has no children. We have been told more than once that we are blessed with a *"good Governor,"* and if *saving* knowledge is requisite for a "good Governor" then I must confess Arkansas is thrice happy in the selection of her chief magistrate.
>
> DEVEREUX.[18]

---

16. For details of the duel, in which Conway was fatally wounded, see Lonnie J. White, *Politics on the Southwestern Frontier: Arkansas Territory, 1819-1836* (Memphis: Memphis State Univ. Press, 1964), pp. 66-81.

17. HLS, C. F. M. Noland to William Noland, 11 May 1829. Univ. of Virginia, Alderman Library, Berkeley Papers, 38-113-32. For details surrounding the appointment of John Pope (1770-1845), third territorial governor, 1829-1835, see White, pp. 88-92.

18. *"Non pudeo dicere quod scio," The Arkansas Advocate,* 15 December 1830.

Three weeks later William Fontaine Pope, nephew and aide to the governor, offered to fight a duel.[19] Noland's answer is curious in that his tone suddenly changes at midpoint. Throughout the first two paragraphs, Noland is courteous, almost bordering on condescension. The final paragraphs, however, are fiery. Noland's mood has changed, and he seems to be goading Pope into renewing the challenge:

> The writer of "Devereux" begs the indulgence of the public while he enters into an explanation of the circumstances connected with a *card*, which appeared as a supplement to the "Arkansas Gazette" of the 5th Jan. 1831.
>
> The *reputed father* of that flowery production is known to be Maj. W. F. Pope, aid, and nephew to the Governor. "Devereux" had not the *pleasure* of an acquaintance with the young Major, until Dec. 24th, 1830. They were both invited guests to a party on the same evening; both attended, and during the first dance, and before it was possible for the Major to get drunk, they had a conversation on the subject of the supposed writer of "Devereux." The Major observed, that he had been informed who "Devereux" was, and that if it was "Devereux's" wish to fight him, &c. The reply was, that "Devereux" could be known by an application at the proper source, that he had never expressed a wish to fight the young Major—and under no view of the subject could he consider himself the aggrieved person. This took place in the presence of a third person, and the Major professed to be satisfied. They spent the two following days in company, apparently in perfect friendship. On Monday, the 3d of January, they met again, and "Devereux" received a cordial shake of the hand from the young Major. He, "Devereux," left town, and did not return until the 5th, when to his astonishment, he saw the Major's fierce card.
>
> This is a true statement of the case, and one which can be proved. A few words young Major, and I will drop you for the present. You have made a considerable display at the chivalrous in your card, but you are not so anxious to fight as one might infer. You well know that you can get a fight—you resemble a barking fice, all noise but no

---

19. "A Card," *Arkansas Gazette*, 5 January 1831. Whether Pope had taken it upon himself to defend his one-armed and aged uncle or whether the governor insisted upon the response is unclear. W. F. Pope had, in October of that year, fought to a draw with John H. Cocke. That he, like Noland, was something of a hothead is apparent.

biting; you are "a sluggard in love, and a dastard in war," and never would have been worthy the notice of any gentleman, had you not been appointed aid to the Governor. You came here expressly to fight Gov. Pope's battles—you avowed this when you first came to Arkansas; you expected to bully every one off the track, but in this you have been woefully deceived. Suffer me to say to you, that I am well convinced, that you would prefer meeting me at "Phillippi," as the time taken up in getting there, and the difficulties attending the trip, would considerably retard the fight; and it is my firm belief, that it is your wish to put it off. I would advise you, young Major, to throw off some of the effervescence of youth, and bear well in mind, that an aidship to the governor, will not make a smart man out of a fool, nor a soldier out of a coward.

I anticipate, Major, a severe *handbilling* in reply, as I know you must be fonder of writing than fighting; but I must take the liberty to inform you, Major, that I cannot notice but *one* more note from you, and that must not be through the medium of a newspaper.

DEVEREUX.[20]

Pope's response was, of course, to challenge Noland to a duel. The challenge was accepted, and the duel occurred on 5 February 1831. The *Arkansas Advocate,* on 16 February, reported the event:

Duel.—A meeting took place in the State of Coahuila, (Texas,) on Saturday morning the 5th inst. between Maj. W. F. Pope, of this Town, and Mr. C. F. M. Noland of Batesville. At first fire, Major Pope was severely wounded, Mr. Noland's shot taking effect in the superior part of the hip bone of his antagonist. An extract of a letter to the Editor, states—"They both behaved with the greatest courtesy and bravery upon the field, and what will be gratifying to the friends of each, they parted reconciled." The distance at which these gentlemen fought, was twenty feet.

Afterward Pope was taken first to the house of Benjamin Milam, then to Washington, Hempstead County, and later to Little Rock.[21]

---

20. *"Governor Pope, and Gov. Pope's Bully," The Arkansas Advocate,* 12 January 1831.
21. Lonnie J. White, "The Pope-Noland Duel of 1831; An Original Letter of C. F. M. Noland to His Father," *Arkansas Historical Quarterly,* 22 (1963), 119.

Several weeks later Noland sent a lengthy letter to his father in which he attempted to explain some of the circumstances surrounding the duel:

Batesville A. Ty.
April 2nd 1831

My Dear Father,
    In my last letter to you, I promised that an explanation would be given in the "Arkansas Advocate" which would place my conduct in my late unfortunate affair in its true colors—Respect for my antagonist (with whom I am now friendly), whose recovery is yet doubtful, owing to the ingratitude of his uncle & the inattention of his friends, forbids that I should do so at this time—I have given below the copies of 3 letters the purport of which are explained on their faces—

No 1

Little Rock Jany. 16th 1831

Sir,
    The undersigned have witnessed with sincere regret the progress of an altercation between yrself and Maj. Pope. The respect which we entertain for you both as well as a firm conviction that no just cause of hostility actually existed in the origin of your controversy, has induced our earnest solicitude that (if possible) a compromise or adjustment of the difficulty might be effected. To promote so desirable an end, permit us to tender our mediation and to ask your permission, to make such suggestions to you as in our opinion would conduce to that object—We confidently indulge the hope, that you will not doubt the sincerity of the declaration that we are prompted by no motive unconnected with your present and future welfare, and that we should consider ourselves dishonored in making any proposition in relation to this subject which would be incompatible with yours. We should be pleased to hear from you on this subject as soon as convenient—A duplicate of this note will be handed Mr. Pope at the same instant you receive this

(Signed)

Mr. C. F. M. Noland
        Present

Very Respectfully
Ben. Desha
Js. Woodson Bates
Robt. Crittenden
William S. Fulton

(C. F. M. Nolands reply, is with Col. Desha. No. 2. is in substance but not exactly worded as his was)

No. 2   Little Rock Jany 17th 1831

To Messrs. Bates Desha Crittenden & Fulton,
Gentlemen
     Yr. note of the 16th inst. was received last evening   I have reflected much on its contents—And alho. I agree with you, "that no just cause of hostility existed in the origin" of the controversy between Maj. Pope and myself, yet *matters* have gone *so far*, that I fear It will be impossible to adjust amicably our difficulty—I will however hear any suggestions coming from you with pleasure—and for the kind feelings which prompted you to this act of disinterested friendship accept the sincere thanks of one who has the honor to subscribe himself

Very Respectfully
Yr. obt. Sevt.
(Signed)   C. F. M. Noland

No. 3

Maj Popes answer
"To Messrs. Desha, Bates,   Little Rock Jany 18th 1831
     Crittenden & Fulton
Gentlemen   your note tendering a mediation on the part of yourselves, in the quarrel between Mr. Noland and myself was duly received. The regret expressed therein that any thing of a nature calculated to disturb the harmony of the scene should have occured, finds in my bosom a most cordial response. A careful examination of the facts which led to this affair have resulted in an earnest conviction that there is on my own part nothing to *ask hope* or *fear,* and in refusing a request so kindly and liberally urged, I do my feelings a violence which nought could atone for but *conscious rectitude* and a deep sense of *injury* and *insult.* To the motives which prompted your communication I accord all the credit due them, and if it comported with my feelings to submit this quarrel to the arbitrators of any board, I could not select one of which capacity candor and honorable award I entertain so high a sense—I beg leave in conclusion to tender to each and every one of you my grateful thanks for the kind expres-

sions of interest in the welfare of one who will always feel proud and happy in saying that he reciprocates those feelings and can not and will not forget your kindness

       With Sentiments of Esteem & gratitude
       Yours &c
(Signed)   Wm. Fontaine Pope

Thus you will see that after this high handed letter there were no hopes of a mediation—Gov. Pope must have seen this letter & he did approve of it—Maj. Pope has said on several occasions since he was wounded, "that he had been pit'd twice" That he had fought other people's fight—And how has his uncle treated him since? He is lying at Washington Hempstead Co. suffering from his wound—pennyless—depending on the *charity* of Strangers And his uncle has not been near him neither has he sent him any money—His sunshine friends have all deserted him—I will now give you the conduct of Robt. Crittenden in that affair—I was not friendly to him before it took place Sevier had poisoned my mind against him—He did every thing in his power to prevent the fight—I found him the high minded honorable gentleman; and Sevier's friends to a man were found missing, when I needed a friend Mrs. C. manifested as much anxiety for me as tho. I had have been her brother—she set up almost the whole night before I started preparing Coffee tea & sugar for me—and when I bid her adieu wept like a child. Robt. Crittenden has been *basely slandered*. His acts have been misrepresented Never did a man rise with such rapidity & gain popularity as fast as Robt Crittenden has in the last year—*Col. Desha approved of my course*—I was vilified and abused without cause by a man with whom I thought I was friendly—And as God is my Judge I never had said ought disrespectful against him—until his card came out—Had I have borne it silently, the next thing would have been his spiting in my face—It grieves me much to give you pain; but my conscience reconciles me to this act. And I hope in time you will look over this act of mine. I would have paid you a visit this spring but Mr. Redmon has gone to Ky. & will not return, till June—I have to attend to the Land office in his absence—a disease *sui generis* but by some said to be the small pox is in this neighbourhood. It has given some alarm but vaccination has been resorted to—My love to the family

      Yr. affectionate & dutiful Son
      C. F. M. Noland

Pope died in early June from the effects of his wound, ending a tragic episode in Fenton's life.[22]

Noland was out of Arkansas for the following five years. He spent time in Fort Gibson, Indian Territory; in Florence, Alabama; and in the Army. Possibly the duel was the motive behind his departure. In light of events, it is surprising that he did not accept Sam Houston's invitation to accompany that distinguished man to Texas.

Noland had met Houston in 1829 while in Little Rock attending to his "lovely claims." Houston, who was acquainted with Major William Noland, was on his way to Indian Territory where, according to Fenton, he would winter with the Cherokees. Despite the considerable age difference, Noland and Houston must have liked one another immediately, for in his letter of 11 May 1829 Noland wrote almost exclusively of Houston's plans. That Houston was fond of Noland is clear from a letter which Houston wrote from Washington, 10 June 1832, to Noland in Fort Gibson:

Dear Noland,

I have returned from New York, and design going to Texas in a few days—I write you to ascertain whether or not you have any thought of going to that country. It will be necessary for me to have some person with me, and to be candid, I would prefer you to any other person. I wish a companion of intelligence, of honor and of first rate moral and physical courage. In all these attributes I am satisfied with you.

Whatever my destiny is, yours shall be the same, so far as I may be able to make it glorious, prosperous or happy. If you can come down and see me, within four or five days, I will be happy to see you, as I will wish to set out ere long by way of Tennessee, and Arkansas and reach there with the least delay possible. If I should see you here, I will make you acquainted with the extent of my hopes and expectations! Write me if you can't come down; but come if you can—Do nothing in violation of your parents' wishes to gratify me; but if we should live, our wealth must be boundless.

---

22. *Arkansas Gazette,* 22 June 1831; and *The Arkansas Advocate,* 22 June 1831.

My most cordial and friendly regards to your father.

Truly your friend
Sam Houston

Noland's reasons for not accepting Houston's invitation are unclear. However, he remained in Fort Gibson for several months. It was there that Noland met Washington Irving, whom he describes in a letter of 4 October 1832:

> The celebrated Washington Irving arrived here a few days since in company with Mr. Ellsworth one of the Indian Commissioners—his object is to ascertain the character of the different indian nations— The opportunity he now has will enable him to give to the public a better history of the manners customs and habits of the different tribes, than any which have yet appeared. In his manners, I thought I could discover something of the foreigner—In his conversation I did not find him as *easy* as I expected—nevertheless I was much pleased with him—he is a plain unassuming man.

From Fort Gibson, Noland joined the Mounted Rangers, receiving the commission of First Lieutenant on 5 March 1833.[23] The reasons for his joining the Army are not clear. One might conclude, given his enrollment in the Academy when Fenton was a youngster, that he was once again pursuing the dream of a military career. If such were the case, however, he should have sought to distinguish himself. He did not. He should also have spoken highly of the Army in his letters home. He hardly mentioned it. Apparently, he held no aspirations for such a career.

More probably Noland's reasons were entirely political. Joining the Army enabled him to earn a living without settling outside Arkansas, while at the same time allowing the situation to cool following his duel. Having killed the Governor's nephew, he was a fairly hot political item. The Army permitted him to bide his time until he could return to Arkansas in a more favorable political light.

The record of his Army career is, at best, sketchy. During the

---

23. Josiah H. Shinn, "The Life and Public Services of Charles Fenton Mercer Noland," *Publications of the Arkansas Historical Association,* 1 (1906), 339. Shinn provides no documentation for his statements and is, therefore, untrustworthy.

spring of 1833 he served in Michigan Territory, from which he was transferred to St. Louis in May.[24] When the Mounted Rangers were turned into the Regiment of Dragoons on 19 September 1833, he continued as First Lieutenant.[25] In a letter to his father, dated 6 October 1833, he speaks of having received orders for recruiting service in either Arkansas or Kentucky. No other data exist until 14 March 1834, when he wrote to his father explaining his reasons for going on inactive duty:

> Jef. Bks. Mo.
> March 14th 1834
>
> My dear father
> I feel pained on your account to write you that I have resigned—the reasons that have urged me to this step are. 1stly the rascally manner in which I have been treated by the Secy. of War. He has made to outrank me not only 2 2nd Lieuts of other regiments but also 3 of my own & also a lieut who served under me all last summer—He has given rank to a gentleman because he was dismissed from the Marine Corps—
> I have protested against his decisions & sent it to Col Sevier—If I can get a furlough on redress I will remain in the Service—I wish you to call on the President & state these facts—My health is improving slowly. I will in the course of a few days give you my views & feelings at length
>
> Yr afft Son
> C. F. M. Noland[26]

Noland received the furlough, and sufficient pressure was brought to bear that a military board was called to review his complaint. The report, dated 8 May 1836, ruled against him.

He evidently spent the remainder of 1834 and most of 1835 in Florence, Alabama, at the home of his brother William. His letters to Virginia indicate that he was awaiting a decision on his

---

24. Worley and Nolte, p. xiv.
25. Report in the Case of Lieutenant Noland, 8 May 1836. Univ. of Virginia, Alderman Library, Berkeley Papers, 38-113-33.
26. Lewis Cass was the Secretary of War. Friendship between Major Noland and President Jackson was sufficiently strong that Jackson occasionally trusted Noland to handle personal matters in his behalf. Fenton apparently hoped to capitalize on this friendship.

military appeal and that he apparently was receiving regular military pay during the entire appeal process. These letters also treat family news and the coming presidential campaign. Noland's political involvement once again was on the increase, for his letter of 17 April 1835 to his father confesses that he has been writing campaign literature:

> I hope you will excuse me when I tell you I have again been scribbling in the papers—My nos. over the signature of "L.B." on the next presidency have had a wonderful effect in behalf of Mr. Van Buren—they have been copied into a great many papers in this State and Tennessee and also in the Globe—I have sent you the papers containing them. "Loos" to Gov. Moore and "Aristides" upon the political opinions and public acts of Van Buren are from my pen.

In three different letters, those of 9 March, 15 May, and 1 July 1835, he speaks of having been quite ill. His 15 May letter also reveals plans to return to Arkansas; sometime late that year he made the trip.

Noland's arrival could not have been at a more exciting time, for Arkansas was in the process of achieving statehood. On 4 January 1836, the Arkansas Constitutional Convention met in Little Rock to draw up a constitution and petition for statehood.[27] On 29 January work was finally completed, and the convention held elections to select a messenger to take official parchment copies of the documents to Washington. Six men were nominated for the position of courier. In addition, pragmatic John F. King of Carroll County nominated the United States mail.[28] Finally, on the seventh ballot, Noland was elected.

On the morning of 5 February he boarded the steamboat *Neosho* at Little Rock bound for Washington with the certified copy of the state constitution.[29] A copy of an *Arkansas Gazette* extra carrying the constitution was mailed the same day.[30] No-

---

27. For details of the convention, see White, *Politics on the Southwestern Frontier,* pp. 183-200; and Margaret Ross, *Arkansas Gazette: The Early Years 1819-1866* (Little Rock: Arkansas Gazette Foundation, 1969), pp. 105-134.

28. Ross, p. 132.

29. *The* [Little Rock] *Times,* 8 February 1836.

30. *The Arkansas Gazette,* 29 March 1836.

Figure 2: Charles Fenton Mercer Noland, from a portrait in the Noland House in the Arkansas Territorial Restoration, Little Rock.

photo by Mark Hoagland

land took what he thought would be the quickest route: to New Orleans and Mobile by steamboat, thereafter overland on horseback to Richmond and Washington.[31] Heavy snows, however, made roads virtually impassable, and he did not reach Washington until 8 March, eight days after the *Gazette* extra had arrived and been submitted to the House on 1 March.[32] President Jackson signed the bill admitting Arkansas as the twenty-fifth state on 15 June 1836.

While Noland was away a special election was held, and on 13 February 1836, he was elected to the Arkansas House of Representatives from Independence County.[33] He was reelected in 1838, 1840, and 1846. He drew directly from his experiences in office as source material for Pete Whetstone's tenure as a "big legislator." He, like Pete, regarded the office with a double vision, at once recognizing the serious responsibilities involved in determining the directions for the new state, and at the same time viewing with amusement the fumbling efforts of himself and his colleagues who had little idea of just what they were supposed to do. In later years he wrote what must have been an accurate description of many early Arkansas lawmakers: "I once travelled from Little Rock in a four-horse postchaise, where I had been *playing the part of legislator*. . . ." [34] Elsewhere he drew a clever analogy between the public's opinions of politicians and race horses:

> After all, your horses and your politicians are much alike; riding on the tide of popular favor, your politician gains an ascendency over the minds of his fellow men, that enables him to wield them at his pleasure, and his every footstep is marked by their homage. Some new theory in political economy is broached, he seizes it, or in an evil hour he forgets his country, and thinks only of self, or, perhaps as

---

31. Wilson Powell, "Only a Marker Recalls One of State's Historic Homes," *The Arkansas Gazette*, 26 January 1969, p. 4E.

32. *The Arkansas Gazette*, 5 April 1836; and *The Arkansas Advocate*, 22 April 1836.

33. Townsend Dickinson had been elected to the post but was chosen a judge of the state Supreme Court. Noland filled the vacancy. See Noland's lecture to the Batesville Lyceum, published in the *Arkansas State Gazette*, 6 March 1844; rpt. *The* [Independence County Historical Society] *Chronicle*, 12 (October 1970), 21-37.

34. "Still Later," *Spirit*, 23 (14 May 1853), 147. The italics have been added.

often the case, he thinks of his country and forgets his party, and then comes a long farewell to all his greatness—curses take the place of plaudits, and he sinks into insignificancy. From different causes, perhaps, yet traceable in a great measure, to the same promptings of the heart, *horse flesh* is doomed to suffer. The gallant *Boston,* that so often has put money into the purses of his backers, tasked beyond endurance, has had his brilliant fame tarnished. The crowd decry him—they swear now he is no part of a horse, and some of them even think him unfit to run for sour apples. The victor and the vanquished are two different animals. The crowd run after the bubble Fame, never once asking or caring why the Hero of a thousand hard fought fields has been beaten.[35]

But Noland's attitude was not entirely cynical. His record reveals careful consideration of the acts and resolutions which came before the House. Although he belonged to the Whig Party and was a powerful voice in its Arkansas efforts, he frequently voted against his fellow Whigs, following what he felt was the better course; undoubtedly it is to this circumstance that his politician-horse analogy refers. One example of his approach to party politics occurred in December of 1837. During a session of the Arkansas General Assembly, House Speaker John Wilson of Clark County and Representative J. J. Anthony of Randolph County became engaged in a heated argument concerning floor rights. Wilson stepped down from his Speaker's table and killed Anthony in a knife fight. At Anthony's funeral Noland served as pallbearer. The following day, when the House voted to expel Wilson, Noland's was one of the few dissenting votes.[36] He was harshly criticized for not voting with the majority, which included both Whigs and Democrats, and for appearing two-faced by serving as a pallbearer for his friend and then refusing to vote to oust Anthony's murderer. Noland felt called upon to explain his actions to his constituency in Independence County:

It is . . . urged against me, that as a member of the last Legislature, I voted against the expulsion of John Wilson. I did so—and my

---

35. "Letter from 'N. of Arkansas,'" *Spirit,* 11 (8 January 1841), 531.
36. See *Arkansas State Gazette,* 5 and 12 December 1836.

reasons for so doing, were, that Wilson's resignation had been received, before the resolutions concerning his expulsion were presented—that the House had not the power to prevent his resignation—and that when they expelled him, he was not a member of their body; and hence, they had no control whatever over him. Wilson was my political enemy, but a stern sense of duty, made me act as I did; under similar circumstances, I should act so again.[37]

Such action, prompted by thoughtful consideration and a strong sense of ethics, was typical of Noland throughout his political career. In many ways it is appropriate that he represented a county named Independence.

Arkansas was a veritable paradise for anyone who enjoyed fishing and hunting, and Noland's interest in these sports began while he was a youngster. In a letter to his sister, written 28 February 1827, shortly after his migration to Batesville, he speaks of the abundance of game:

The hunting and fishing in this country are much better than they are at any place I have ever seen. Mr. Bracken and myself gigged at two gigs a cat fish weighing 50 and a buffalo weighing 23 pounds. There are a great many turkey this season and I have got completely sick of all kinds of hunting except fox hunting. We have caught several foxes with Leader. There are but 2 or 3 hounds in the neighborhood besides him—Victor runs very fast—he caught a fox the other morning in running through an open space of about an hundred yards. I often wish I could send you some of our fine venison turkeys and ducks.

Letters throughout his life were sprinkled with such references.[38] His first love, however, was horse racing, and he became a recognized authority on the subject. It was this love of the breed which brought him into association with the *Spirit of the Times,* and his earliest known piece to appear there was a survey

---

37. "To the Voters of Independence County," *The Batesville News,* 27 September 1838. [p. 26].

38. One survey of this aspect of Noland's life is Ted R. Worley, "An Early Arkansas Sportsman: C. F. M. Noland," *Arkansas Historical Quarterly,* 11 (1952), 25-39.

of southern racing stables.[39] Throughout the twenty years following that first appearance in 1836, Noland contributed well over 300 sports reports to the *Spirit*.[40] Most were like the first: straightforward accounts of his favorite horses, of particular races, or of various other sporting events and experiences. Many, however, are spiced with humorous quips:

> I had, the other morning, while I was lying in bed, one corner of my office knocked into *bug mouthfuls* by a flash of lightning. It was a close fit—a perfect *three feet* affair. The *good folks* tell me it is a "warning." I admit it, but don't much admire the style in which the hint was given.[41]

The frequent occurrence of such passages indicates that Noland's motive in creating Pete Whetstone was not merely to provide an outlet for his keen sense of humor; that outlet already existed in his own letters to the *Spirit*. As will become apparent, his purpose in the Whetstone letters was considerably more complex.

Meanwhile Noland's personal life prospered. He had been admitted to the bar in 1836, and in 1837 he formed a lucrative law partnership at Batesville with William F. Denton.[42] He also engaged with reasonable success in land speculation. Writing home 7 April 1838, Noland speaks of a scheme for forming a town on Black River in northern Arkansas near the present site of Black Rock. He and his partner—possibly Denton—had sold half of their town, named Berkeley, to a German who planned to sail to Europe and bring fifty families. "Berkeley will be the finest town in all of North Arkansas." However, the venture apparently failed, for the proposed town received little further attention.

---

39. "A Glance at Southern Racing Stables, etc.," *Spirit*, 6 (26 March 1836), 45. The abrupt opening of this letter suggests that Noland had previously written for the *Spirit*. No earlier appearance has been located; however, files of the early years are quite incomplete.

40. Masterson, p. 29, places the number of pieces at 228, but there are a great many which he overlooked.

41. "Matters and Things in Arkansas," *Spirit*, 7 (29 July 1837), 188.

42. Shinn, p. 342.

In 1838 Noland was reelected to his seat in the Arkansas House and was, at 28 years old, clearly emerging as a major political voice in the state. In December he was elected one of three delegates to represent Arkansas at the Whig National Convention to be held in Harrisburg, Pennsylvania, in December 1839.[43] For unknown reasons, he did not attend the convention, but, by 16 November 1839, was back in Batesville after a lengthy stay in the East.[44]

His first letter to Virginia following his return (20 December 1839) was addressed to his mother; it is unusual in that it juxtaposes completely different moods. The first portion of the brief note displays the "saddest gloom" spoken of by Arrington: "I was much grieved to hear that sister had lost her baby, and deeply as I sympathise with her, can not but rejoice for the poor baby, who was taken from this world of care and grief." The following segment, however, is joyful:

> I have a secret for you—I am going to be married to a sweet pious girl—She is the most amiable being I have ever known and her mild and sweet disposition will be the very thing for my hot and wayward temper—I need not add her name—she was with you last summer and you doubtless then guessed of my feelings towards her—I have not yet fixed the period.

His bride-to-be was Lucretia Ringgold—"Luty" he called her—the daughter of John Ringgold, a powerful Whig state senator from Batesville. Noland had roomed with the Ringgold family since his return to Batesville in 1835-1836, and the couple continued to reside in the house after their wedding on 12 December 1840.[45]

Little is known of Lucretia. She probably was only 15 years old at the time of their wedding.[46] Fenton regularly spoke of her in letters to his family, and in one letter to his sister Frances, she

---

43. *Arkansas State Gazette,* 19 December 1838.
44. See " 'N.' at Home," *Spirit,* 9 (14 December 1839), 486.
45. See note by William T. Porter, *Spirit,* 10 (2 January 1841), 523.
46. Lucretia's tombstone in Mount Holly Cemetery gives her age at death in 1866 as 41 years, placing the year of her birth at 1825.

added a brief, inconsequential note giving instructions for making a child's apron.[47] He seldom mentioned her in his published pieces, however, and none of her own correspondence is known to survive. After Fenton's death she married James B. Keatts. She and Noland had one son, Lewis Berkeley, who was born 15 May 1844.[48] Berke served in the Confederate Army as a sergeant in the Third Arkansas Cavalry, was wounded, and was twice promoted for gallantry. He died 26 February 1870, survived only by his wife.[49]

By 1841 Noland's health had begun to fail. He was never a strong, robust person; at one point he gave his weight as 129 pounds, "six pounds more than ever before."[50] The humid Arkansas climate took its toll. With increasing frequency he noted chills, fever, and a sinister cough. Malaria tormented him regularly during the last fifteen years of his life, and tuberculosis, which eventually caused his death, plagued him throughout most of his adult life. In spite of his illnesses, however, he maintained his sense of humor: "I have again been laid flat by an attack from chills and fever, but by the aid of Dr. Sappington, I am rising like fog from a fish pond."[51] Neither did he lose his interest in horses, dogs, and hunting. In the same letter, he asks, "Will you ask G. W. P., of N.O., if he knows any thing of a certain dog left for me in April last with him by Lieut. N.? Come P., fork over that 'ar dog,' if he aint died of 'yaller jack,' or been minced up into 'sassinges.' " He was not, however, as healthy as this tone suggests.

Early in 1842 he traveled to New Orleans where he hoped to attend the spring races, but illness forced him to leave before the season opened.[52] Later that spring his health worsened, but by May he had begun to improve and to plan a trip east:

---

47. This and another letter to Frances Berkeley, neither of which carries a date, are incorrectly filed in the Berkeley Papers as being dated 7 April 1838. This date is impossible, however, since Noland speaks of his son who was not born until six years later.

48. HLS, C. F. M. Noland to Catharine Noland, 8 January 1845.

49. Worley and Nolte, pp. xxvii, xxx.

50. "Letter from 'N. of Arkansas,' " *Spirit*, 23 (8 October 1853), 403.

51. "Latest from 'N. of Arkansas,' " *Spirit*, 11 (20 November 1841), 450.

52. "Visit to New Orleans by 'N. of Arkansas,' " *Spirit*, 12 (19 April 1842), 66.

I have been very ill—close to death's door, but am able to walk about the house—19 days flat on my back. I shall leave in a few days for Virginia, with a view of restoring my health.[53]

As circumstances developed, the trip to Virginia was hazardous, for on 16 June the stage in which the Nolands were riding met with an accident. Lucretia narrowly escaped being killed, receiving severe cuts and bruises about the head. Noland listed his own injuries as "a 'shocking bad hat,' a 'punk knot' on the head, and a few bruises." [54]

The Nolands remained in Virginia until late that year. On their return trip to Arkansas they stopped in Louisville, where Noland was given a hunting dog:

> I know not when I have met with a compliment so flattering, as one I received while in Louisville. A gentleman whom I had never before met, learning I was anxious to get a setter or pointer, presented me with a magnificent dog, saying that he had derived much pleasure from my contributions to the "Spirit." I felt deeply and gratefully obliged to him, both for the dog and compliment.[55]

The trip had improved Noland's health. Early in 1843 he terms it "pretty good again," and mentions that he was able to hunt with the dog, named Dash.[56] In the same piece, he speaks of an earthquake:

> We have had a *tolerable shake* of an earthquake here—a harder one would have upset us pretty generally. 'Tis the first I have witnessed, and I confess myself fully and abundantly satisfied. To see a large house shaken after the fashion of a man's catching a boy by the collar of his jacket, and racking the breath out of him, is not as pleasant as it might be.

The years 1844 and 1845 were quiet ones in Noland's life. His letters to Virginia indicate that he was busy with his land specula-

---

53. "Letter from 'N.' of Arkansas," *Spirit,* 12 (11 June 1842), 174.
54. "Accident to 'N. of Arkansas,'" *Spirit,* 12 (25 June 1842), 198.
55. "'N. of Arkansas' on His Way Home," *Spirit,* 12 (3 December 1842), 477.
56. "Sporting Epistle from 'N. of Arkansas,'" *Spirit,* 12 (4 February 1843), 584.

tion, farm, and law practice. In May of 1844, Berkeley was born.

During the week of 12-17 November 1845, Noland attended the National Whig Convention in Memphis as one of Arkansas' delegates.[57] He served as the party's first secretary and described the convention, in a letter to his brother on 2 December 1845, as "the most magnificent assembly, both in number, talents, and respectability . . . that ever congregated before in America." Indeed, he must have been in high spirits, for, according to one newspaper account,

> The most amusing incident that occurred during the session of the recent Convention at this place, and which threw the gravity of the whole body topsy turvey to indulge in unrestrained and repeated bursts of laughter, occurred just before its adjournment, on the adoption of Mr. Topp's resolution respecting the Arkansas Military Road. A gentleman from Ohio proposed an amendment to the effect that the government should prosecute the extension of the Cumberland road through Ohio, Illinois, Missouri, &c.; at the proposition of which amendment, C. F. M. Noland, Esq., of Arkansas, (the veritable "Pete Whetstone") rose and begged the privilege just to be heard *two* words. "The gentleman from Arkansas," said the Speaker, accomplished with a keen rap with his hammer on the table.
>
> "Mr President," said the gentleman from Arkansas, "that amendment, sir, will kill the resolution; it is intended to do it, sir; it is packing down more weight than it can carry sir. And it reminds me, sir, of an anecdote of Gen. Roger Clark, who, being taken by the Indians, was packed down with a heavy load of pots and skillets to carry for the Indians. The next morning, when they were about to renew the tramp, they began to load him down again with skillets, whereupon the General mounted a stump close by and made the following speech: 'Gentleman Indians, I move that every man packs his own skillets.' And Mr. President, I move now that every *state* shall pack its own skillet." It is unnecessary to state that the Convention, amid the most hearty peals of laughter, and such as we are quite sure were never before heard within these sanctified walls, knocked the skillets into a "cocked hat," and passed the resolution.[58]

---

57. [Memphis] *American Eagle,* 18 November 1845.
58. [Memphis] *American Eagle,* 20 November 1845; rptd. [Van Buren, Arkansas] *Western Frontier Whig,* 9 December 1845.

Hard work, little rest, and exposure during his trip took their toll; on 27 January 1846 he wrote his father, "My health has been decidedly worse this winter then ever before, and I am determined on abandoning Arkansas—I have fool like stuck here, until my constitution is all but ruined & my money in a great measure exhausted—I have enough to live on, if I can ever regain my health, but I have ceased to hope for such a thing." His physical condition evidently improved; he did not leave the state but instead was reelected to the Arkansas House.

In 1848, a special election was held in the Arkansas General Assembly to fill the three-month unexpired term of Ambrose H. Sevier, who had resigned as United States Senator to become Commissioner to Mexico. Noland was the Whig nominee for the position. At that time the party in Arkansas was torn by disunity and weakened by apathy. Noland viewed his nomination as having little hope of success; his frequent, sharp criticism of other Arkansas politicians had severely damaged his public image. In January he wrote of his willingness to yield the nomination to any other candidate having a better chance of election:

If we harmonize, we will have a fine prospect of success—What is there to prevent us? I will be in no mans way—If my chances are deemed inferior to those of other Whigs, I will submit cheerfully and willingly & will do service as freely in the ranks as I would have done elsewhere—If Newton or any other is preferred by the Whigs to me, I will cheerfully yield—we must have the man who is most likely to make a good race.[59]

In February he complained, "The Whigs of Arkansas seem very indifferent to politics—I shall do my duty—battle for the cause if I stand alone."[60] In November, when the General Assembly met to select a senator, Noland did stand almost alone. The vote was

---

59. HLS, C. F. M. Noland to Jesse Turner, 12 January 1848. Duke Univ., Perkins Library, Turner Mss.
60. HLS, C. F. M. Noland to Jesse Turner, 23 February 1848. Duke Univ., Perkins Library, Turner Mss.

74 to 19 in favor of Solon Borland.[61]

By May of 1850 he reopened his law and real estate office in Batesville. Earlier that year he had been urged to take charge of a Memphis newspaper, but declined because of his health which, indeed, must have been very poor, for on 18 June 1850 he wrote to his brother. "Nothing but the mercy of God will make me last more than a year or so—and you may expect at any time to hear of my death." Although his health improved somewhat, he was never free of his cough. On 24 January 1851 he wrote, "I am living under a violent cough, my constant companion for many years—yet my general health is I think, better than for many years." His business also was good, and his finances were in excellent condition; $21,000 had been deposited and another $4,000 was on hand. He evidently continued to reside and engage in business in Batesville until early in 1855, when he was elected Swamp Land Commissioner and moved to Pulaski County.[62]

The early part of 1855 apparently was both busy and happy for Noland. In February he was preparing to move to Little Rock, but still he found time for a hunting trip, described in a letter of the 17th:

> I am improving in health—I have taken a great deal of horseback exercise in the way of hunting—use Berkeleys colt; old Simon being down at the mill to spend his winter in the Cove—I went out tuesday evening & at 9 shots, killed 6 mallards 3 flying & 3 sitting, & an old fox squirrel—next day the 15th broke an old mallards wing & after a long struggle she dived down, & I do not believe has come up yet, & I got a shot at some turkies, killed two fine ones on the ground with my

---

61. Ross, p. 258. Ross states that every political figure in Arkansas knew that Borland was to be elected and that Noland's nomination served only to block other possible opponents. Noland's correspondence, however, suggests that he was unaware of any such manipulation and considered himself a serious candidate. An arrangement such as Ross describes would explain the lack of Whig support of which Noland complains.

62. Worley and Nolte, p. xxviii. The United States Congress, in 1849, transferred ownership of about 8,600,000 acres of "swamp and overflowed" lands to the state. A board of three Commissioners was appointed by the Governor to oversee these lands. It was to this board that Noland was appointed. See John L. Ferguson and J. H. Atkinson, *Historic Arkansas* (Little Rock: Arkansas History Commission, 1966), pp. 101-102.

first barrel & wounded a third flying with the other—on Thursday I was out. Killed but a solitary wood cock, & caught the hardest kind of a fall from my horse Dr. Allen who was with me, was riding by my side, in passing round the corner of a fence, a great white hog, ran out suddenly between my horse's legs & he jumped it seemed to me 15 feet right up in the air & over I went—my foot hung for a moment in the stirrup—the Rocks were as thick as they well could be, & yet neither I or my gun hit one—It was a most narrow escape—I felt no inconvenience until just before sun down, when I could not walk—bathed it in hot water, applied Mustery linament & took ¼th of a grain of morphine—I suffered a good deal till eleven or twelve & wished for Cousin Lucy's poultice; was confined to the house on yesterday but am as sound as a trout to day.

Once Noland and his family moved to Pulaski County, they lived with James B. Keatts, an affluent bachelor friend whom Noland had known as early as 1840, when Keatts had given him half interest in a filly.[63] Keatts, a quiet and sophisticated plantation owner, was devoted to Noland, opening his home to the family for the three years prior to Noland's death. After Noland's death, Keatts gave one of the lots in the Keatts family plot in Little Rock's Mount Holly Cemetery for his gravesite.

Late in February of 1855, Noland assumed the duties of editor of the *Arkansas State Gazette and Democrat* while its regular editor, C. C. Danley, recovered from an eye ailment.[64] He continued his association with the newspaper on an irregular basis throughout that year. He seems to have delighted in newspaper work, writing numerous editorials and letters. His age, health, and good humor mellowed the tone of his pieces to the point that they became casual and chatty. Only two subjects aroused his wrath: Know Nothingism and abolitionism.

In April he resigned his office as Swamp Land Commissioner to take a position as receiver for the Real Estate Bank. He thought the job would be nonpolitical and, therefore, secure. In a letter to his sister, dated 10 May 1855, he listed the salary at

---

63. See "Col. Whetstone again in the Field!" *Spirit*, 10 (11 April 1840), 63.
64. Ross, p. 327.

Figure 3: The Noland House in the Arkansas Territorial Restoration.

photo by Mark Hoagland

$2,700 plus "an excellent dwelling, outbuildings and garden," and he was excited about buying furniture. It is unclear whether this house is the one known today as the "Noland House" in the Arkansas Territorial Restoration. More tradition than evidence attaches the building to the person. He never owned the house, although he may have rented it. Built sometime in the mid-1840s, it was advertised for sale in 1850 as renting for $150 per year. It was bought in 1852 by Dr. Roderick L. Dodge, although he did not live in it.[65] Possibly this was the house supplied by the state which Noland looked forward to furnishing and occupying.

By November of that year, however, he had, for reasons not quite clear, been removed from his office in the Real Estate Bank and was planning a general land agency in Little Rock.[66] Thereafter his health was in steady decline. Despite that fact, he remained in general good spirits and was optimistic about the future. In the summer of 1856 he wrote, "I am stouter than I used to be yet have a bad cough—I weigh but 113—I am not determined what I shall do in the future—Have some idea of Memphis or Louisville as my future residence—I shall never be well, yet I have a good deal to be thankful for—a merciful Providence has spared me while the stout and robust have fallen around me."[67] He did not relocate, but remained in Little Rock. By the end of August 1857 his weight was down to 103, yet he expected to be "good as new" within a week.[68] He was never to recover. As early as February 1858 Noland knew that death was certain, and he was making efforts to complete a home for Lucretia and Berkeley. He wrote to his friend, Jesse Turner, asking him to sell off property:

> I am very feeble, & write from my bed— . . . My dear Turner, I am so anxious to improve my little place near here & wind up my busi-

---

65. Ross, p. 328, n. 116. See photograph, Figure 3.

66. HLS, C. F. M. Noland to Jesse Turner, 16 November 1855. Duke Univ., Perkins Library, Turner Mss.

67. HLS, C. F. M. Noland to Jesse Turner, 29 August 1856. Duke Univ., Perkins Library, Turner Mss.

68. Ross, p. 329, citing *Arkansas State Gazette and Democrat*, 5 September 1857.

ness that you must excuse my troubling you—I know not how soon the sounds of my life run out, & I am anxious to fix up my little home.[69]

His last letter to Virginia was dated 13 April 1858, and was written aboard the steamer *H.D. Newcomb* while he was en route to New Orleans, desperately hoping to save his life. The trip failed, however, and, back in Little Rock, the "sounds of his life" ran out on 23 June 1858 at the home of his friend James B. Keatts.[70]

This brief narrative of Noland's life contains several characteristics which repeatedly present themselves, almost as themes in music: his frail health, his passion for sports and outdoor life, his independent and readily expressed political opinions, his unfailing and robust sense of humor. Interestingly, all of these are also characteristics of Pete Whetstone. Noland's persona is clearly derived from his own life; to know Pete is to know Noland. Generally, the Southwestern humorists carefully remained but observers of the characters and activities about which they wrote, but in the Pete Whetstone letters such is not the case. In many ways, Pete Whetstone is the backwoods alter-ego of the Virginia gentleman, Fenton Noland.

Little is known about the actual composition of the Pete Whetstone letters. Although Noland was prolific and treated many subjects, he wrote almost nothing about his own writing. None of his earlier work foreshadowed the appearance of Pete.[71]

---

69. HLS, C. F. M. Noland to Jesse Turner, 26 February 1858. Duke Univ., Perkins Library, Turner Mss.

70. For obituaries, see "Metarie," *Spirit,* 28 (31 July 1858), 291; and [C.C.] D[anley], "The 'Old Settlers' 'Passing Away,' " *Arkansas State Gazette and Democrat,* 10 July 1858.

71. Richard Boyd Hauck, in his "Literary Content of the *Spirit,*" does not share this opinion, but rather sees Pete as the result of a gradual process in Noland's development from a reporter into a humorist. He concludes (p. 171): "Noland's assumption of the character of Pete for the purpose of relating yarns and backwoods opinions was not a sudden development. Before February, 1837, Noland often included in his N. of Arkansas turf reports tall yarns, scraps of dialogue, or short narratives about hunts." What Hauck fails to note is that these items appear throughout Noland's career, and cannot, therefore, be seen only as groundwork for Pete Whetstone. Furthermore, in none of his pre-Whetstone pieces does Noland adopt a persona. In fact, nothing in Noland's earlier work anticipates the appearance, full grown like Athena, of Pete Whetstone.

The first Whetstone letter begins abruptly, "Excuse my familiarity, for you must know us chaps on the Devil's Fork, dont stand on ceremony." That opening, with its marked absence of prefatory remarks, aptly characterized the apparently spontaneous origin of the letters themselves.

Once Noland began the Whetstone letters, however, he at once became intensely involved. Twenty, almost one-third the total, were written in 1837; eight were produced in 1838; eleven were done in 1839. Thus, during the first three of the nineteen years within which the letters were published, well over half were composed. Additionally, numerous other brief references to Pete appeared in the letters published under Noland's own name. Doubtless the remarkable consistency of character and event found in the letters is at least partly due to many of them having been written within a short interval.

But such a view hardly presents an adequate account of Noland's success. Consistency is not limited to those letters produced in the first three years, but is also found throughout the canon. Particular traits, habits, and attitudes of the characters are maintained; Pete, Jim Cole, and Dan Looney are of the same nature in 1856 as they were in 1837. Even the minor characters and their expressions, such as Giles Scroggins' five-fold classification of mankind, are consistent. The fact that Noland maintained this coherency in the letters not only indicates some measure of his ability but also suggests his commitment to literary endeavor.

Such well-sustained coherency produces realistic scenes and characters, and scholars have tended to focus attention upon the realism of Southwestern humor. For Clement Eaton, realism is a chief attribute of the humorists, who "found around them the racy and individualized characters of the cracker and the yeoman, whose uncouth language and provinciality afforded substance for mirth. They could therefore create a native American humor based on realistic observation and illuminated by many sidelights of local color."[72] Constance Rourke goes

---

72. *The Mind of the Old South* (Baton Rouge: Louisiana State Univ. Press, 1967), p. 133.

further, claiming that the tales may be viewed as history filled "with such close and ready detail as to provide something of a record of the time and place."[73] John Q. Anderson, however, wisely judges the realism of Southwestern humor as "the realism of art, not of factual reporting." Anderson makes his emphasis clear: "Consciously or not, the Southwestern humorists responded to the demands of entertainment imposed upon the storyteller and observed the primary dramatic requirements of fiction."[74]

Such is the case in the Whetstone letters. Those elements which collectively result in the "realism" of the letters were very carefully worked out and were the work of a writer rather than a reporter. Noland's techniques were so effective that many of his readers were misled into believing that Pete Whetstone was an actual correspondent. In one instance, an anonymous contemporary writer reported having seen Pete at a Washington horse race:

> I forgot to tell you I saw your old friend and correspondent, PETE WHETSTONE, to-day.— [Doubtful, but hope it may be so—Ed.]. I am certain it was he, though I never saw him before. When I read his late epistles in the Spirit, I made up my mind as to what sort of a looking chap he was, and to-day he stood up naturally before me. That there may be no mistake, I will tell you how he looked: he looked all the time at some very pretty girls in the stand and carriages, and never once thought of Decatur and Fanny Wyatt. He is a very tall well-made gentleman, with sandy whiskers, prominent nose, and large mild blue eyes, with one of nature's best countenances. I am sure 'twas Pete. He wore a light green coatee with yellow buttons, and pantaloons of the widest stripes you ever saw. I had a notion to say "how are you Colonel Whetstone?" but my hear[t] failed me. He stood pretty close to Mr. HENRY CLAY of Kentucky and Gov. DAVIS of Massachusetts. He will write you by this mail no doubt.[75]

---

73. *American Humor: A Study of the National Character* (New York: Harcourt, Brace, 1931; rpt. Garden City, New York: Doubleday, 1953), p. 64.
74. "Scholarship in Southwestern Humor," p. 77.
75. "Match for $10,000 Aside—Decatur vs. Fanny Wyatt," *Spirit*, 8 (5 May 1838), 93.

Many such reports were composed by writers who sincerely believed that Pete was an actual backwoods friend of Noland. But certainly many others were written by Noland and his friends in order to reinforce Pete's reality. Several such reports occurred in the *Spirit*; they substantially contributed toward its over-all humor.

As a matter of fact, an actual Pete Whetstone did once live in the Batesville area. His name was listed in the Independence County tax list of 1824.[76] Josiah H. Shinn was certain that Noland and Whetstone were old friends:

> In 1832 or 1833 he [Noland] made the acquaintance of Pete Whetstone, a typical hunter and trapper, who lived on Devil's Fork of the Little Red River, then in Conway County, but now in Van Buren County, and where he had lived since 1819. A warm friendship sprang up betwen Noland and Whetstone, which was never broken until death carried Whetstone away. With Whetstone Noland took many a hunting jaunt and soon became a master of the backwoods philosophy, idioms and humor. Noland conceived the idea of giving these to the world over the *nom de plume* of Pete Whetstone, and arranged with the New York *Spirit of the Times* for their publication. For more than ten years, under the caption "Scenes and Characters in Arkansas," Noland delighted readers of the *Spirit of the Times* with his wit and humor, as well as the people of Arkansas, who read the articles as they were regularly reproduced by the Arkansas press (pp. 342-343).

Shinn, however, overlooked at least two important facts: Noland was out of Arkansas at the time Shinn said he became friends with Whetstone. Furthermore, Whetstone's name did not appear in later records; evidently he either died or left the area shortly after the 1824 list was compiled.[77]

In any event, all that Noland took from the historical Pete

---

76. "Territorial Tax List Independence County, 1824," ed. Duane Huddleston, *The* [Independence County Historical Society] *Chronicle*, 11 (October 1969), 42.

77. Other errors occur in Shinn's account: The Whetstone pieces span nineteen rather than ten years; only the first letter carried the title, "Scenes and Characters in Arkansas." Such weaknesses cast doubt upon his entire undocumented account and suggest he was perhaps more interested in writing a good story than in adhering to fact.

Whetstone was the name.[78] The other people, places, and activities were drawn directly from Noland's own experiences and imagination. These products of Noland's artistic prerogatives do far more to reinforce the realistic qualities of the letters than does evidence of Pete Whetstone's existence. The apparent authenticity of the Whetstone letters, then, rests primarily upon four elements which are carefully maintained throughout: the historical actuality of certain people and events, the detail and nature of characterization, the vernacular speech, and the first-person narrative technique.

Sprinkling the Whetstone letters with references to people and events well known to readers of the *Spirit* enabled Noland to create the illusion that the letters were drawn from reality. If Pete spoke of Martin Van Buren, who obviously was real, then Dan Looney, whose personality was more clearly evident than Van Buren's, must also be real. The authentic appearance of the letters also had another advantage; Noland was able to hide behind a mask where he could voice ideas and opinions otherwise unutterable.

Noland's references to Van Buren make a good example of this double purpose. Van Buren was not a popular president. His difficulties, many of which stemmed from his fairly blunt and unfriendly manner, were compounded by his following such a strong and well-liked figure as Andrew Jackson. Adding to Van Buren's problems were several widely disfavored policies, some of which were inherited from Jackson's administration.[79] Noland capitalized on these circumstances. Like many others on the frontier, he had been a firm supporter of Jackson. He had, as has been mentioned, also supported Van Buren early in the

---

78. Both Worley and Nolte (p. xxxi) and Hennig Cohen and William B. Dillingham, *Humor of the Old Southwest* (Boston: Houghton Mifflin, 1964), p. 109, reach this same conclusion. The latter state that Whetstone appeared in Arkansas as early as 1816; however, they offer no evidence for this assertion. That they have been misguided by Arrington's work can be deduced from their statement that the historical Whetstone "later became something of a legendary figure in Texas." See n. 6 above.

79. One enlightening account of Van Buren's tenure in office and the difficulties he faced is James C. Curtis, *The Fox at Bay: Martin Van Buren and the Presidency, 1837-1841* (Lexington: Univ. Press of Kentucky, 1970).

campaign. But sometime prior to the election he switched his allegiance to the Whig Party. Pete accurately expressed Noland's opinion when he wrote that he "always went for Old Hickory, but can't swallow Marting Van Buring or Buck Woodruff" (Letter 4). This displeasure was widely shared; surely Pete met with popular approval when he wrote, "Now, Van Burenism is so close to thieving, that to save time we use them for each other" (Letter 6).

Allusions to the contemporary political scene fill the Whetstone letters, so much so that at one point Porter issued a warning that such abundant and strong opinions be avoided or else the letters would not be published.

> We wish Amos Kendall would drive up his Arkansas Postmasters a little, for we are persuaded that our worthy friend Pete Whetstone cannot have received the several letters we have written him. Pete is getting regularly *wolfish* in his politics, and we, early detecting the premonitory symptoms, thought it worth while to drop him a line, hinting at various remedies which we thought might mitigate them. But really Pete's late letters seem to indicate a hopeless state. We do beg some faithful friend at the far West to wait on him and endeavor to soothe his declining hours, for we are persuaded his friends will see little more of him unless the progress of his malady is arrested. To say nothing of "our feelings" upon so melancholy an occasion, we would not for the world lose a correspondent so staunch and clever.[80]

Pete took Porter's advice, and, although political references continued, they were not so "wolfish."

Such use of authentic political figures was not Noland's only method of weaving a realistic quality into the Whetstone pieces. Equally effective was the incorporation of other *Spirit* material. When, in letters 4 and 6, Pete spoke of being "as bad off as a small varmint in 'Sharptooth's' grab," and of having lost his money to Sir William, the readers of the *Spirit* recognized his

---

80. *Spirit,* 7 (18 November 1837), 316. The political nature of the Whetstone letters is explored a bit further in my article, "Charles F. M. Noland: One Aspect of His Career," *The* [Independence County Historical Society] *Chronicle,* 10 (April 1969), 52-58.

reference to a race between Sir William and Independence which Noland reported in the same issue. Furthermore, Noland's report included a paragraph about Pete, reinforcing the realistic illusion of the entire situation. The horses and the race *were* real; Pete's predicament seemed to be. Over and over in the letters, Pete spoke of horses, jockeys, hotels, steamboats, and racing stables which were familiar to his readers.[81] When he wrote of fictitious horses, people, and events in the same manner, the reader must have assumed they too were actual. Noland's fictional fabric was carefully woven to achieve this apparent reality.

Moreover, when Pete spoke of matters which, in all probability, had their source in Noland's own knowledge, he did so in a manner which caused them to appear authentic. Pete's description of a backwoods frolic, related in letter 12, was so complete and so accurate that it has been cited as a contemporary account of this folk custom.[82] Undoubtedly any number of Pete's other depictions of life in frontier Arkansas were equally accurate.

But the realism of the Whetstone letters did not end with allusions to contemporary figures. The characterization of fictional persons was also treated in such a manner as to convey their apparent authenticity. Jim Cole is an example. The portrait given of him was so detailed that the reader came to know him quite well; his character was fully realized.

Jim was introduced in the first letter, where several traits—his readiness to bet on horses, to drink, and to fight—were given. In his next appearance he became involved in a political argument, telling an outsider that "the Devil's Fork boys didn't want any chaps from *Chapel Hill Township* to come and tell them how to vote" (Letter 7). He voiced his dislike for dishonest politicians and then whipped the outsider for calling him a liar. In letter 8 Pete spoke of Jim's marriage to Pete's sister Sal. He praised Jim's

---

81. The number of actual people, horses, and other items identified in the glossaries provides some indication of the extent to which Noland employed this technique.

82. See my "An Early Arkansas 'Frolic': A Contemporary Account," *Mid-South Folklore*, 2 (Summer 1974), 39-42.

prowess as a fighter: "He is all *horse*, I tell you, and when it comes to real hard fighting, give me Jim." Pete's comment on Jim's vanity, once he was dressed in finery for the wedding, was a splendid touch: ". . . the way he struts now is sorter *peacocky*." Later Jim's actions revealed that he was not above cheating on horse races (Letter 9). Such suggestions were made at intervals throughout the letters and served to underscore his humanity. He was no hero; he was exactly like any real person.

Eventually the reader found that Jim and Sal had children, that he continued to bet on horses, that he remained a good hunter, and that he finally was elected to the Legislature. When Pete made a trip East, he wrote back to Jim giving his impressions of the sights. Jim was the author of letters answering Pete. Interestingly, Jim's letters were slightly less literate than those of Pete. Noland subtly and realistically distinguished between the two men.

In later years Jim gave up drinking. However, in a weak moment, "he got drunk." As a result, he almost lost an eye in a fight. He had, Pete hopes, learned his lesson and "will fall back on the good principles of temperance" (Letters 49, 50). When the California gold rush occurred, Jim was "fool enough to think he could make his everlasting fortin, by going way out yonder to dig gold" (Letter 56). He was unsuccessful. In one of the last letters, Jim had returned to resume life on the Devil's Fork, which had changed but little (Letter 61). The composite portrait was well developed. Sustained throughout the letters, Jim became a believable character, one which any reader of the *Spirit* might expect to meet. He, like Pete, Dan Looney, and Lawyer McCampbell, was thoroughly credible.

Noland also used vernacular speech as another effective means of providing a realistic quality to the Whetstone letters. The fact that Pete wrote as if he were a product of the backwoods aided in making him appear to be.

Indeed, the use of language has been viewed as one of Southwestern humor's outstanding features. James M. Cox offers the suggestion that early in the rise of this literature, these humorists discovered that "the future and ultimate power of Southwestern humor lay in discovering through dialect the direct experience of the frontier." [83] Kenneth S. Lynn finds in the language a "wonderful, lifesaving freshness." He feels that the dialects of the characters with their "spontaneous metaphors and original images generate laughter and renewed hope" in a world which at times must have appeared frightening.[84] Cohen and Dillingham view this "earthy vividness" of metaphoric language as "the most striking feature of vernacular language as it was used by the Southwestern writers." [85] Their conclusion (p. xviii) is important: "Although the use of local dialects was not new, this kind of language was. It combined the wild imagination of the frontiersman with the concreteness of poetry."

Walter Blair explains that this dialect was appropriate for humorous effect because it employed the idea that education had little to do with knowledge and because it made frequent use of indirect statement. "A throwaway comment can be funny when a frontal attack cannot." [86]

All this is, of course, directly applicable to the Whetstone letters. They are among the earliest sustained uses of backwoods vernacular, one of Noland's true achievements. Worley and Nolte note that the way Pete wrote was a fairly correct rendition of actual dialect. They assert (p. xxxv) that the best evidence indicates that many of Pete's characteristic expressions remain in fairly current usage. While this is hardly *prima facie* evidence, it is not far from the fact. Norris Yates praises Pete for his "semiliterate dialect which is 'heavy' enough to be distinctive but not so pronounced as to afford awkward reading" (p. 65). While Noland's innovation undoubtedly paved the way for later

83. "Humor of the Old Southwest," in *The Comic Imagination in American Literature,* ed. Louis D. Rubin, Jr. (New Brunswick, New Jersey: Rutgers Univ. Press, 1973), p. 108.

84. *Mark Twain and Southwestern Humor* (Boston: Atlantic-Little, Brown, 1959), p. 138.

85. P. xvii. Cohen and Dillingham also note (p. xviii) the frequency with which the humorists employed animal similes. The half-man, half-horse or alligator is one popular example.

86. " 'A Man's Voice, Speaking': A Continuum in American Humor," in *Veins of Humor,* ed. Harry Levin (Cambridge: Harvard Univ. Press, 1972), p. 192.

humorists, such as Harris in his Sut Lovingood yarns, it served a more immediate purpose: Pete's language established him as a unique and credible character.

The principal device Noland employed as a means of achieving apparent realism, however, was the first-person point of view. Pete told most of the stories completely in his own language. This technique is not one characteristically found in Southwestern humor. Most other writers enclosed virtually all their stories in a framework, a device which Noland used only occasionally. Stories using this structural frame typically begin from the point of view of the author, who sets the scene, describes the teller of the tale, and sketches the circumstances of the telling. Then the tale itself is reported, frequently by the tale's protagonist in his own dialect. Once the story has been related, the author-narrator reappears with his own cultured language and ends the sketch.

Walter Blair feels this box-like structure is especially useful for the humorous Southwestern yarn:

> It was admirable because it effectively characterized the story-teller, through direct description, through indirect description (i.e., the description of the effect he had upon his listeners), and through a long and highly characteristic dramatic monologue in which, revealingly, the imagination of the yarn-spinner was displayed. The vividness of the presentation of the narrator gave the narrative illusive power. It was also admirable because, as it was used, it seemed artless. The realistic setting given at the beginning, the detailed description of scene and narrator, gave an impression of naturalness just as it does when Kipling or Conrad presents a tale in such a framework (*Native American Humor,* p. 92).

Blair concludes that this framework is effective in Southwestern humor because it emphasizes the various incongruities which are the basis of the tales' comic appeal.[87]

---

87. Kenneth S. Lynn argues that the humorists employed the framework structure for quite another purpose than those Blair suggests. He says that this "frame was a convenient way of keeping their first-person narrators outside and above the comic action, thereby drawing a *cordon sanitaire,* so to speak, between the morally irreproacha-

Although Noland made some occasional use of this frame technique, it is not typical of the Pete Whetstone letters. When used, as in letter 3, it not only served those purposes outlined by Blair, it also reinforced the idea that Pete was an actual friend of Noland. In most cases Noland permitted Pete to speak for himself without the intrusion of a gentlemanly author-narrator. Pete was a whole-hearted participant in the life he described, and, as a result, his activities as well as his personality took on a reality as vivid as any in Southwestern humor.

Once Noland had achieved the appearance of two distinct figures as correspondents to the *Spirit,* he further pursued Pete's actuality by including in his own letters a number of references to Pete's sayings and doings. Often these were sufficiently substantial to warrant inclusion in this edition, e.g., letters 3, 5, and 9. Here Noland sometimes employed the frame structure. Frequently, however, these references were only one or two sentences in length and added little substance; their only apparent function was to reinforce the idea that Pete was a friend of Noland—a friend who also wrote to the *Spirit* and was well enough known to readers that news of him would be interesting.

One example of such a passage appeared at the end of a report of races held in Batesville. After a description of the meet, Noland added, " 'PETE' and JIM COLE are here. The former told me he was going to give you a *'prime letter.'* "[88] A week later Pete's "prime letter," number 13, appeared in the *Spirit*; Noland's note had prepared the way.

Another instance of Noland's occasional mention of Pete occurs when Noland made one of his several visits to Virginia. In a postscript he added, "Pete is along, his eyes are nearly popped in gazing at curiosities. He keeps a journal for lawyer McCampbell. I will try and *steal* it for you." [89] If Noland actually had plans to

---

ble Gentleman and the tainted life he described" (p. 64). Lynn is, of course, out to prove that the humorists were really satirizing the life of the frontier which they hated, a thesis which, at least when applied to Noland, is ridiculous.

88. "Batesville (Arks.) Fall Races," *Spirit,* 7 (4 November 1837), 302.

89. "Tour of 'N. of Arkansas,' " *Spirit,* 9 (27 April 1839), 91.

have Pete write a journal, he evidently dropped them. He did, however, compose several letters in which Pete spoke of his experiences and impressions. Thus through numerous references, both brief and substantial, Noland added to the apparent reality of his character.

William T. Porter, always quick to recognize a good thing, also contributed to the illusion of Pete's reality. Following a junket through the racing circuit, which he made during the closing weeks of 1837, Porter spoke of Pete as he might of any rising political figure:

> There are strong reasons for believing that our facetious and spirited correspondent, *Pete Whetstone,* will be elected to Congress from Arkansas, at the next election. He is not only the most able speaker in the State Legislature, but can out-shoot, dance, sing, fiddle, any man in the state; while at racing, preaching, or telling a story, nobody there is a huckleberry to his persimmion. We saw a steamboat and half-a-dozen flat-boats on the Mississippi, bearing his name, and "shouldn't be surprised" if he was elected as the Western candidate for the Presidency one of these days. Go it, Pete![90]

To unsuspecting readers this sketch, which, interestingly enough, foreshadowed Arrington's hyperbolic thumbnail biography of Noland, might well have spoken of an actual figure; nothing in the note suggested otherwise.

A bit later Porter added a note, following one of Noland's letters, that is even more explicit in its treatment of Pete as an individual correspondent:

> He [Noland] has arrived in N.O. accompanied by his friend [William F.] DENTON, of Batesville, and the celebrated Col. PETE WHETSTONE, the universally popular correspondent of the "Spirit of the Times" and the London "New Sporting Magazine," etc. Col. Whetstone hailed the "Pawnee" just as she was clearing the Devil's Fork of the Little Red, when she rounded to and took him on board, with his famous hunting jackass "Levi Woodbury," so famous as a

---

90. "On Dits in Sporting Circles," *Spirit,* 8 (17 February 1838), 4.

racer on the Snakebite Prong. We shall address the Colonel to-day, a letter of congratulation upon his arrival at New Orleans, where he will be "the big dog of the tanyard."[91]

This note, undoubtedly written to prompt a Whetstone response, enhanced the reality of Pete. The appearance of letter 47, which incorporated features from Porter's note, carried the entire guise one step further.

This whole fictional Whetstone network was elaborated upon by a letter from Albert C. Ainsworth of New Orleans, a friend of Noland, who wrote under the pseudonym of "Trebla" and spoke of Pete in a half-dozen contributions to the *Spirit*. His note following Pete's trip to New Orleans is especially significant for several reasons: It solidified, perhaps more than any other external material, the character of Pete Whetstone; it underscored the real importance of the Whetstone letters in Southwestern cultural history; and, finally, Ainsworth was actually speaking of Noland:

> I have seen "PETE WHETSTONE" since I wrote you. Pete is a "phurst wrate" boy—rather thin but the way he *walks* into your affections is worthy brogans and a shame to prunellas. Pete's *memory* is what I look at. I don't know how old he is, (he looks thirty-five,) but he talks about horses, women, wine, catfish, country jokes, accidental adventures—scrapes with the Long Waisted, and a whole frying-pan full of *eat*-ceteras, with as much confidence and precision, as though they had all happened on Monday. I love to hear such a man. He is the inpersonation of a gone time—the impress of an age passed away. He is a living, moving, speaking record, and one that never gets musty at any age. I was introduced to him *as* "Pete," and he to me *as* "Trebla!" We shall henceforth read each others "scratches" with an "Arkansas *interest*"—that is to say "use-YOU-rious!" How'd ye like that?
>
> But "Pete" is gone, and our city to some folks looks rather gloomy. I parted [from] him with only ordinary ceremony, but I hid my real feelings under a cloak. His honest phiz, easy manners, sensible talk,

and good feeling, will remain in my memory until my mind takes the "benefit of the bankrupt law." [92]

The telling passage in this letter is, "I was introduced to him *as* 'Pete'. . . ." Here it becomes evident that Ainsworth was actually writing about an introduction to Noland rather than to Pete. Having known Noland and Pete through the *Spirit,* he was aware that Pete was a product of Noland's imagination and he used the fictional name to apply to the actual person. He was identifying Noland as Pete; only such a reading is sensible.

This use of Pete Whetstone as a sobriquet for Noland occurred at other times. The Memphis *American Eagle* account of Noland's address to the Whig Convention parenthetically identifies him as "the veritable 'Pete Whetstone.' " [93] In several accounts of horse races, Pete's name was used when actually Noland was the person to whom the writer referred. William T. Porter, in reporting a match race between Wagner and Grey Eagle, stated, "Even our friend Col. WHETSTONE, of the Devil's Fork, declared that he had never seen 'the beat of it' out in 'the Arks.,' and he has 'seen sights—some!' " [94] Presumably the writers of such accounts knew that Noland was the author of the Pete Whetstone letters and saw no reason for avoiding the switching of names.

And, indeed, Noland must not have given reason; none of these cases drew an unfavorable response from him. Apparently he was fully content to allow himself to be identified as his character. His attitude, of course, was unlike that of most other Southwestern humorists. More often they avoided such identification with their narrators—one possible motive behind their frequent use of the frame structure. Richard Boyd Hauck suggests that the almost universal use of the pseudonym sprang

---

92. "Sayings and Doings in New Orleans," *Spirit,* 12 (26 March 1842), 37.
93. See n. 57 above.
94. "The Louisville Races," *Spirit,* 9 (4 January 1840), 522. Wagner and Grey Eagle were two of Noland's favorite horses, and he follows their careers throughout his correspondence. Recall also that Noland was a virtual walking encyclopedia of racing information.

from the writers' desire to prevent such identification.[95] W. Stanley Hoole relates circumstances in which Johnson Jones Hooper was angered when he was addressed as Simon Suggs.[96] With few exceptions, the humorists shared to varying degrees Hooper's attitude.[97]

One obvious explanation for Noland's willingness to be identified with his character lies in the fact that Pete, to such a great extent, was drawn from Noland's own life. Indeed, Noland might well have considered Pete as himself without refinement, social or political images to uphold, or hesitancy to indulge in the wild and raucous life on the Arkansas frontier.

Both Noland and Pete shared a passion for hunting and horse racing and were recognized authorities on the subjects. Both were Representatives in the Arkansas General Assembly and held similar views of their roles. Pete's political enemies—Sevier, Ashley, and Woodruff—were Noland's. When Noland traveled to "the Rock," New York, Virginia, or New Orleans, Pete also made the trip. A high regard for Jackson and little respect for Van Buren were common to both. The list could continue indefinitely; throughout Pete's letters his interests, attitudes, and activities paralleled those of his creator. It thus was appropriate that Noland was introduced to Ainsworth "*as* 'Pete.'"

Although Noland used Pete as an alter-ego through whom he could speak more openly, his motive underlying the composition was much more complex than that of merely creating a mouthpiece for his opinions or an outlet for his sense of humor. Pete was a fully developed fictional character.

Some measure of Noland's success with the Whetstone letters is indicated by the contemporary acclaim given them. Ainsworth

---

95. *A Cheerful Nihilism: Confidence and "The Absurd" in American Humorous Fiction* (Bloomington: Indiana Univ. Press, 1971), p. 41.

96. *Alias Simon Suggs: The Life and Times of Johnson Jones Hooper* (University, Alabama: Univ. of Alabama Press, 1952), pp. 102-103.

97. Two notable exceptions, other than Noland, are George Washington Harris, whose friends frequently addressed him as Sut (see M. Thomas Inge, *High Times and Hard Times: Sketches and Tales by George Washington Harris* [Nashville: Vanderbilt Univ. Press, 1967], p. 41); and Thomas Bangs Thorpe, who was widely known as "the author of 'Tom Owen, the Bee Hunter.'"

was one of those who frequently applauded the "scratches." Once, when Pete was silent for several weeks, he wrote, "Give my compliments to 'Pete Whetstone,' and ask him to finger his goose feather a little oftener—if he don't, we've got a club here will give that *whetstone* a knife!" [98] When thus prompted, Pete responded with letter 45. Ainsworth was pleased, but he warned that the letters must continue: "I notice that 'Pete Whetstone' 'came to taw' after I *raked him down,* and gave you a letter afterwards. If 'Pete' doesn't write you oftener, he may expect to be *toasted* on the 'Devil's *fork*'—a *knife* 'wouldn't phase him,' because he's a *whetstone.*" [99] Ainsworth was, of course, one of Pete's greatest fans; evidently many others looked with equal anticipation for the letters.

Most readers, however, were interested in the humor of the letters. And therein lies their chief claim to popularity: They are funny. A brief note in which Porter reprinted a passage from a New Orleans writer, possibly George Wilkes Kendall, must have expressed the feelings of a great many subscribers:

> The New Orleans "Picayune" thus apostrophizes Col. PETE WHETSTONE's late letter to us; they are always 'hard to beat,' but several of the latest ones 'can't be beat no how you can fix it!':—
>
> Tall Son of York, thou are hereby commanded to close the columns of the "Spirit of the Times," henceforth and forever against the letters of one PETE WHETSTONE, of Rackensack. The last letter cost us much more than we can afford in these hard times. We desire to be paid for three buttons and one suspender strap. Compensation is required, likewise, for injury done two false teeth shaken out by laughing over the letter aforesaid.[100]

As the Whetstone letters became increasingly popular, Porter and his correspondents began to drop Pete's name wherever possible as a means of kindling interest. The official report of the 1839 spring races held at Trenton, New Jersey, is typical. It was a

---

98. "Trebla," "Life in New Orleans in the Dog Days," *Spirit,* 11 (11 September 1841), 325.

99. "Trebla," "Sayings and Doings in New Orleans," *Spirit,* 11 (1 January 1842), 517.

100. *Spirit,* 12 (21 May 1842), 135.

long account, giving detailed descriptions of each race together with the official record, but in one short paragraph, Porter tantalized the reader:

> The last heat of the third race yesterday was not over until near six o'clock, and as we did not reach our office until midnight, we had not leisure to make our report as full as we should like; however, our friend and correspondent, "KURNEL WHETSTONE, of the Devil's Fork," has kindly volunteered to "do the clean thing" in our next.[101]

In letter 35, Pete "does the clean thing" and describes the race. Presumably writers sought to capitalize upon the widespread fame of Pete Whetstone as a means of attracting attention to whatever horse race, cock fight, or dog show they were promoting. What is important is that the name Pete Whetstone must have been enormously popular to have carried such an impact.

This widespread popularity is further indicated by the number of horses, dogs, and even mules named after the characters in the letters. The fact that one race horse was named Hard Times might be credited to circumstance; [102] but another named Fent Noland is an obvious tribute.[103] Another similar compliment came with a horse being named Pete Whetstone; while not as fast as Pete predicts in letter 4, he did win several races.[104] An even greater compliment occurred when a race at the Baltimore track was named the Pete Whetstone Stakes.[105] Undoubtedly the most delightful event of all, however, occurred on Friday, 10 September 1837 when a mule named Pete Whetstone lost a race at Hoboken, New Jersey.[106]

Significantly, with no other Southwestern correspondent to the *Spirit* does a similar fame exist. Evidently Noland was, during his own time, more widely read and more popular than any of

---

101. "Trenton (N.J.) Spring Races," *Spirit*, 9 (1 June 1839), 151.
102. See *Spirit*, 9 (20 April 1839), 79.
103. The horse was owned by David Thompson of Van Buren, Arkansas; see *Spirit*, 9 (16 March 1839), 19.
104. See lists of winning horses in *Spirit*, 9 (16 March, 13 April, and 20 April 1839), 19, 68, and 80.
105. See *Spirit*, 11 (24 July 1841), 246.
106. See *Spirit*, 7 (11 November 1837), 308.

the *Spirit*'s other writers. Only T. B. Thorpe approached Noland's popularity, and even he was a distant second.

This widespread popularity of the Whetstone letters prompted other writers to pattern their correspondence after Pete's, a
point which Richard Boyd Hauck emphasizes.[107] In fact, the
extent of Noland's influence on other writers was so great that
Norris Yates terms the whole series the "Noland Cycle." [108] In
some cases the results exhibited rather thinly veiled plagiarism,
as in "Sporting Epistle from 'The Swamp' " reprinted in Appendix 1. In most instances, however, Noland's techniques and subject matter were adapted to the particular needs of the individual
writer. Frequently these correspondents admitted that Pete was
their inspiration, as in the case of a Virginian who called himself
"Boots." His first letter began: "Well, Mr. Porter, seeing as how
Mr. Pete Whetstone has not rubbed agin the steel lately, so as to
put forth some of those bright scintillations from 'the Devil's
Fork of the Little Red,' that used to illuminate your pages, I takes
occasion where the big lights ain't a-shining to let my little taper
glow some. . . ." [109]

Through such imitation and adaptation, various innovations
and characteristics first found in the Whetstone letters may well
have become the stock-in-trade of much Southwestern humor.
Certainly Noland was the earliest of these humorists to appear in
the *Spirit*.[110] He was also an innovator, using many of the key
features of Big Bear humor for the first time. Norris Yates em-
phatically states,

> It should be clear that Noland in 1837 had created the first sustained
> character of the southwestern frontier to tell a story entirely in his
> own person. He was thus the first southwestern author to eliminate
> his own cultivated personality entirely from the story as far as direct
> presentation of character and atmosphere was concerned (p. 66).

---

107. "Literary Content of the *Spirit*," p. 32.

108. P. 75. Yates (pp. 68-75) offers an enlightening discussion of Noland's influence
upon other contributors to the *Spirit*.

109. *Spirit,* 7 (2 December 1837), 333. The letter carried no title. Ironically Pete's
letter 16, one of the best of the canon, appeared on the same page with Boots's letter.

110. Hauck, "Literary Content of the *Spirit*," p. 32; Cohen and Dillingham, p. 108;
and Masterson, p. 30, all agree with this assertion.

Important features in Southwestern humor—realistic characters, racy action, outrageous boasts, dialect speech, detailed descriptions of local scenes—all appeared in the Whetstone letters
some time before they were used by Harris or Thorpe.[111] Certainly Augustus B. Longstreet, Davy Crockett, and Joseph G.
Baldwin cannot be overlooked as important forces in the birth of
Southwestern humor. But, without a doubt, the *Spirit* was the
primary instrument in its development. William T. Porter encouraged writers to submit humorous frontier yarns for publication; C. F. M. Noland's Pete Whetstone letters served as models.

Whether Noland ever intended to collect the Pete Whetstone
letters in book form can probably never be determined, although
internal evidence suggests he did. He is known to have been
pleased with their popularity and the wide circle of acquaintances they helped bring him. Noland's father, writing to another son, speaks of their acclaim:

> Your brother Fenton has been with us; but is now in New York; He
> has had great attention paid him in New York by the first men in the
> City. He writes for "The Spirit of the Times," (a paper published in
> New York,) under the signature of "Pete Whetstone" and "N. of
> Arkansas." These pieces are much sought after and have given him
> much celebrity.[112]

Fatherly pride aside, this letter presents firm evidence that Noland readily acknowledged authorship, indeed, enjoyed the
celebrity. When his pieces appeared in London, Fenton was delighted:

> I have contributed to the "N.M.S. Magazine" printed in London for
> some time past—I recd. a most beautiful letter from its editor, highly
> flattering & complimentary— In its January No. I have a "Pete

---

111. Harris and Thorpe clearly took Southwestern humor to its finest heights. However, they learned much from their predecessors. Thorpe did not appear in the *Spirit*
until 1839; Harris's first appearance was in 1843. See also Inge, pp. 34-35.
112. HLS, William Noland to Callender Noland, 30 July 1839. Univ. of Virginia,
Alderman Library, Noland Papers, 6463-1.

Whetstone" and Turf matters in America by "N. of Arkansas"—This
is complimentary—.[113]

Noland was clearly proud of his Pete Whetstone letters. Furthermore, he did not object to being addressed as his character,
one more indication of pride in his work. A writer pleased with
his material would surely wish to seek more permanent publication than that offered by newspapers and magazines.

When the canon of Whetstone letters is examined, at least one
other indication of Noland's intention to publish a book is
apparent: their remarkable degree of consistency. Such consistency is hardly the work of a writer only incidentally and occasionally interested in his fictional community. The letters suggest
that he either held a full file of the stories and constantly
referred to them, or else he possessed a truly phenomenal memory. To save such a quantity of material for use only as reference
for later stories hardly seems reasonable. In fact, little purpose,
other than collecting them in book form, could have been served
by such retention.

Regardless of what Noland's intentions might have been, no
Whetstone book appeared. Perhaps his frail health and busy
schedule postponed such plans. Any hopes he may have had
were, of course, cut short by his early death. Changes in the
editorship of the *Spirit,* the remarriage of Lucretia, and the Civil
War combined to frustrate possible posthumous publication.

For more than a century the Pete Whetstone letters lay buried
in the periodicals in which they appeared. Occasionally a few of
the letters were reprinted, and James R. Masterson's *Tall Tales of
Arkansaw* included excerpts from many of them. Masterson believed strongly in the need for a complete edition:

> If the Whetstone letters are ever collected in a volume, it may well
> take its place on the same shelf with *Georgia Scenes, The Flush Times of*

---

113. HLS, C. F. M. Noland to William Noland, 4 March 1841. Univ. of Virginia,
Alderman Library, Berkeley Papers, 38-113-33. The abbreviated title of the magazine
is incorrect; it should read "N.S.M." [*New Sporting Magazine*]. The Whetstone letter
mentioned is number 40.

Alabama and Mississippi, The Adventures of Captain Simon Suggs, and other chronicles of a hard-racing, hard-drinking, hard-fighting era (p. 54).

Unfortunately, the Worley and Nolte edition did not achieve distinction near that which Masterson predicted. In fact the edition is so incomplete and inaccurate that it may well have prevented serious and significant attention being afforded the letters.[114]

Hopefully, this text will bring Fenton Noland the recognition he deserves. Even though the Devil's Fork now lies beneath Greer's Ferry Lake in north-central Arkansas, Pete Whetstone, like Simon Suggs and Sut Lovingood, is as fresh and lively as he was a century ago. What Albert C. Ainsworth wrote is still true: "He is the inpersonation of a gone time—the impress of an age passed away. He is a living, moving, speaking record, and one that never gets musty at any age."

The Pete Whetstone letters are not only an important chapter in what might be called "Unofficial American Literature," they are also the history of an age and place. It is indeed appropriate that most of them originally appeared in a journal named *Spirit of the Times.* They are collected here so that once again one may find Jim Cole, Dan Looney, and Pete Whetstone cavorting on the Devil's Fork.

---

114. In the first Whetstone letter alone, the Worley and Nolte edition, which was announced as being both accurate and complete, contains 72 textual errors, including several word changes and omissions. A comparison of the list of letters contained in that text with those appearing here will reveal the incomplete nature of the earlier edition.

Cavorting
on the Devil's Fork

Figure 4: Map of the Devil's Fork area

[1] SCENES AND CHARACTERS IN ARKANSAS

Peter Whetstone's real estate operations–The "Benton's mint drops" currency–The "chaps" of the Devil's Fork and the Raccoon Branch of the War Eagle–Peter Whetstone's rifle, dog, and sister–Red-headed Jim Cole–Race between "Warping Bars" and "Bussing Coon"–The Banter, the Acceptance, the Treat, and the Consequences.

DEVIL'S FORK, OF LITTLE RED RIVER, (Ark)
Feb. 14, 1837.

DEAR MR. EDITOR,—Excuse my familiarity, for you must know us chaps on the Devil's Fork, dont stand on ceremony; well, week before last, daddy sent me down to the Land Office, at Batesville, with a cool hundred shiners, to enter a piece of land—I tell you, it took all sorts of raking and scraping to raise the *hundred.* 'Squire Smith let him have forty, but he would'nt have done it, but for a monstrous hankering he has, after sister Sal. Dad has got right smart paper money, but the great folks at Washington have got so proud they turn up their noses at the best sort of paper now-a-days.[1] While I was at Batesville, I saw your *paper,* and the way I did love to read *it,* was nobody's business. Captain _____ lent them to me every day, and I just made

---

Text: *Spirit,* 7 (18 March 1837), 36.

1. As a result of President Andrew Jackson's issue of the Specie Circular on 11 July 1836, payments for public lands were required to be made in gold or silver. This caused considerable difficulty in the frontier areas of the country where bank notes were plentiful and specie was scarce.

up my mind, that no matter what Daddy said, I would take *it* myself.

I just wish you could come to the Devil's Fork. The way I would show you fun, for I have got the best pack of bear dogs, the closest shooting rifle, the fastest swimming horse, and perhaps, the prettiest sister you ever *did* see.[2] Why, those fellows on the Raccoon Fork of the War Eagle, ain't a priming to us boys of the Devil's Fork. They aint monstrous friendly to us, ever since I laid out *Warping Bars,*[3] with the *Bussing Coon.* I tell you, we used them up that hunt—red headed Jim Cole drove home twenty-four of the likeliest sort of cows and calves, and Bill Spence walked into a fellow for three good chunks of horses.

I'll tell you how that race was made. Monday evening of the election, I was standing talking to Squire Woods—we were just outside of the Doggery, when I heard somebody cavorting—I stepped right in—There stood big Dan Looney the Raccoon Fork Bully. I said nothing, but stopped right still—Says Dan, "I say it publicly and above board, the Warping Bars can beat any nag from the Gulf of Mexico to the Rocky Mountains, that is now living and above ground, that drinks the waters of the Devil's Fork, one quarter of a mile with any weight, from a gutted snow bird to a stack of fodder!"

Before I had time to say a word after Dan got through, in jumped Jim Cole—Says he, "Dan, the Bussing Coon can slam the Warping Bars this day three weeks, one quarter of a mile, with little Bill Allen's weight on each; for fifty dollars in cash, and two hundred in the best sort of truck."

"It is wedding," said Dan, "and give us your hand."

---

2. The boast was a standard device in frontier humor. Thomas D. Clark attributes the origin of such boasting to river men; see *The Rampaging Frontier,* pp. 34-36.

3. Although undoubtedly used here fictionally, a horse named Warping Bars was raced in the Batesville area. See N[oland], "Batesville (Arks.) Fall Races," *Spirit,* 7 (4 November 1837), 302, which states that such a horse, owned by T. Denton, won a race in Batesville on 5 October 1837. Pete, in letter 13, reports the same event, naming the owner as William F. Denton. See also N[oland], "Races at the Salt Sulphur Springs, Va.," *Spirit,* 9 (7 September 1838), 319. For a definition of the term "warping bars," see Nancy McDonough, *Garden Sass: A Catalogue of Arkansas Folkways* (New York: Coward, McCann and Geoghegan, 1975), p. 48.

They shook hands and agreed to put up two good horses as forfeits. No sooner was the race made, than the boys commenced drinking and shouting. Dan said Jim Cole owed a treat—Jim Cole said Dan owed a treat. They agreed to leave it to Squire Woods; now Squire Woods is up to snuff and makes no more of belting a quart, than a methodist preacher would of eating a whole chicken, so says he, "boys, taking all things into consideration, I think it but fair that *both* should treat to a gallon, and sugar enough to sweeten it." "Hurrah for 'Squire Woods," roared every chap except Dan and Jim.

It did'nt take more than twenty minutes to make some of them feel their keeping. I knew what was coming, and you may depend I kept my eye skinned.—Dan soon became uproarious, and made out he was a heap drunker than he was—After a little while he could'nt hold in—Says he, "I can pick the ticks off of any of you hell-fire boys," (meaning the Devil's Fork chaps)—the words were hardly out of his mouth before Jim Cole cried out, "you are a liar, Dan," and *cherow* he took him just above the burr of the ear—Dan reeled, and 'ere he recovered, several persons rushed between them.—"Come boys," says one, "there is Squire Woods, and have some respect for him." "Damn Squire Woods," says Dan, "a Squire is no more than any other man in a fight!"

The physic was working—there was no chance to control it—coats were shed—hats flung off—shirt collars unbuttoned[4]—but one thing was needed to bring about a general fight—that soon happened, for Bill Spence jumped right upon the table and shouted "hurrah for the Devil's Fork!" Dan answered him by yelling "go it my Coons"—the Doggery was on about half way ground, and the two settlements were about equally represented. The fight commenced—I tell you there was no time to swap knives—I pitched into Dan—'twas just like two studs kicking—we had it so good and so good for a long time—at last Dan was using me up, when Squire Woods (who had got through whipping his

---

4. The rough and tumble nature of frontier fighting necessitated the removing of ties and unbuttoning collars to prevent strangulation. For additional details of frontier fighting, see Thomas D. Clark, *The Rampaging Frontier,* pp. 34-36.

man) slipped up and legged for me, and I *rather* think gave Dan a slight kick—Dan *sung out* and the Devil's Fork triumphed.

I reckon there were all sorts of 4th July's cut over the fellows' eyes—and bit noses and fingers were plenty.[5] We started home just about dark, singing Ingen all the way. I did'nt want Daddy to see me that night, so I slipped to the stable loft—next morning I started out bear hunting, the particulars of which I will write you some of these times.

Ever yours, PETER WHETSTONE.

[2] PETE WHETSTONE'S BEAR HUNT

DEVIL'S FORK OF LITTLE RED RIVER, (Ark.)
Feb. 15th, 1837.

DEAR MR. EDITOR,—Being that this is a rainy day, I thought I would write you about the bear hunt.[1] Well, next morning after

---

5. Biting, tearing, and gouging became so widespread and so vicious during the early 1800s that several states enacted legislation forbidding mayhem, the term collectively applied to all such methods of fighting. Thomas D. Clark, citing Kentucky and Indiana statutes, lists penalties of imprisonment from one to fourteen years and fines up to $1000; see *The Rampaging Frontier*, p. 35.

Text: *Spirit*, 7 (25 March 1837), 46.

1. The bear hunt was one of the standard subjects of Southwestern humor; there are dozens of such tales. Thomas D. Clark concludes that one reason for the telling of such a large number of these tales was that "bears and their habits figured prominently in the life of the frontier." See *The Rampaging Frontier*, p. 42.

James M. Cox writes: "The . . . ultimate power of Southwestern humor lay in discovering through dialect the direct experience of the frontier. The most dramatic example of that direct experience was the bear hunt. First emphasized by Davy Crockett, the bear hunt in one form or another [became] the subject of innumerable stories. It remained for Thomas Bangs Thorpe, a Northerner who came to Louisiana, to realize the full possibilities of the bear hunt in one triumphant sketch, 'The Big Bear of Arkansas' [which first appeared in the *Spirit*, 9 (27 July 1839), 247]." See Cox, "Humor of the Old Southwest," p. 108.

The bear population of northern Arkansas remained large well after Noland's time. Details of bear hunting in the White River area during the 1870s are given in John Quincy Wolf, *Life in the Leatherwoods* (Memphis: Memphis State Univ. Press, 1974), pp. 75-80.

the fight with Dan Looney, I started out. I was mighty sore, I tell you, for Dan had thumped me in the sides till I was blue as indigo. I saddled my horse, got my wallet, and fetched a whoop, that started my dogs; they knew what I was after, and seemed mightily pleased. I took six with me, as good dogs as ever fought a bear. *Sharp-tooth* and *General Jackson,* if there was any difference, were a little the best. I struck for the Big Lick, where Sam Jones and Bill Stout were to meet me. I found them there—they had a good team of dogs. We had heard of great *sign* up the dry fork, and there we determined to go. It was about thirty miles off, and as we did not wish to fatigue our dogs, it took us until the middle of next day to reach it; we rested that evening, and put out by day-break next morning.

In about half an hour, old General raised a cry: I knew then we were good for a bear—the other dogs joined him. The track was cold; we worked with him till about ten, when they bounced him. Bill Stout was ahead, and raised the yell—such music, oh lord, and such fighting. I got the first shot; my gun made long fire, and I only slightly wounded him. At the crack of the gun the dogs gathered; he knocked two of my young dogs into the middle of next week before you could say Jack Robinson—the others kept him at bay until Bill Stout could shoot: his ball struck him too far back. He was a tremendous bear, and just lean enough to make a good fight. He made two other dogs hear it thunder, shook off the whole pack, and got into a thicket, and the next moment plunged down a steep cliff. I listened only for an instant, to hear the clear shrill note of Sharp-tooth, as he plunged in after him, and then socked the spurs into *Dry-bones,* and, with Bill Stout on *Fire-tail,* and Sam Jones on *Hard-times,*[2] dashed round the hill. We rode for our lives, for we knew that many of our dogs would suffer if we did not relieve them. When we overtook them, they had him at bay; two dead, and three crippled dogs told of the bloody fight they had had. Sam Jones fired: the wound was that time mortal. At the crack of the gun, the dogs again clamped him; with a powerful reach of his paw, he

---

2. Although fictional here, a gelding named Hard Times was foaled in 1832; he was by Redgauntlet out of an unnamed dam by Tartar and was owned by J. Maxwell.

grabbed the old General, and the next moment fastened his big jaws on him; [3] this was more than flesh and blood could stand: I sprung at him with a butcher-knife, and the first lick sent it to the handle.[4] He loosened his jaws, and Sam Jones caught the old General by the hind legs and pulled him away. I gave him one more stab, and he fell dead.

I examined the old General, and found that he was not much injured. We lost seven dogs that day, and many of the others were so badly crippled, as to render it necessary for us to lay by a few days. Sam found a bee tree, and I killed some fat turkies; with them, and the ribs of the old *he*, we had fine times. It has stopped raining, so I must stop for the present.

Ever yours, PETE WHETSTONE.

---

3. Owing to the fact that hunting dogs were trained to attack the prey at the sound of the gunshot, countless dogs were lost to wounded bears. This circumstance gave rise to a great many tall tales which eventually found their way into American folk humor. John Lawson, Surveyor-General of the province of North Carolina, wrote, in 1709, of the bears of Carolina: "If a Dog is apt to fasten, and run into a Bear, he is not good, for the best Dog in *Europe* is nothing in their Paws; but if they ever get him in their Clutches, they will blow his Skin from his Flesh, like a Bladder, and often kill him; or if he recovers [from] it, he is never good for anything after." *A New Voyage to Carolina*, ed. Hugh T. Lefler (Chapel Hill: Univ. of North Carolina Press, 1967), p. 122, as cited in William A. Dobak, "An Eighteenth-Century 'Bear Story,'" *Journal of American Folklore*, 85 (July-September 1972), 275.

4. The method of killing the bear and the hunt itself anticipate William Faulkner's treatment of the subject in "The Bear." Several studies have examined the influence of Southwestern humor on Faulkner's fiction; see, for example, Carvel Collins, "Faulkner and Certain Other Southern Fiction," *College English*, 16 (1954), 92-97; Frank M. Hoadley, "Folk Humor in the Novels of William Faulkner," *Tennessee Folklore Society Bulletin*, 23 (1957), 75-82; Cecil D. Eby, "Faulkner and the Southwestern Humorists," *Shenandoah*, 11 (1959), 13-21; and M. Thomas Inge, "William Faulkner and George Washington Harris: In the Tradition of Southwestern Humor," *Tennessee Studies in Literature*, 7 (1962), 47-59. None of these studies treats a possible Noland-Faulkner relationship.

[3] BULLETIN FROM ARKANSAS [Excerpt]

BATESVILLE, (Ark.)
May 1st, 1837.

DEAR P.,—I have just returned from Van Buren County;—had the exquisite pleasure of seeing your correspondent, "Pete Whetstone." He says you ought not to call him Peter—but Pete.[1] Settle this, or you will raise his dander; Pete is a jewel in his way. He made all sorts of a speech to the sovereigns while I was over. The commencement was much after this fashion:—

"We, the people of Van Buren, are shut out from the candle of light by the cloud capp'd hills that surround us;—though we drink of the purling streams that flow at their foot—though we were sown in the whirlwind, and reap'd in the storm, yet, fellow citizens, we are the true democracy of the land.—[Hear him, hear him.]—Who is this Marting Van Buring, who comes from the State of York, riding on the suburbs of posterity in the open atmosphere?—[Go it, my Pete.]—I ask him no boot; and if he does not let us have land for paper money, we will make him smell hell!—[Hurrah, Pete.]—You have known me from the time I killed the wild cat on Devil's Fork until now,—you know I am real grit,—well, I now say publicly and above board, that when the lark rises on his rectum, and soars aloft, before the sun has dried the dew on his feathers, I generally make him fling up

---

Text: *Spirit,* 7 (27 May 1837), 117; signed "N."
1. The first Whetstone letter appeared in the *Spirit* over the name "Peter Whetstone." The same error occurred much later when Porter issued *Porter's Spirit;* there Pete's first letter was headlined "Peter Whetstone's Reception of the Spirit." See letter 62.

his tail.—A wink is as good as a nod to a blind man;—so look out, Marting Van Buring.—[Hurrah for Pete.]—It is my treat, boys, so come up."

This is all I can recollect of Pete's speech; he is good for the Legislature.

[4] PETE WHETSTONE ALIVE AND KICKING

BATESVILLE, (Ark.)
May 5th, 1837.

Dear Mr. Editor,—Well, here I am, used plum up—as bad off as a small varmint in *"Sharptooth's"* grab.—Old *Sir William* cleared me out—they acted as foul as a buzzard's nest, or I would have been "in town" with my pocket full of rocks. There is no use to cry over a "lost bear," but I will make some of them think day is breaking next Fall. This here place aint much for feeding man or brute; the "green tree" finished me—I hadn't enough left to buy a half-pint.[1] *Dry Bones* like to have had the big head; but I would have had him out, or burst a shoe-string.

Well, I have had an all sorts of a time since my last letter;— knocked the hind sights off from old *bess*—used up two *painters,* and made a mash of lots of little varmints. I tell you, they have had me in a tight place: I tell you how it was—Squire Woods came over to my house, and says he, "Pete, you must run for the Legislature." Well, now, the Squire has a hankering that way, and he thought I would say *no,* and then ask him; but he warnt smart. Says I, "Squire, I don't care if I do." [2] This here sorter

---

Text: *Spirit,* 7 (3 June 1837), 121.

1. Pete's displeasure over his trip to Batesville and the results of the Sir William-Independence race is detailed more fully in letters 5 and 6.

2. Pete's experiences in campaigning for office and in serving in the state legislature roughly parallel those of Noland.

took him by surprise; but he acted like a man, and is doing his best for me. Says he, "Pete, you must make a stump speech at the 'log rolling' on the middle fork." [3]—"Well," says I, *"good."* I went to the "log rolling;"—I found my opponent there. He was cutting a wide swarth among the sovereigns. I guess I used him up; for the moment I rode up, I called for a "gallon and sugar." "Hurrah for Pete!" shouted the hell-fire chaps, "he is the man what don't care for a dollar." I stirred among the boys; presently some fellow cried out, "A speech from Pete." I tell you, I began to have the thumps; says I, "Look here, lawyer McCampbell, arter you is manners." Up jumped lawyer Mac, and bowing low, addressed the crowd:—

"Friends and fellow citizens,—I am an unambitious man—I never sought office; I belong to a party that are modest and unassuming,—I am a disciple of the Van Buren, Amos Kendall, Tom Benton, Buck Woodruff school.[4] I have been always a democrat—one that loves the many, and hates the few;—I am a professional man. I have spent a patrimony in preparing myself to be useful to mankind, and you ought to elect me. I hold this doctrine to be correct, that a representative should vote as his party directs. I pledge myself to vote as Chester Ashley and Buck Woodruff tell me. Who is Pete Whetstone? Why, he is an uneducated man—he knows nothing of the immortal principles of Lindley Murray [5]—quem deus vult per dere priusque

---

3. John Quincy Wolf, p. 116, describes the early Arkansas log rolling:
When a settler cleared new ground and saved the best logs for his house, kitchen, barn, or smokehouse, a great deal of brush and a good many scrub logs were always left. Eventually he passed the word to his neighbors that on a certain day he was having a logrolling, and most of them came with their families, bringing horses or mules, grab hooks, crowbars, and other tools that would be useful. While the women chatted and prepared food and the children played games, the men piled the brush and logs into great head-high heaps for burning.
Pete, thus, would have a large audience for his speech.
4. Noland, an active Whig, was, of course, very much opposed to all four of these Democrats.
5. Lindley Murray's "immortal principles" were those of English grammar. By 1850, between one and one-half and two million copies of Murray's grammar texts were in circulation.

dementat[6]—yes, fellow citizens, I say, sic transit gloria mundi[7]—which means, that the higher a monkey climbs, the plainer he shows his tail."

Down he sat. "What larning," says one.—"He is a great man," said another. I swallowed a horn of bald face, and riz up. "Boys," says I, "Pete's out for the Legislature; Pete is an ambitious man—but his is an honorable ambition. Pete always went for Old Hickory, but he can't swallow Marting Van Buring or Buck Woodruff. Pete's a democrat, according to the old fashion meaning. Lawyer McCampbell says he has spent a fortune to make himself useful. All Pete can say is, that he laid out his money badly. He asked who Pete is?—Why, he is a professional bear-hunter, and a scientific bee-hunter.—Pete is no orator; but when it comes to killing a bear, or finding a bee tree, he is *there*. Pete aint good at figures, but he can read big print. If he goes to the Legislature, he will do his best for you. Pete *tracks* no man. As to that strange tongue that lawyer McCampbell speaks, I can say nothing; it aint Shawnee, Creek, or Cherokee;—maybe it is Dutch. Pete never flies higher than he can roost. You all know him, and if you don't want him to go to the Rock, just say so. Pete has a "couple of gallons" over at the doggery;—step over and drink."

"Hurrah for Pete!"—"He is my chap," shouted about three-fourths. This is the lawyer's strong hold, and I have him safe. I expect he has been taking some pulls on me since I left; but if he has, I will make him think a Rhode Island jackass had kicked him. To-morrow I put out for the Devil's Fork, and I will tell you more about my election when I get home.

Ever yours, PETE WHETSTONE.

P.S Look here, don't call me Peter—my name is Pete. I have a monstrous notion of that Mr. JOHN STEVENS, and tell him if he

---

6. "Quem Deus vult perdere priusque dementat." Trans.: "Whom God wishes to destroy he first makes mad."

7. Trans.: "Thus passes the glory of the world."

wants to have a colt a little faster than the Bussing 'coon, why, call him Pete Whetstone.[8]

[5] MATCH, SIR WILLIAM vs. INDEPENDENCE [Excerpt]

"Pete" dropped his pile, and was sour as vinegar.[1] He says he will make some of them smell hell yet with the *"Bussing coon."* [2] He says he could have stood the race, but the landlord of the "Green Tree" used him right up—$2.50 a day for man and horse; nothing but "corn dodgers" for the former, and no fodder or "rub down once a day" for the latter. The last I saw of "Pete," he was hunting a bacon rind, to grease the tavern, for the purpose of making the dogs eat it up. He says he is going to give you a small sprinkle about, prehaps one of the greatest fights.[3]

---

8. Not John C. Stevens, but a Mr. Murfree of Murfreesboro, Tennessee, took Pete's advice and named a colt "Pete Whetstone." The horse did not prove to be as fast as Pete's prediction, though he did have a fairly successful season in 1838.

Text: *Spirit,* 7 (3 June 1837), 125; signed "N."
1. Pete's wrath is kindled as a result of a race between Joseph D. Thompson's Sir William and Thomas T. Tunstall's Independence, which was run in Batesville, 4 May 1837. Sir William was the winner. The full details of this race are given in the letter from which this paragraph is excerpted. Pete alludes to his ill treatment in letters 4 and 6.
2. Bussing Coon's fame as a race horse stems from his race against Dan Looney's Warping Bars, reported in letter 1.
3. Reference is to a bear fight Pete had before he went to Batesville. Although this is mentioned in letter 6, Pete never relates the whole story.

[6] PETE'S VERY LAST

DEVIL'S FORK OF LITTLE RED RIVER, (Ark.)
May 8, 1837.

MY DEAR MR. EDITOR,—Well, I got home last night. Old *Dry Bones* is all horse—knocked off 40 miles a day, and never blowed at it. Just as I expected, the *lawyer* has been Van Burenising. Now, Van Burenism is so close to thieving, that to save time we use them for each other. But that aint here nor there. He has been among the religious women, telling them with a long face that I am a sinner—that I play cards, horse race, and drink whiskey. Well, now, all this is true; but I'll make him think the earthquake has come, just for telling the truth. He has gone up to New Dublin and told the Irish Van Buring was born in old Ireland, and they believe it. Now, can't you contradict this?—Just do, and send your paper quick. I am in a tight place, and if I once get out of it, I am done with politics—I won't be a great man. I have written a circular, and am going to put a copy up at New Dublin, one at the Doggery, and one at the Dry Fork. Here it is:—

"Pete's got home. He has seen all sorts of times over at Batesville. They won his money, and gave Dry Bones no fodder. He aint in a good humor no how. Now, he just wants to say, if lawyer McCampbell don't take care, he will find himself in a bark mill. You all know Jim Whetstone—Pete's father; he has fought, bled, and died for his country.[1] He was a democrat; Pete is a strap of

---

Text: *Spirit,* 7 (3 June 1837), 121.
1. In his first letter, Pete informs the reader that his father sent Pete to Batesville to register a claim. Jim Whetstone was, at that time, very much alive. No mention is made of his death.

the same leather. Lawyer McCampbell says Pete's a sinner. He tells a lie: Pete loves God, fears the devil, and hates snakes. He doesn't play cards, except when the truck is up. He doesn't horse race, except for fun, and when there is a sure chance to win. He doesn't drink liquor, except bald face whiskey, just to encourage our own 'stil houses. Pete don't wear two faces—lawyer McCampbell does. Pete don't go in the altar at camp-meeting and hug the gals—lawyer McCampbell does—Marting Van Buring aint an Irishman—he is a Dutchman, and the Irish and Dutch are always fighting. Who is lawyer McCampbell? Nothing but a mischief maker. Didn't he persuade Dan Looney to sue Jim Cole for the cows and calves he lost on the *Warping Bars*? Dan dars'nt deny it. He can't kill a bear. Why, he would starve to death in the woods, with a good rifle, and old General Jackson and *Sharptooth* to keep him company. Now, if you want to run the thing in the ground, just elect him. Pete don't ask any man for his vote; all he asks is fair play.

PETE WHETSTONE."

I guess that will bring them to their senses. I am going to make a stump speech at the county court, and the way I'll use up that lawyer won't be slow.

Don't tell anybody: *sister Sal is going to be married;* but she will put it off till *after the election.* I tell you, Sal is a great gal;—she makes all her sweethearts believe she is going to have them, and they go their death for me. There will be a fuss when the thing leaks out; but I don't care.

I aint no time to tell you about a big bear fight I had before I went to Batesville. So, good bye; but don't forget to say Marting Van Buring aint an Irishman.

Ever yours, PETE WHETSTONE.

[7] PETE WHETSTONE AGAIN

DEVIL'S FORK OF LITTLE RED RIVER, (Ark.)
May 15, 1837.

Dear Mr. Editor,—We have had fun of the right sort; Jim Cole gave a fellow hell—I'll tell you how it was. Lawyer McCampbell sent word to Little Rock that if they didn't do something for him, he was a *gone 'coon.* Soon as they got the letter, they writes to Fayetteville to lawyer McK. *Blue-belly,* telling him he must bring in some fellows from *Benton county.* This being arranged, they sent over *Coffee-vault* to see how the *thing* was working. Well, now, last Saturday, at the muster, he and Jim Cole came together. Jim told him that the Devil Fork boys didn't want any chaps from *Chapel Hill Township* to come and tell them how to vote. Says he,—"I have hearn tell of you fellows on *Cravat Creek,* and I know if Pete goes to the Rock, he won't *steal checks* from a *faro bank.*" I guess *Coffee-vault* turned mighty pale, for *he* is the *chap* what brung in the *"beef bones* for the *pure ivory"* on old Asa last year, when the Legislature was in session.[1] So says he, "Mr. Cole, if you mean me, you are a liar." The next minute Jim was on him like a duck on a June bug, and in less than no time made him sing out.

Text: *Spirit,* 7 (10 June 1837), 132.

1. "Coffee-vault" is probably Noland's name for William G. H. Teevault, the Prosecuting Attorney for the northwestern portion of Arkansas; "Asa" was Asa Thompson, a gambler and member of the Arkansas General Assembly. In a capsule biography of Thompson in "Early Settlers of Arkansas.—No. 4," *Spirit,* 19 (12 January 1850), 559, Noland repeats this episode: "He [Thompson] was terribly taken aback by an honorable member, whom he had just aided in electing Prosecuting Attorney [Teevault], attempting to slip in false checks upon his book. Old Asa detected and exposed him, by telling him, he 'could'nt wring in his beef bones, for the pure ivory.' "

I just want to get hold of lawyer McCampbell—I'll make him think a buffalo bull has horned him. He has put out a circular—I know it was made at the Rock—*Thieving Talleyrand, preposterous Buck and Pukee, of cow-hided memory,* wrote it for him. Here is a copy:—

"To the Democratic Citizens of Devil's Fork—Fellow citizens,—The attack made upon me by Pete Whetstone calls for a few remarks. All great men have their enemies; how, then, can I hope to escape? Pete asks who I am: I will give him my history. I was born of democratic parents—I was brought up democratically—the democratic State of Virginia gave me birth—I moved to the democratic State of Missouri, and now live in the democratic State of Arkansas. I have ruined a good constitution in the great cause of democracy. Pete Whetstone is an aristocrat,—yes, he was in favor of the United States Bank.[2] And if such men as Pete had have administered the government, instead of the 'Hero of Orleans, and the savior of his country,' why, what would have been the consequence? I'll tell you what you would see: why, the same distress and derangement in money matters that you witnessed eight years ago;—you would have seen rail-road banks put down[3]—yes, fellow citizens, it took the democracy to learn the people to bank without specie capital. Look at the results—New Orleans is in a most flourishing condition, so is New York, and all the other big cities; cotton is worth 18 cents, and every kind of produce is high; the banks have confidence in each other, and so have the merchants in them all. Eight years ago, when that vile institution, the United States

---

2. The Second Bank of the United States was granted a twenty year charter in April, 1816. When, in 1832, Congress passed a bill to recharter the bank for another ten years, Jackson vetoed the measure, touching off a controversy which lasted for years. Excellent treatments of the difficulties surrounding the Bank are Arthur M. Schlesinger, Jr., *The Age of Jackson* (Boston: Little, Brown, 1953), pp. 74-114; and Arthur Cecil Bining and Thomas C. Cochran, *The Rise of American Economic Life* (New York: Scribner's, 1964), pp. 210-219.

3. During the depression of 1837, many railroads and other businesses issued their own currency. Usually this currency took the form of promissory notes and were frequently severely discounted or rejected altogether. This, like many other statements in McCampbell's circular, is a clear distortion of fact. Contemporary readers would, of course, recognize the fallacious nature of McCampbell's statements.

Bank, had full sway, these very cities were almost bankrupt; nobody would receive its notes, and cotton could scarcely be given away. Such are the fruits of democracy. And because I am an advocate of those immortal principles, will you desert me? I have stood side by side with the great Tom Benton,—I have fought the good fight in company with Wm. C. Rives, Amos Kendall, Frank Blair, and Reuben Whitney. All that story about Benton and the cravat, and Whitney and the treasury, is false.[4] They are innocent, persecuted men. The enemies of General Jackson abuse them just to hurt his feelings; that is the reason they abuse me.

"Can Pete Whetstone frame a law?—I guess not. Look at my digest—(though that story about the stray law coming under the head of *Judicial proceedings* is rather agin me, I confess)—aint that a nice book? [5] Vote against me and you show yourselves enemies to General Jackson."

Well, now, the lawyer beats hell amazingly. All that are stuff about the banks is lies. Nobody won't take rail-road money, and I saw right in the last paper where most everybody in Orleans was broke. Now I have hearn people from North Carolina say, that "Tom Benton learnt a curious fashion of *wearing a stiff cravat* while he was at college."

I'll catch the lawyer at the doggery next Saturday, and I'll try him on the stump. I have got three or four newspapers laid by, and I'll prove him a *liar* right before all the people. Now, I don't know much about *banks,* but I do know that these *democrats* are

---

4. Specific details concerning Benton and a "stiff cravat" have not been uncovered; however, he has frequently been described as extremely arrogant, conceited, and vain. See Claude G. Bowers, *The Party Battles of the Jackson Period* (New York: Octagon, 1965), p. 319; and Schlesinger, p. 60. His vanity may well account for this peculiar fashion note; however, the number of such similar allusions to Benton's cravats suggests a more specific origin. Whitney, one of the early directors of the Bank of the United States, was a spokesman for state banks. He apparently wanted to organize the state banks into a substitute for the Bank. Such a move would have relocated government treasury deposits.

5. This sentence suggests that Lawyer McCampbell might be based upon James McCampbell of Jackson County, who, with John Steele, digested the laws of Arkansas Territory. All other features of his character, however, are fictional.

always mighty *hungry* after *notes* with *Nick Biddle's* name on them.[6]

In haste, ever yours, PETE WHETSTONE.

[8] LETTER FROM PETE WHETSTONE

DEVIL'S FORK OF LITTLE RED RIVER. (Arks.)
June 5th, 1837.

DEAR MR. EDITOR,—I am as safe as a *Limmon,*—I have laid out old McCampbell.[1] Here is the result:—

	WHETSTONE.	McCAMPBELL.
Raccoon Fork Township	...9	27
Devil's Fork Township	39	 4
Owl Creek Township	18	12
Kinderhook Township	14	16
Total	80	59

If the election had have come on three weeks ago, he would have beat me. But Tom Jones and Bill Hightower got from Orleans about ten days before the election. They carried down a flat boat of steers and hogs, and got a tolerable fair price. But they were real ranting, roaring democrats, and took their pay in paper money, such as the *Planter's Bank of Mississippi,* because Martin Van Buring and Gen. Jackson both said this sorter

---

6. The United States Bank currency carried the signature of Nicholas Biddle, the president of the Bank.

Text: *Spirit,* 7 (8 July 1837), 166.

1. In a letter appearing on the same page with Pete's letter, Noland comments on the election: "I saw 'Pete' a few days ago; he is safe in his election, as some of McCampbell's friends brought from Orleans lots of paper on the pet banks, and the people won't take it, and the way they curse *Van* is about right."

paper was better than U. S. Bank notes.[2] When they got home, they found the newspapers full of dreadful accounts about broken banks, and the *Planter's Bank* was on the list. They have tried to get off their money, but the boys are too smart to take it; so they turned right into abusing Van Buring and old McCampbell, and the way they spread themselves for me was a caution.

Sister Sal was married two days after the election;—now just guess who she took? Why, Jim Cole, I don't like the color of Jim's hair, but he didn't make it, and it aint his fault.[3] He is all *horse,* I tell you, and when it comes to real hard fighting, give me Jim. He whipped two fellows from *Cravat-stuffing* Creek. Bill Spencer was sick, and didn't go to the election. Jim went down to the Rock to get some finery for Sal's wedding. Lord, you ought to hear him tell about what he saw; he heard them trying a fellow for murder. He says the lawyers made all sorts of speeches, and that lawyer McCampbell aint no more to them than a *pole cat* to an old *he.* He said one of them that they called the State's Feliciter, told the jury that "he warnt *arter blood,* but he wanted the prisoner, if he was guilty, to die the *ignominious* death we all had to die—for, gentlemen of the jury, he hurried a man of good *kerrecter* into the presence of an *unjust God.*"

Jim bought him a *long-tail blue,* and a sure enough fur hat, and the way he struts now is sorter *peacocky.* I guess Jim will be running for a *militia officer* before long.

Bill Spencer and Dan Looney have made another race; they run three hundred yards, with 60 pounds on each. Bill Spencer runs the "Hyena" against the "Charmed Bullet." [4] They bet four cows and calves, and 1000 pounds of *mast-fed* pork. I think the

---

2. The Planters' Bank of Mississippi was established in Natchez by action of the Mississippi legislature in 1830. During the panic of 1837, it refused to honor the notes of the United States Bank. The Planters' Bank, which had extreme difficulty in remaining open during the panic, failed completely in 1840. See Porter L. Fortune, Jr., "The Formative Period," *A History of Mississippi,* ed. Richard Aubrey McLemore (Hattiesburg: Univ. and College Press of Mississippi, 1973), I, 251-283; and Ben B. McNew, "Banking, 1890-1970," *A History of Mississippi,* II, 312-333.

3. In letter 1, Pete mentions that Jim's hair is red.

4. In "Races at the Salt Sulphur Springs, Va.," *Spirit,* 9 (7 September 1839), 319, Noland applies the name "Charmed Bullet" to a horse running in one of the races.

Hyena can lay him a dot. I am going over to Batesville this Fall to see the big races, and I mean to go my death on "Independence." I got your paper t'other day for the first time, and before I could read it through, somebody packed it off.

Changing the subject, there has been a heap of scandal started in the *rattlesnake neighborhood,* all growing out of a camp-meeting they had about six months ago. Old aunt Peggy Sims told me t'other day, with a sorter of smile, that the *rattlesnake gals* had out-*fattened* anything she ever saw; and, says she, what else could be expected when they make a *circuit rider* of such a handsome young fellow. Let me tell you one thing. "Pete," says she, "I am now seven-and-seventy years of age. I have been used to camp-meetings all my life, and I never knew it to fail, that *nine months after them* there was *three times as many babies born* as at any other time of the year."

Ever yours, PETE WHETSTONE.

[9] BULLETIN FROM ARKANSAS [Excerpt]

They have had a great quarter race on the Devil's Fork, between the *"Burnt Blanket"* and the *"Busted-shot-gun;"* Jim Cole made it with a travelling man. He rode a ketch on the Burnt Blanket to 140 on the Busted-shot-gun. They broke it up in a squabble, and had half a dozen fights; they beat, bruised, and amalgamated the stranger till his head was big as a bushel. He was good pluck, and fought manfully. Pete writes me the particulars, and I rather think Jim practised off the *Van-ism.*[1] *Burnt Blanket* got about two feet start, and beat out about 9 inches. Jim

---

Text: *Spirit,* 7 (8 July 1837), 171; signed "N."

1. Recall that in letter 6 Pete equates "Van Burenism" with thievery. The implication here is that Jim's actions were less than honorable.

had wrung in a *foul judge,* and he swore enough to cover the case—they at length made it a *draw* race.

[10] MATTERS AND THINGS IN ARKANSAS
[Excerpt]

I shall visit "Pete's" neighborhood in a few days, and will spur him up to give you a letter. He writes me, that if the *Legislature* don't interfere with him, he will slay the varmints this winter in the right way. He is going to revenge the death of poor Stephen Harris, who was killed a short time since by a bear at the mouth of White River.[1] This was a most melancholy accident. Harris was a good fellow, and has left a wife and large family. It is the only instance in which I have known an Arkansas hunter killed by a bear. H. was an excellent hunter, and met his death in his anxiety to release his dogs, who had the bear at bay; in approach-

---

Text: *Spirit,* 7 (29 July 1837), 188; signed "N."

1. The newspaper account of Harris's death differs slightly from that of Noland. The *Gazette* of 13 June 1837 reported the event thus:

Horrible Encounter with a Bear.—On Monday the 5th inst., near the Mouth of the White River, STEPHEN HARRIS, (the keeper of a public house on the river), went out with a friend, Mr. F. J. Keen, on a bear hunt. It was not long (after they were out) until Harris encountered one of the largest and fiercest bears in the forest. He fired on his game two or three times, wounding him badly, but not mortally for the moment; seeing his antagonist still struggling, and making fight, he determined to close in on him with his large knife, in preference to shooting again, at the risk of killing some of his dogs, who were surrounding the bear; but when he advanced pretty close, he found he had lost his knife, and in this posture his enemy sprang at him, taking out a portion of the bowels, almost at the first grasp. In a few seconds, he tore loose and parted the *femoral artery* and he bled to death instantly, only having time to exclaim, "I am killed."—His companion came up at the time, but all efforts to save him, were in vain. He has left a large family, and was esteemed a good citizen.

This is truly a melancholy end to one of our oldest hunters! He has been one of our hardy and sturdy pioneers of this wilderness; and heretofore, has always made these denizens of the forest cower to him, having slain his thousands in his day.

It is impossible to determine which report is the more accurate.

ing, his foot caught in a vine, and he was precipitated into the very jaws of the animal, who at one *hug* made a perfect mash of him.

[11] PETE WHETSTONE'S VERY LAST

DEVIL'S FORK OF LITTLE RED RIVER, Arkansas,
July 10, 1837.

DEAR MR. EDITOR.—Well, I reckon some of them horses, way over the Mississippi, can beat shot out of a shot gun. I read JIM COLE all about *Mingo,* and his cutting off a 3rd heat in 7:47.[1] He wont believe it.

I have just got through with my crop—may be I aint got a big show for corn.

Since the election, the lawyer's as mute as a wild cat, with his head cut off. We have all sorts of fuss here, about our *bank.*[2] Here is just about the way the thing stands. The last Legislature made a bank—they elected an officer of the army, a Capt. Brown, President of it. There was a mighty fine man run against him—one that come here when the buffalo were thick on White river.[3] But he and Brown barked up different trees. He took

---

Text: *Spirit,* 7 (19 August 1837), 212.

1. The report Pete says he read to Jim Cole is in the 24 June 1837 issue of the *Spirit,* p. 148. It revealed that Mingo won 15 out of 20 starts and had the 7:47 for a third heat. The writer, probably Porter, concludes that Mingo is among the best horses of his time.

2. The Arkansas Constitution of 1836 provided for the incorporation of a state bank. Considerable controversy and difficulty surrounded the bank for the first ten years of statehood. See Ted R. Worley, "The Arkansas State Bank: Ante Bellum Period," *Arkansas Historical Quarterly,* 23 (Spring 1964), 65-73.

3. Brown's opponent in the race for the state bank presidency was apparently not as clearly a candidate as this letter suggests. The contemporary press does not mention another contender for the position. Pete is possibly referring to John Ringgold of Batesville, Noland's father-in-law, who was one of the chief advocates of a state bank. He and Anthony H. Davis of Chicot County drew up the bank charter; see the Batesville *North Arkansas,* 6 September 1843, p.n.n.

White Oak, Brown *Slippery Elm.* Of course Brown beat him. Well, Brown's friends said he would quit the army—but he hasent done it.[4] He has been away East, and we cant find out what he has done. The papers say he got a *cashier at $3,000 a year!* (Oh lordy, hold my hair.) It has been well nigh 9 months since he was elected, and we aint no nearer a BANK *now* than we were *when we started.* I dont know much about the banks, but when I get to the Legislature I must look wise and say something.

I must tell what a pedlar said here the other day. Why he said Uncle Sam was *broke.* Well now, was'nt that a big lie. Why he could buy all Devil's Fork and have a pocket full of money left. These pedlars are cute chaps—one of them got a *pack of peltry* out of Dan Looney once, by selling him a little box of *Bengal salve,* swearing it would *heal up a wound in a day, and hair it over in twenty-four hours.*[5] Dan would have knocked him into a crackling if he could have laid hands on him after he found out he was cheated.

Is *Alicum Guiacum* so heavy that four ounces weighs a pound? Old Thorp of Batesville says so, and he is a snorter. The way he trims apple trees is a caution. He works by the job and has his *board* thrown in. You ought to see him *shovel victuals* into his mouth. Eating dont take away his appetite—three corn dodgers, four big biscuits with grease to make them go down, and a quart of coffee dont make a meal. He is one of your *crane* built fellows, and walks with his head hung down as though his mammy weaned him too early.

I shall go over to Batesville races. Jim Cole has a "bite" that he thinks he can "wing in" on some fellow, and make all our expenses. Bears are getting plenty as blackberries, but it wont do to hunt them now, for they are too poor for meat, and they use a

---

4. The fact that Jacob Brown retained his commission as Captain in the United States Army at the same time he served as president of the state bank caused numerous outbursts from his opponents. A public meeting in Fayetteville denounced him; see *Arkansas Gazette,* 14 November 1837, p.n.n. Several Whig newspapers also condemned this situation. Eventually the opposition became so great that Brown was forced to resign on 20 November 1837; see *Arkansas Gazette,* 21 November 1837, p.n.n.

5. In Pete's letter of January 1841 (number 40), a similar experience is reported. In that case the wonder drug Dan Looney purchases is called "Holloway's Ointment."

dog plump up this hot weather. I'll show them sights this fall, after the Legislature breaks up.

We are rigging up for the camp meeting, so I must cut this off in haste.

Ever yours, PETE WHETSTONE.

[12] LETTER FROM PETE WHETSTONE

DEVIL'S FORK OF LITTLE RED RIVER, (Arks.)
Sept. 10, 1837.

DEAR MR. EDITOR,—Well, I suppose you think PETE's forgot you. It ain't so. The fact is, I have been monstrous busy;—I have had a *heap of fodder* to pull, and then I had to go to Batesville to enter a 40 *acre tract.* I tell you I'm mighty proud to hear "Pete's" put in the "Sporting Magazine" *over the Big Waters.*[1] When I read JIM COLE what you say about "Pete," I tell you he danced like a pea on a hot griddle.[2] I had 'bundance of fun over at Batesville. Your friend "N." carried me down to Capt. TUNSTALL's to see all his race horses.—I tell you I saw some crowders.

First and foremost I saw *Charline,* the mare that is to run against *Old Bill.* She belongs to Capt. TUNSTALL & C. F. M. NOLAND, Esq.[3] I tell you she is a nice cretur, about 15½ hands high,

Text: *Spirit,* 7 (7 October 1837), 265.

1. Letter 8 was reprinted from the *Spirit* in the September 1837 issue of the London *New Sporting Magazine.*

2. Evidently Pete refers to a note appearing under the title, "To Readers and Correspondents," *Spirit,* 7 (15 July 1837), 169, in which Porter says the *Spirit* is always delighted to receive letters from Noland, Pete, and others. He concludes, "The truth is no poor devil of an Editor ever was gifted with a more intelligent, entertaining, or excellent a circle of correspondents than him who pens this grateful acknowledgement."

3. The stable of Capt. Thomas T. Tunstall of Batesville almost completely dominated the Arkansas turf from 1835 to 1845.

of a deep rich bay, with black legs, mane, and tail, with one grey foot, the finest stifle and thigh I ever saw, beautiful thin shoulders, nice bony head, big nostrils, good back and loin. I tell you she is a nag for my money, and if Old Bill beats her Pete Whetstone is a *"ruined woman."* Then I saw *Ella Wickham,* a clean limbed brown, 3 yrs. old, by Volcano, out of a— I don't know what. She is a clinker, and the way she runs is a caution. She is old Volcano out and out, and if Charline don't break me I drop my *kit* on her. Then I saw *Margaretta,* a great big sorrel 3 yr. old filly. She is full of wild oats and vinegar, runs like a little steamboat burning pine knots; she is by old Bertrand. These were all the nags in training. I saw old *Volcano*; the way he used to run was about right, and the way his colts, out of all sorts of mares, run is pleasing to those that breed from him. I think if he had a fair *shake* with Eclipse, Priam, and the other big cattle, they couldn't make their bread come off of him.

Then I saw some great mares and colts; a Stockholder mare, belonging to Col. RECTOR and Capt. TUNSTALL. She is a large, well-formed brown mare. She has a great two year old called *Bob Crittenden,* by Volcano, and a sucking colt by Tom Fletcher, called *Ben Desha. Southern Belle,* by Mercury, and full sister to *Coahoma,* has a fine sucking colt by Tom Fletcher; it is small, but made like a deer. *Rebecca,* by Palafox, has a 2 yr. old colt and a yearling filly, both by Volcano. The colt is called *Lycurgus.* Then there is a nice 2 yr. old out of Zephyr (full sister to Southern Belle), called *Little Red*; he is by Volcano. A large, fine looking mare by Randolph's Rob Roy, called *Emeline*; she belongs to Capt. Tunstall & C. F. M. Noland. These were all I saw. I must tell you something about CULLEN MANLY, that trains for Capt. Tunstall. He is a free *yaller* man, but honest and honorable as any *pale face.* He is a great trainer, and then he is so polite and attentive when you go to see his horses. He is mighty careful and industrious, and his employer has unbounded confidence in him.[4]

---

4. The facts presented here appear to be true. Manly was Tunstall's trainer, and Tunstall, as Pete notes, had great confidence in him. Noland, in *Spirit,* 11 (27 March 1841), 42, mentions that Manly had transported Tunstall's horses to northwest Arkansas for the spring races. Manly was in complete authority; Tunstall did not make the trip.

Upon the whole, I was mightily taken with my visit. On our return to Batesville, we went by the *Springs*, a brisk place, I tell you. Why, the doggery where Jim Cole and Dan Looney raised the fuss about the *Warping Bars* and the *Bussing Coon* ain't a priming to it.

We lit and took a *horn*. I never see such a *cardy* place before— old *sledge, poker,* and *three up,* all going on. As I stept up, says one fellow, "I'm a mighty man to bet."—"Yes," says another, "I'm a mighty man to anty."—"Fifty cents," says one.—"Two and a half better," said a quiet, steady looking fellow.—"Out and gone, like Grouger's eye," said the first fellow.—"Six bits blind," said a sorter cross-eyed looking fellow; "go in if you dare," and then he commenced singing—

> As I walked out by the light of the moon,
> So merrily singing this old tune,
> I come across a big raccoon,
> A sittin' on a rail.
> A sittin' on a rail, sleeping very sound.[5]

"D____n your raccoon—I'm in for your blind mighty man to see blinds."—"I make it good," said the cross-eyed fellow, "on *two small pair*."—"*Three little ones*," said the other fellow.—"Good as hell," said the cross-eye. I went over to the "*Seven up*" fellows. "That sets me four times," said a fellow with a head like a *hurrah's nest*. "Not quite so fast," said his opponent, who was a double-fisted fellow, with shoulders like an ox, though the way the *figure of fun* was cut over his eyes showed he had been in a *hornet's nest*. "I'm a mighty man to count," said the first fellow.

At this I left them, and joined friend "N." Says he, "Pete, there is a *frolic* here to night, and they say we must stay."[6]—"Good,"

---

5. This song is probably the same as "Old Zip Coon" (compare Pete's letter 28), which appears in a list of fiddle tunes from rural Alabama appearing in Carl Carmer, *Stars Fell on Alabama* (New York: Literary Guild, 1934), p. 276. The title also appears in a list compiled by John Q. Anderson; see *With the Bark On*, p. 130. "Zip Coon" was composed in 1834 and quickly became a classic of the early minstrel show and one of the earliest successful popular songs about the Negro. It was introduced by the minstrel Bob Farrell at the Bowery Theatre in New York on 11 August 1834. See David Ewen, ed., *American Popular Songs: From the Revolutionary War to the Present* (New York: Random House, 1966), p. 468. The melody survives as the classic "Turkey in the Straw."

6. This writer has reprinted the following excerpt of this letter, pointing out its accurate depiction of a frontier play-party, in "An Early Arkansas 'Frolic': A Contemporary Account," *Mid-South Folklore,* 2 (Summer 1974), 39-42.

says I.—"Well," says he, "we must go and put our nags up and give them their oats." "Now," says he, "Pete, we will step over to the quilting, and I'll show you some great gals." Over we went. Says he, "Ladies, I'll make you acquainted with my friend Mr. Pete Whetstone, of the Devil's Fork." Says I, "Ladies, I hope you are all well;" and with that I sidled off to one corner where a mighty *putty* gal was setting. The way I talked to her was about right. After a little, says I, "Miss, did you ever see Sally Jones?"— "No, Sir," says she.—"Well," says I, "she is prehaps the puttiest gal on all the Forks of Little Red; and what's more," says I, "she is the pictur' of you!" I tell you, this made her blush. So after a while they asked us out to dinner; we had all sorts of good things. Soon as dinner was over, they rolled up the quilt, and called on the *fiddler.* I led out the putty gal. "What shall I play?" asked the fiddler. One wanted *"All night there,"* another *"She wouldn't and she couldn't, and she wouldn't come at all."*[7] Says the fiddler, "I can't please you all, so here goes *'My Roaring River.'* "[8]

Well, we kept the floor hot till about ten. "N." then proposed a play; so at it we went. May be you never saw one of these plays, so I'll just try and tell how we fix things. First and foremost they set a chair in the middle of the floor, then they set a gentleman in it, a couple walk round the chair, singing as follows: [9]—

A little boy *sot* down to sleep,

---

7. "All Night There," probably a popular song of the day, is now unidentifiable. "She Wouldn't and She Couldn't, and She Wouldn't Come at All" was apparently widely known. George Washington Harris mentions the same title twice in his Sut Lovingood yarns; see "The Knob Dance—A Tennessee Frolic," *Spirit,* 15 (2 August 1845), 267; rptd. in Inge, *High Times and Hard Times,* pp. 44-53; and "Sut Lovingood's Big Music Box Story," [Chattanooga] *Daily American Union,* 11 December 1867, p. 1, and 12 December 1867, p. 1; rptd. in Inge, *High Times and Hard Times,* pp. 184-189.

8. "Roaring River" appears in a list of Ozark fiddle tunes, taken from the work of Vance Randolph, published in Duncan Emrich, *Folklore on the American Land* (Boston: Little, Brown, 1972), pp. 128-135; Randolph's original list appeared in *Midwest Folklore,* 4 (1954), 81-86.

9. The melody for the first portion of this game-song is that of "Nancy Dawson," a popular ballad in eighteenth-century England; see William Chappell, *The Ballad Literature and Popular Music of the Olden Time* (1859; rptd. New York: Dover, 1965), pp. 718-719. The melody was used in "The Beggar's Opera," where it was a hornpipe among the thieves. The tune is still sung in children's games such as "Here We Go Round the Mulberry Bush." The remainder of the game may be related to "Marching Round the Levee." See Newman Ivey White and Paul F. Baun, eds. *The Frank C. Brown Collection of North Carolina Folklore* (Durham: Duke Univ. Press, 1952), I, 119-122.

Sot down to sleep,
Sot down to sleep,
A little boy sat down to sleep, so early in the morning.

He wants a little gal to keep him awake,
To keep him awake,
To keep him awake,
He wants a little gal to keep him awake, so early in the morning.

Sugar is sweet, and so is she,
And so is she,
And so is she,
Sugar is sweet, and so is she, so early in the morning.

What do you say her name shall be?
Her name shall be,
Her name shall be,
What do you say her name shall be, so early in the morning.

Miss _____ her name shall be,
Her name shall be,
Her name shall be,
Miss _____ her name shall be, so early in the morning.

Then the gal he chooses takes his place, and he joins the singers. They repeat as above, except "that vinegar is sour, and so is he," &c. We work on this way until we get all the young folks into the snap; then comes the cream of the thing. The first person chosen sets down in a chair, then we all join hands around him and sing:—

Come brothers and sisters and join us in marching,
Every one his true love *sarching*,
   Fal, lal, de lal, de la.
Call your true love now or never,
Call her by her name and tell her how you love her,
   Fal, lal, de lal, de la.
It is oh my honey, and oh how I love you,
None on earth I adore above you,

> Fal, lal, de lal, de la.
> My heart you have gained and my hand I'll give you,
> One sweet kiss and then I'll leave you,
> Fal, lal, de lal, de la.

At the second verse you pick out any gal in the ring, and she sits down by you; at the last verse you smack her lips the right way.

Well, we played and danced till just afore day, when "N." and me put out for Batesville. I believe I sorter fell half in love with that putty gal; her breath is just like new honey-comb, and the way she is smart is about right. I kinder hinted to her that she had made a hole in my heart. "May be, Mr. Whetstone," says she, "you have got a *tarrapin egg heart.*" This sorter bluffed me. Says I, "Miss, Pete has a *rale watch crystal heart,* when you once knock a hole in it, the *dog's dead.*"

I was tickled during the night at a little thing that happened. We were redeeming pawns—selling them over "N.'s" head. Says the auctioneer, "Say, what shall be done with the owner of this?"—"Why," says "N.," "he shall get down on his knees to the gal next to him and say—

> I'm down on my knees,
> I'm up with my paws,
> I'll thank you, kind Miss,
> For a smack at your jaws.

Well, it so happened that the pawn belonged to Christopher Ivings, and he was sitting next a gal that he was going to marry in two or three days. All eyes were turned on Christopher, and he swore "he would die fust." So they had to let him off.

Well, I am now at home. What do you think of lawyer McCampbell's turning Whig? I tell you he is warm in our cause. I believe he will stick to the track, and I told him I would give way to him next time. It made him as proud as a dog with a bunch of red roses tied to his tail. My paper has gin out.

Ever yours, PETE WHETSTONE.

[13] LETTER FROM PETE WHETSTONE

DEVIL'S FORK OF LITTLE RED RIVER, (Arks.)
Oct. 13, 1837.

MY DEAR MR. EDITOR,—Don't think Pete has forgot you because he hasent writ you often of late; the truth is, he has been monstrous busy. He has been to the Batesville races, and had lots of fun there. As he has a heap to write, I reckon the best way is sorter to put it under different heads, touching first on things in general, and secondly, on horse racing in particular.

Well, while I was away, the President's message came: [1] all wanted to know what was in it; and as a good many of the Devil's Fork chaps can't read small print, Jim Cole moved that lawyer McCampbell mount a stump and read it to the crowd. The lawyer read it out in all sorts of style, and when he got through, give his sentiments. He is right agin it plum. He said if the United States Bank was a *monster,* the Treasury bank would be a *double monster,*—that the former was no more to the latter than a wild cat to a painter. What killed the critter the deadest of all was that the old law of gold and silver for land still remains. [2]

Well, just about this time two keen chaps from New Hampshire, came into the settlement with a load of clocks. They said they were cousins of Isaac Hill, a great big man in that State.

Text: *Spirit,* 7 (11 November 1837), 305.

1. Pete's reference is to President Van Buren's address to both houses of Congress at the opening of the twenty-fifth session, 4 September 1837. The text was published in the *Arkansas Times and Advocate,* 25 September 1837, [pp. 1-2]; and *Arkansas State Gazette,* 26 September 1837, [pp. 1-2]. In his message Van Buren specifically rejected the concept of a bank and espoused what was later to be known as the Sub-Treasury Plan.

2. Van Buren continued the effects of Jackson's Specie Circular of 11 July 1836. See letter 1, fn. 1.

They commenced persuading the Devil Fork boys that they were all in the dark; told them that there was a new party called loco foco, (I think that is the word,) that was worth all the parties. Well, Dan Looney asked them to tell him how they worked it. Jim Cole said he wanted to know. Bill Price said he would like to hear, and lawyer McCampbell insisted on his being let into the light. They up and tells how that the *loco focos* were the *real friends of the people*—that they went in for *equal rights*—that *all men were born equal,* and that the word equal meant that *every man* was entitled to an *equal share of property.* Well, this here took with every one except lawyer McCampbell. So next day they agrees to commence the business with Dan Looney; over they went. "Now," says Isaac Hill's cousins, "we will show you practically what loco focoism means." So they asked Dan how many horses, cows, sheeps, hogs, &c. he had? Dan up and tells them. "Now," says they, "we will divide them out equally among all of us that are here." Says Dan, "I be d____d if you do." Says Jim Cole, "This aint the clean thing." "I think they are swindlers," cried Bill Price. "Let us give them hell," roared all. I tell you they used them awfully; they beat, bruised, and amalgamated them until they looked like the last of an ill-spent life. They have sneaked off. Their experiment failed, and loco focoism is knocked into a cocked-hat on the Devil's Fork.

They have had all kinds of times in Jackson County at their late election. Such chat about a *white bull* and a *sow and pigs*; and then there was a *heifer* and a *steel trap.* I tell you it beat all; like to have been fifty fights—the Vans were used up. I don't think the *white bull story* was the sole cause of it. You ought to have seen the boys when their blood was up: the way they shed their shirts was sinful. An old fellow that was present told me he "never seed so many yaller hides in all his life."

Well I reckon it is time I was saying something about the races.[3] You have heard how *Charline* used old *Bill* up. I tell you,

---

3. Noland's official report of the Batesville races had appeared one week earlier in "Batesville (Arks.) Fall Races," *Spirit,* 7 (4 November 1837), 302. That account is parallel with Pete's. Charline, owned by Noland and his friend Thomas T. Tunstall, won almost $2500 as a result of defeating John Safford's Sir William.

she just run right away from him without any sorter trouble. Old
Bill had the track when they first started, and his friends thought
he would run right off from the mare. They barked up the
wrong tree; for the Roman Senator on the mare nailed him in
less than two hundred yards from the starting-post.

The track was mighty heavy in some places, and the time was
good—6:24—6:20. Nearly all the crowd were on old Bill, and
when the mare came out ahead there was no shouting, not like
when Bill beat Independence. The mare is a great animal, and
can beat old Bill always; she would be a troublesome customer
anywhere. The mile day was poor fun; the Bertrand filly
brought here by a Mr. Broadfute was beaten. She is a tolerable
mare, but Volcano has lots of three year olds, from dung-hill
mares, that can beat her from a—b, ab to crucifix. By the by, this
Mr. Broadfute sold a br. 4 yr. old horse by Bertrand, and *represented him as never having been trained,* but *Bob Smith* says he *distanced him.* I tell you Volcano never got a colt that can't distance
him. All Mr. Broadfute's Bertrands turned out badly.[4]

For the two mile day, Mary Ellen, by Sir Charles, dam by
Contention, and Ella Wickham, 3 yrs. old, by Volcano, out of a
Scrub, contended—both off; but Ella in a manner dead. Time,
4:34—4:10, Mary winning both heats—Ella close at her heels.

The saddle races created abundance of fun. Mr. Frazier's b.g.
won the $50 saddle in two heats; four entries, two distanced the
first heat.[5] For the second saddle we had a beautiful race, put up
and put up on each. Once round, lacking 110 yards of a mile; 2d
nag to receive martingale and bridle.

Maj. Wm. F. Denton's r.g. *Warping Bars* 1
Col. C. F. M. Noland's s.f. *Kate Longworth* 2
John S. Loring's g.f. *Ozark* ....dis
Time, 1:51.

---

4. Pete's comments concerning "Mr. Broadfute" and Bertrand's colts prompted an
angry response from James H. Bradfute of Franklin, Tennessee, apparently the person
to whom Pete refers. The long letter appeared as "Look Out, Pete Whetstone," *Spirit,* 7
(6 January 1838), 372. Pete's rejoinder is letter 23.

5. Noland's account gives the name of Ephram Frazier's gelding as Tom Benton.
Defeated in the race were a horse named Fork of the Devil and another named Devil's
Fork.

A close race between Kate and the Warping Bars. Jim Cole wrung in his *bite,* and the way the Devil's Fork won money was a sin to Moses. But I havent time to tell you all, so I'll put it off for another letter.

I leave for the Legislature in a few days, and I'll give you a letter from the Rock. Jim Cole says he will call his first boy arter you.

Ever yours, PETE WHETSTONE.

[14 UNTITLED]

DEVIL'S FORK OF LITTLE RED, (Arks.)
Oct 14, 1837.

DEAR MR. EDITOR—I writ you on yesterday, but being as how I have some leisure time to-day, I thought I'd give you another letter.

There has been the mischief to play over in Pope county. Lawyer Coffee Vault[1]—the man what swung in the beef bones on *Old Asa* last winter, and the same man that is Prosecuting Attorney, elected by the _____ *Legislature,* has got himself into a tight scrape. Here is about the way the thing was: his animal passion—I believe that is what the scholars call it—got the up-hand of his prudence, and he tried to indulge on a thirteen year old gal, whether or no. She made oath of the fact, and he is now in as tight a place as a varmint in a steel trap. Lawyer McCampbell says he is mighty sorry of this indignity to the pro-

---

Text: *Spirit,* 7 (11 November 1837), 305.
1. Pete speaks of Coffee Vault (William G. H. Teevault) in letter 7. No mention of his having been charged with rape appears in the contemporary press.

fession; but thank God he left the ranks before the accident happened.

Now for the varmints:—bears are thick, and JIM COLE has the best team of dogs I ever saw; he swears he will make the fur fly this winter. Jim is a mighty hunter, and when he starts a bear the thing is certain. There is 'bundance of bitter mast this year, and by this time three weeks bears will be fat; but then I shall miss all the good hunting this Fall—so much for being a *Vig Legislator*. They do say we are to have lots of fun at the Rock; and then the races come on during the session, and old Bill is in soak for *Charline*. DICK HAUKINS has got a hard string to beat; and then MAJ. RECTOR's *Metamora* is a caution; and the way the Major stands up to his horse is the right way. Maybe you don't know the Major? He is a gentl. in any crowd, with a heart as big as a barn door: he will hit a lick in a minit for a friend. I tell you he is all sorts of a good fellow.

Ever yours, PETE WHETSTONE.

[15] LETTER FROM PETE WHETSTONE

DEVIL'S FORK OF LITTLE RED RIVER, (Arks.)
Oct. 21, 1837.

MY DEAR MR. EDITOR,—Well, I have had a great chace with an old *he*—fought *him* from the dry fork to the Brushy Lake— the way Jim Cole's dogs made the fur fly off him was about right. He was good meat, and his ribs were right slick I tell you.

Lawyer McCampbell liked to have had a fight with a big fellow that moved in from old South Carolina. It commenced about John C. Calhoun and the banks. Lawyer McCampbell said he

---

Text: *Spirit,* 7 (18 November 1837), 316.

was fearful *Mr. Calhoun was going to join the tory ranks.* No sooner did he say it, than *South Carolina* walked right up to him, and looked him full in the face—the Lawyer went on to say, that he was afraid *Mr. Calhoun was growing jealous of Henry Clay, and that he wanted to run for the Presidency himself.* Right at that I saw South Carolina double his fist. McCampbell kept on—says he, *"Calhoun has shaken hands with Benton;"* this was more than South Carolina could stand, and he blazed right away at the Lawyer, but I fended off the lick, and stept right between them. "Come gentlemen," says I, "don't fight." The blood of South Carolina was up, and it was no small matter to calm him. Says he, "Pete, I hated to hear Calhoun accused of joining the tories, but I stood it—and then to say he was jealous of any man; but I stood it and said nothing—but when he said *John C. Calhoun shook hands with Tom Benton,* I couldn't stand that." "Come, friends," says I, "make up." "Well," says the Lawyer, "I didn't mean to hurt any body's feelings." At that South Carolina gave him his hand, and the thing was made up on the spot.

Lawyer McCampbell went home with me that night. After supper we had a long chat. He gine me some good advice when I go to the Legislature. Says he, "Pete, the United States is in a bad old way—I have been reading Mr. Secretary Woodbury's report, and I tell you it is a mystified document.[1] I can't make head or tail of it—I think, Pete, he is troubled with a *kimerion* of the brain, as old Culp said of Squire Archy. He is no more fit to be Secretary of the Treasury than a *tumble bug* for a lady's pet. Whetstone," says he, with great emphasis, "nothing can save us but *Old Tippecanoe*—the people believe strong in him, and I don't think they will give him up. Then we must have a bank of the United States—one whose notes are good every where. Now, Mr. Whetstone," says he, "what sort of money have you got to carry to the Rock?" "Rail Road," says I—"one ten, two fives—one of them a little ragged—and two dollars and five bits in shin plasters." Says he, "they will shave you, Pete." Says I, "I carry my

---

1. Woodbury's complicated treasury report, dated 5 September 1837, was published in the *Arkansas State Gazette,* 3 October 1837 [pp. 2-3].

own razor." Says he, "you don't understand me—I mean they will discount your paper." "Do what," says I. "Why," says he, "they will take twenty cents out of every dollar you have got." "Well, if they do," says I, "some of them 'll get shaved with a bone razor." "Keep cool," says he. "I will," says I. Well, the Lawyer went to bed, and next morning started early.

I shall have some more talk with him before I go to the Rock. We will have a right smart fuss about our own banks—the President of the mother bank is ordered to the Florida wars—at least that is the news here—and you must know he is a captain in the army, and *bound to obey instructions,* even if he wornt a democrat.[2] So I expect we will have to get somebody else in his place.

Old McCampbell has been a trip to Izard, Lawrence, and Randolph—he says his heart bleeds to think of the ignorance he found—*nigh on one half of them think Gen. Jackson is still President.*

Ever yours, PETE WHETSTONE.

[16] LETTER FROM PETE WHETSTONE

DEVIL'S FORK OF LITTLE RED RIVER, (Arks.)
Oct. 30, 1837.

DEAR MR. EDITOR—Our Court is just over—'bundance of lawyers—lots of fun. Jim Cole took sister Sal up; they gave us a big *blow out:* the way we had kissing and dancing was about right. The Racoon Fork said they could beat the Devil's Fork dancing: right at that Tom Blackjack led out sister Sal, and Jim Cole Miss Bittry Brewerton—Dan Looney led out his partner, and Sam

---

2. Details of the circumstances surrounding Captain Jacob Brown's presidency of the Arkansas State Bank are given in letter 11. Brown's resignation occurred on 20 November 1837.

Text: *Spirit,* 7 (2 December 1837), 333.

Jones led out a nice little gal; the fiddler struck up "all night there," and Nicholas *Hard-to-beat* and Esquire *Up-to-snuff*, were chosen as judges. I tell you, it was real shuffling—so good and so good for a long while; at last the judges said they had decided. "Who wins?" says I,—"Devil's fork," says they; "for," says Nicholas, "that *last shake* of Mrs. Sally Cole took the corn;" the Coons didn't like it at first, but they soon got reconciled, and every thing went off well—I tell you them Clinton chaps go in for pie-doings, and I heard one of the loungers say that they fed him so high he had lost his toe nails.

Lots of business in Court—every fellow that had struck a lick was tucked up; State *vs.* Old Hombuckle was one case;[1] the States Attorney wrote his name Cormbuckle—the Defendant's Attorney plead not guilty and *misnomy*, I think; the jury said as how they thought the States Attorney had a right to spell as he pleased, because they said Judge Screviner, our member of Congress, spelled *Bowels* with a *K*—so poor Hombuckle was found guilty. One fellow came in scared to death, and acknowledged the crime like Deck Cornwell did when he jined the church—says he, "Oh, Lord! I knows I am a sinner, and one of the meanest sort." Wiley, *a-perfect-case*, was at Court; he has hair about a foot long. Nicholas says he has known a *louse* to swim the Devil's Fork to git to his head for *winter range*. Lawyer McCampbell is at the Rock; I got a letter last mail from him— here is a copy:

LITTLE ROCK, Oct. 24, 1837.

Dear Pete—I thought I would write you a few lines to-day. Well, I went over to Buck's office yesterday. He was mighty polite, and soon commenced abusing you. It made my blood boil, but I said nothing; presently in comes Wapponoca: says he, "Buck, I want the last Spirit of the Times"—says Buck, "take it and welcome, for I have struck the vile paper from my exchange list;" at that I felt my dander rise, but said nothing. Soon as Wapponoca went out, Buck commenced: "Lawyer

---

1. Noland gives a delightful account of a trial in which Uncle Tommy Hombuckle is a witness in "Bulletin from Arkansas," *Spirit*, 7 (8 July 1837), 166.

McCampbell," says he, "we must beat Whetstone next time, because he is a bold chap and tells too much truth; do you think," says he, "a thousand dollars in gold and silver will do the business?" says I, "may be so," for I still was playing possum. Says he, "lawyer, why didn't you tell about General Jackson and the great democratic principles?" says I "*that* was what used me up;" at that he begin to smell a rat—so he twists and turns about a good deal; at last says he, "are you a Whig, Lawyer McCampbell?" Says I, "if the truth must be told, *I am*." "You traitor," says he; "softly" says I, "don't call hard names Buck, for you know what I know— besides you know *what happened right in this office once:*" at that Buck turned pale and began to apologise: says he, "Lawyer McCampbell, you would have been appointed minister to Texas if you haden't left our party." Says I, "Buck, I went with you hand and heart as long as I believed your conduct was honorable, and that the good of the people was your aim—I scorn your offices—I believe you are corrupt, and wash my hands of you." Wasent that the right way to lay it down to him?—right then in walks *Pukee.* Says he, "Mr. McCampbell, how do you do? I hope you are well—cheering news—the Democracy are triumphant:" at that Buck winks at Pukee: this sorter put him to a stand. Says he, *"I'm coming,"* and went right out. "Excuse me a few moments," says Buck; this was hint enough, and I put out. You must come down a few days before the Legislature meets; board is high and the town crowded: you will have a heap of business to do. The Coddifiers are ready to report[2]—they have adopted the New-York code in honor of Martin; I don't think it ought to be adopted, because the people expected the laws were to be digested, not a new code introduced. The Bank pays out a little

2. In 1836 the Arkansas legislature authorized the codification of the state's laws. This massive volume was prepared by Samuel Calhoun Roane, president of the Senate, and William McKissick Ball, a member of the Senate, under appointments by the governor with the approval of the Senate. Instead of making a systematic arrangement of the laws passed by the Arkansas General Assembly, Roane and Ball drew upon the laws of other states as well, so that action by the legislature was necessary to put several of the laws in force in Arkansas. Some legislators, including Noland, voiced strong objections to the content of the new code of laws. See Ross, p. 152.

silver; their notes aint as good as Nick Biddle's paper—for you can't get Nick's paper for gold or silver. No more at present. Best respects to Jim Cole and Sally.

Your friend, McCAMPBELL.

To Mr. Pete Whetstone, Devil's Fork.

I start to the Rock to-morrow, and will give you all the news. Old *Tom Fletcher* distanced *Shakspeare* the first heat.

In haste, ever yours, PETE WHETSTONE.

[17] LETTER FROM PETE WHETSTONE

LITTLE ROCK (Arks.)
Nov. 16, 1837.

DEAR MR. EDITOR,—Pete has been here a week and better, but he has been so busy that he couldn't write to you. This is a great place, and we can have lots of fun every day. Legislating don't suit Pete's genius—he has found that out. I have been prowling about pretty considerable, and the way I have seen some right sights is about right. And would you believe it, the Circus is here. I went last night. I tell you what, that spotted fellow they have along made fun. If they would just go to the Devil's Fork, I reckon they would make money. The way them chaps ride is a caution. I guess they would be great on a bear hunt. Then there was one fellow lifted three great big anvils at once; may be he aint all horse; I reckon he could knock the filling out of Jim Cole; and they laid an anvil on his belly and hit it with a sledge hammer; Spot said it settled his supper. I guess it did. And then the way a big nigger did sing Jim Brown and Raccoon on a rail. Oh, I tell you it was funny.

Text: *Spirit*, 7 (16 December 1837), 348.

"There was a little pig, and he lived in clover,
And when he died—he died all over."

But I am going again to-night. Well, they invited me to a party—I didn't like much to go, because I was afraid I wouldn't know how to act—but lawyer McCampbell said I must go. Well, I got me a new coat, and spruced up pretty slick, I tell you.

I started about 7—I tell you I never see such sights before— the way there was nice looking ladies was right. The finery Jim Cole carried sister Sal wasn't a priming to it—and then such dancing. Says one gentleman, "Mr. Whetstone, don't you dance." "I reckon I does," says I. "Well," says he, "let me get you a partner." "I am much obliged to you," says I. At that he led me up to the prettiest sort of a gal. "My friend Mr. Whetstone, of the Devil's Fork," says he. "I hope you are well, Miss," says I. Oh, Lord, may be she didn't smile sweetly on me. Says she, "Mr. Whetstone, how did you leave your sister Sal?" Says I, "mighty well, Miss, I thank you." Just right at that, up comes a ghost-looking chap, and says he, "Miss, will you allow me the pleasure to dance with you." She bowed, and he led her off, leaving me standing like a widow's pig on a cold morning. Thinks I, you'll catch it, Mr. Ghost, for your smartness, when a fellow tapped me on the back. "Come, Col. Whetstone, (he was a candidate) and take some apple toddy." "I don't care if I do," says I. I told him how Ghost used me. "Oh," says he, "that is a small matter, and you must not get mad." I asked him how I could get to dance, for I wanted to show them a few Devil's Fork steps. He said he would introduce me to a partner. "What must I do then?" says I. "Bow to her, and ask the pleasure of dancing with her," says he. Well, he introduced me to a nice little critter, I tell you. Says I, "Miss, will you allow me the extreme pleasure of dancing with you." She said she would. Out we went. Well, the first motion after the fiddlers struck up, showed me I wasn't in the right place. I got scared, and couldn't get the figure; says one of them, in a whisper, "Mr. Whetstone aint up to *kertillions*;" at that says I, "ladies and gentlemen, excuse me if you please, I am in the wrong row now, for I never got higher than a reel in all my life;" at that they all commenced giggling: this made me mighty mad.

After a while they said supper was ready; I tell you I never set down to such good things before—I just wish Cole could have seen it.

Well, Capt. Brown is going to resign his office in the bank: he has made a good President, and I go in for giving the devil his due.[1] Well, the fuss about the State Bank aint a primin to what is going on about the *Real Estate Bank.*[2] B.B. couldent get to be President, and the way Tallyrand and Buck are mad is awful. I went into the Senate yesterday; the way Z. was preaching agin it was a sin: Wapponocca answered him, and said he, Z., was a stockholder, and jist because he couldent be a *director* he got mad. It all won't do; the Bank will flourish, for it has got into *honest hands.* In a great hurry,

Your friend, PETE WHETSTONE.

[18] LETTER FROM PETE WHETSTONE

LITTLE ROCK, (Arks.),
Nov. 29, 1837.

DEAR MR. EDITOR—Well, Pete is worn out *making laws.* Bear hunting is another sort of fun to what is going on here. The circus have put out; I couldn't get them to go to the Devil's Fork, tho' I told them what lots of money they could make. I got a letter from Lawyer McCampbell last night: he gives me lots of

---

1. Pete speaks of the Brown controversy in letter 11.
2. The 1836 Arkansas Legislature, in addition to creating the State Bank, also created the Real Estate Bank. It was owned by individual stockholders who mortgaged land to the state in order to buy bank bonds at $1000 each. Its main branch was at Little Rock, with branches at Washington, Helena, Van Buren, and Columbia (Chicot County). It began operations on 12 December 1838 and was soon in financial difficulty. It stopped paying in specie in 1839 and failed altogether by 1844.

Text: *Spirit,* 7 (30 December 1837), 368.

news.—Sister Sal has had a fine boy, and Jim Cole is proud the right way; Jim sends word to me to make haste back—he says the *bear* are thick on the *dry fork.* My ambition is satisfied. I have seen more villains here than would hang a regiment in a civilized country.These here pure democrats are cautious: the way they talk about the honest mechanic, and worthy farmer—the bone and sinew—and all such stuff—and at the same time they wear the best of broad cloth, fur hats, and the like. I tell you it is all a mistake about these sort of people loving the people: some of them come under the head of General Jackson's description of Reuben Whitney—they are *"persecuted patriots."*[1]

Well, I guess the *porter flew* in the big race at New-York.[2] If that Lady Cliffden aint all horses, I am mistaken, and Picton and Fanny Wyatt are jewels; Old Mingo being lame was a great misfortune. If he aint the best horse in the world, my name aint *Pete Whetstone.* Why John Bascomb has had the slime knocked clean off him by this *big race*—7:44—7:43½—7:56½—

"Oh, where did you lay last night—
Oh, where did you lay last night?
I lay behind the bed,

To see that *fat gal* shake her leg.—Oh, little boy—little boy, get out the way."

I expect we are going to see horses run the four miles in 7:37—7:40.

Well, I am mighty sick of this place; I want to be in the woods—this here sort of life they live here, is killing *Pete.*

They have got me in a frolic two or three times: they had the *curiosest* sort of cider I ever see;[3] when they pulled the cork out of

1. If Jackson actually made this statement, it has not been located. He is, in fact, quoted as saying quite the opposite. ". . . He [Whitney] is as true a patriot as ever was. . . ." See Bowers, p. 458.

2. Pete's comments concern the report of the New York Jockey Club Second Fall Meeting held at the Union Course, Long Island. The complete account of events is contained in the *Spirit,* 7 (4 November 1837), 300. The race was termed, "the most splendid race ever made in America." It drew a crowd of 30,000. Four horses were involved: Lady Cliffden, the winner; Picton, second place; Fanny Wyatt, third place; and Mingo, which was lame at the beginning, having a swollen right foreleg, and was unable to finish the race. It was run on Friday, 3 November 1837; the purse was $1000.

3. The "cider" to which Pete refers is, of course, champagne. He provides more detail of its appearance and effect in letter 21, where he uses the same simile.

it, it cracked like *Dry Bones* drawing his foot out of a *mud hole*—I tell you it's great cider; I thought after a while that I was a horse—I tell you I felt big: the way some of them got funny, and the way they told good stories, was about right. It is a great drink to knock *possum* out of a fellow. Well, when they got through, some went to fight the tiger, and the way the tiger scratched their eyes out was spiteful.—They aint had any parties here since I wrote last, tho' Capt. Pendyerit, of the steamboat *Little Rock*, gave us a great *blow out:* the *brass band* with Jim Brown at their head were along. The way they danced and had fun was right. The captain is cut the right way of the leather; that wan't slow, I tell you.—Well, we have some big speeches in t'other House: the way they say "Banks are contrary to the genius and spirit of republican institutions, and subversive of the great rights of the Democracy, as secured to them by blood spilt by our forefathers, who fought and bled in the revolution." *N.B. I picked up that scrap.* I am in a hurry, so good bye.

Ever yours, PETE WHETSTONE.

[19] LETTER FROM PETE WHETSTONE

DEVIL'S FORK OF LITTLE RED, (Arks.),
Dec. 24, 1837.

MY DEAR MR. EDITOR,—Well, here I am, safe at home. The Legislature adjourned for a month, on account of the *small pox.* They were tired, and only wanted a good excuse. Well, I aint writ you for a long time. We had a bloody fight in our house—I tell you it was dreadful slaughtering—the way the big knives were

---

Text: *Spirit*, 7 (27 January 1838), 397.

pulled out, and such a slashing—it was awful.[1] But I reckon a man has to pay now for toting a knife, pistol, or other dangerous weapon. Well this here is a mighty fluxible world, as Dr. Kraft said—perhaps you dont know Dr. Kraft. Well, he is a perfect crumpification of cases, and the way he figured at Randolph Court was a sin to Moses—lots of inditements for gambling—just playing a small game. Well, Kraft was a witness in every case, and they do say he and the States Feliciter were in Cohoot. Kraft made as high as $13 one day by being witness.

Well, what do you think? Some of my enemies up about the blowing cave, are trying to injure me—they say I am too hard on the Methodists—that's a lie—Pete dont crowd on any body—he believes strong in the Methodists, but he scorns a possum wherever he finds him.[2] Pete don't apologise. He wishes to hurt no man, woman, or child's feelings, but like the Jack-ass dancing among the chickens, tells every body to look out for their own toes.

Well, after all, bear-hunting is another sort to legislating, and the way we are going to make the fur fly is funny. I came to Batesville, and saw N.'s rifle—the way she is a slick gun is right—I just wish I had sich a one, for if I had, I'd make the varmint see sights.

Pork is as high as six dollars, and scarce at that—nothing but a little *bitter mast*. Lawyer McCampbell is mixing strong among the people. He is bound to be elected.

---

1. Pete refers to a knife fight which occurred on the floor of the Arkansas House of Representatives. A brief note by Thomas J. Pew in the *Arkansas State Gazette*, 5 December 1837, reports the incident: *"Unfortunate and fatal recontre!*—Yesterday, about 1 o'clock, an affray occured, between Col. John Wilson of Clark County, (Speaker of the House of Representatives), and Maj. J. J. Anthony, (late a member of the same house, from Randolf county,) which resulted in the instant death of Maj. Anthony." On 6 December the Speaker submitted his resignation in the House chamber. Action on this resignation was tabled, and "so as such undignified behavior would not be forgotten, a resolution was passed to expel said speaker." Noland was one of the few who voted against expulsion, feeling that Wilson's resignation was valid. See *Arkansas State Gazette*, 12 December 1837.

2. Possibly the reference to Methodist preachers in Pete's first letter is the source of the complaint against him. In that letter he says, "Squire Woods . . . makes no more of belting a quart [of bald face], than a methodist preacher would of eating a whole chicken." No record of any such complaint exists.

The New York elections have reached the Devil's Fork—such a gitting off the fence I never did see—Turkies sliding, as Dr. Kraft would say. By the bye, Dr. Kraft used to be in the big Legislaturs—he is a perfect knight of the blue riband, and the way he drank Muscat for Buck when he was at the Rock, was sinful—when they handed him biscuits at a party, says he, "I thank you, sir, these will do me," and the way he handled the sweet bread was awful. He is going to try agin—if he fails, he starts for the State of Greene.

To-morrow is Christmas, and I have lots of eggs. The way I'll walk into a bowl of nog in the morning will be nice. Sister Sal and Jim Cole are well, and their boy is a bulger. I forget to tell you—the citizens gave us a splendid ball at the neck—it was in the State House—four sets dancing at one time—reels for the benefit of the Sub County Members—the way Pete went it was a caution—he got as high as cotillions. Such pretty ladies I never did see. Lots of good things at supper. Well, there is no mistake, but cotillions are a huckleberry above reels. I am sleepy now, so good night.

Ever yours, PETE WHETSTONE.

[20] LETTER FROM PETE WHETSTONE

DEVIL'S FORK OF LITTLE RED,
Dec. 30, 1837.

MY DEAR MR. EDITOR,—Pete's in a passion—the way his dander is up is nothing to nobody. I have just heard from Batesville, that some of the people are mad about that letter what I

Text: *Spirit,* 7 (3 February 1838), 405.

writ you about my trip to the Springs, way last summer.[1] If any body says I meant a slur on any body, he tells a big lie, and what's more, I'll thrash the ticks off him in a minit, if I can find him out. I know how it is come about. Ever since I talked of leaving the Devil's Fork, and settling in Independence, the Van Burenites have been trying to injure me.[2] I reckon I guess I know who they are, although, while they are cutting deep, they stand mighty far from the blood. One of them tried *twenty-seven* times hand running to get in the Legislature. He got in once—next to his partner, he is the greatest man, in his way, west of White river. He is a perfect thing—lays *two eggs* every day—on Sunday *three,* and occasionally drops a *nutmeg*.

Pete would look well making fun of people who treated him as well as they did at the Springs—besides, Pete has been on the Devil's Fork these twelve years, and is real Arkansas every inch of him.

I will start over to Batesville to-morrow, and I'll make some of them smell a worse smell than the Kentuckian did.

Well, I have had one bear fight since I come back—it wan't much of a fight—Jim's pack nailed in half an hour's run, and pinned it so close that Jim killed it with his butcher knife. It was an old she, not very fat, but tolerable eating. There is but little frost this year, and bear will be scarce, except in spots—the way deer and turkeys are fat is a caution—they always thrive best when there is but little *acorn mast*.

We are to have a big quarter race on New Year's Day, 'twixt the *Biling Pot* and the *Chawed Bullet.* Jim Cole and Dan Looney

---

1. Pete's reference is to letter 12, in which he speaks of attending a frolic at the Springs. N[oland], "Letter from Arkansas," *Spirit,* 7 (27 January 1838), 396, refers to this situation: "Well, Pete came up [to Batesville] with me—he is much improved by his trip [to Little Rock], and his prejudices against *certain men and horses* have been laid a-side. By the bye, some *trifling scoundrel* came well nigh ruining Pete, by inducing the good people to believe that his description of the Springs and the frolic there, was intended as a slur on them; but I went down to a big frolic in the bottom on Christmas, and squared everything. If Pete cotches the chap, I reckon he will pay dear for his politics." Whether anyone actually voiced a complaint is unknown.

2. Today the Devil's Fork is situated in Cleburne County; when the Whetstone letters were written, Cleburne had not yet been created, and the area was located in Van Buren County. The "Van Burenites" are the natives of that county.

made it—they carry 100 lbs. on each. The Devil's Fork chaps are going it with a rush on the Biling Pot, though from what I can learn, the Chawed Bullet picks it up like mice a-fighting. I am persuading Jim to pay the forfeit, for the Biling Pot gets so full of wild oats and vinegar, that there is no dependence in him— but Jim won't listen to me, for he says he's a mighty man to bet on horse racing.

Ever yours, PETE WHETSTONE.

[21] PETE WHETSTONE AT A FARO BANK

DEVIL'S FORK OF LITTLE RED, (Arkansas)
Jan. 8, 1838.

MY DEAR MR. EDITOR.—This is the 8th of January—a day that wont be forgot soon, I tell you.[1] Maybe Old Hickory didn't give the British the hot end of the poker. He was jest the chap what could do it; and tho' he aint great at cyphering, when it comes to hard fighting, he was always there. If Pete's prayers could give him many years of quiet enjoyment, he would have them, for Pete always stuck to Old Hickory like a brother.

Well, I never told you about a little circumstance at the Rock. One night I was asked out to a wine party;—well I went. I found lots of fellows; they were all standing round a table, on which were placed long black bottles with lead on the top of them, and great long glasses, something like a wine glass—but they warnt wine glasses neither. Says one gentleman, "Col. WHETSTONE, the pleasure of a glass with you;" "My compliments to you," says I,

---

Text: *Spirit*, 8 (17 February 1838), 6.
1. Pete is commemorating the anniversary of Andrew Jackson's defeat of the British in the Battle of New Orleans, 8 January 1815.

and at that he pulls out a long cork. I tell you, it went like *Dry Bones* pulling his foot out of a mud hole. He filled up my glass; I swallowed it. "Very good cider," says I; at that they commenced tittering. "Another glass with you, Col. Whetstone;"—"I don't care if I do," says I, for I was always fond of cider. At that one whispered "be careful Pete, for that is *sham pain.*" "What?" says I, "sham pain," says he. "I reckon I knows cider," says I, and presently they commenced singing and telling stories. Give us *"Mr. Beeswax,"* says one—"yes, Mr. Beeswax," says another—and we got Mr. Beeswax.[2] It is a great story. I tell you that cider begin to work on me, and the way I felt sorter big was nothing to nobody; I just thought I could thrash an old *he,* fist and scull; I tell you the company begin to get mighty mouthy: one fellow was spouting some sorter strange language.—"What's that fellow saying?" says I: "Oh, he is talking Latin," says another: "Damn Latin," says I: "What do you mean?" says he, looking fierce as a wild cat grinning out of a black Jack—"I mean," says I, "that you had better neck your bullits, for that are chat you are spitting out all comes in one piece." At that one gentleman sees my veins rising, and he knew it was time to interfere, so he steps in between us. "Come, gentlemen," says he, "one more glass, and let us go and *'fight the tiger:'* "—"Fight the tiger!" says I—"If I cant thrash the ticks off the tiger, or any other varmint, my name aint Pete Whetstone.—Go it, my Devil Forks!" says I. Well, out we put, and at length came to a room—"Now," says one, "I'll shew you the tiger." In we went.—Well, what do you suppose they meant by the Tiger? why it was a *'Faro Bank'* on one side, and a 'Roll the Bones, and fair play,' on the other. The way they were going was a sin to Moses. "Bar Hock," says one fellow, "and I'll go it"—"Cant do it," said a queer looking genius, who was sitting bent like a keg hoop drawing cards out of a little silver box. "Has that man got the *cramp cholic?"* says I[3]—"No," says one, "it is a

---

2. Evidently "Mr. Beeswax" was a popular humorous anecdote of the time which was known to readers of the *Spirit.* Like several other titles in the Whetstone letters, it is now unidentifiable.

3. The physical appearance of the dealer may well be based on Asa Thompson, who is similarly described by Noland in "Early Settlers of Arkansas.—No. 4," *Spirit,* 19 (12 January 1850), 559; see Appendix 2.

natural way he has," and adding in a whisper "that aint the side of the table that is subject to the *cramp.*" The way they did pile up the *'bones'* was awful, and they were the *pure ivory,* none of your *beef bones.* I looked on awhile. It did seem a mighty nice game. Thinks I, I will risk just one dollar; so I pulls out a shin plaster and pokes her quietly, right flat-footed, on the ace. I watched her, I tell you: presently my heart begin to sorter beat quick: at last up she comes, and I won her; I sorter reached over to grab her, when one fellow said, "Col. Whetstone, the ace is a popper, let your bet sweat:" I'll take a fool's advice, thinks I: the next time up comes the ace: "I'll take them four dollars." Says I, "Mister, will you take something to drink?" "No, I thank you, sir," says he, "but I would like to borrow a $5 till morning, and upon the honor of a gentleman, I'll pay in the morning." Well, I pulled her out and give it to him. I tell you a gentleman's honor at a Faro Bank comes up missing sometimes—*I never got my* FIVE!

I walks around where a fellow was rolling a little marble in a wheel.—"27 Black," says he:—"Roll your bones," says a fellow who was "going it blind" agin him. I slips *a quarter* on the red— the little old wheel stopped—"single O by chance," says he, and at that he just swept the platter. I slips *a half* on the red—agin he whirled his wheel—up it comes—"double O" *by chance.* I tell you I begin to feel stuck, but laid up a dollar this time. He whirled agin—up she came—"Eagle," *by chance,* and he scratched over and raked off the whole pile. This raised my dander. "Mister," says I, "if you fling another O, I'll fling you, and if you fling *a buzzard,* I'll pitch you out of this window!" "'Pon my honor," says he, "it is all accident—them things will happen sometimes, gentlemen; I know I have a bad game for myself: why, at Orleans, one man won $18000 in one night playing against the game:— will you drink something, gentlemen—brandy, choice whisky, wine—some fine cigars." "Look here, Mister," says I, "bring in your cider in long bottles with lead corks, and I'll try some." "Jerry," says he, "tell Mr. Johnson to send me a couple bottles of the 'Fly brand';" right at that, some one tapped me on the shoulder—"Pete," says he, *"beware*—give me your pocket-book." I did so, and told him Pete was wide awake.—Well, the way they were going it was funny. "Damn that *coleu nine*," says a little fellow, that looked as if he was smelling something that warnt a rose. "She flung me for a pile." "I touched them that time," said a fellow with a frosty head:—"give us your bone on that—Dr. _____ always said I played them higher than any living man!"

"Tom, cant you give us *"All around my hat?"*—"Yes."

Young men they are so preciously deceiving,
Coaxing on the young gals, and leading them astray,
And when they deceives them, they runs away
And leaves them,
 And it is all around my hat, and
 I vears a green villow, all around my hat,
 For a twelve month and a day.[4]

"G____d damn your *hat*, Tom; how do you think I can keep the cases when you are keeping such a d____d noise?—where is my *bowyer*? Derringers for two!" "Last deal, gentlemen," said the crooked fellow that was pulling them out—"you must play the cases high to get out—crackers and gals at eleven—stewed fawn at ten."[5]

"The 'Fly brand' is coming—where is Col. Whetstone?" "I am here," says I. "Come, Tom, let us give this fellow's cider Hell;" "Certainly, friend," says he: "Shut the doors! there is a pocket-book lost." "I reckon, Tom," says I, "there is a heap of pocket books what is lost their bowels."—"You are right," says he. "Mighty good cider," says I, as I took the third glass of the *'Fly brand.'* Tom whispered to me. "Never mind," says I—"fool Pete if they can." "Come up, gentlemen—now is the chance to get back your losings—the more money you lay down the less you will take up," cried the fellow as he brought a whirl with his wheel:

4. The comic dialect song "All 'Round My Hat," was composed in 1838 by John Hansell (words) and John Valentine (music); see David Ewen, ed. *American Popular Songs: From the Revolutionary War to the Present* (New York: Random House, 1966), p. 12. A poem by the same title appeared without indication of author or source in the *Spirit*, 7 (3 February 1838), 408.
5. In Noland's biographical sketch of Asa Thompson, he describes Thompson as having advertised in the House of Representatives that he would be serving "stewed fawn and crackers at 10" as a means of encouraging other representatives to visit his Faro games. See "Early Settlers of Arkansas.—No. 4."

"Col. Whetstone," says he, "I'd rather you wouldent bet, I don't like the looks of your eye, but if you see something, say nothing!"—"Look here, Mister, none of your coming over me in that are style; I likes your cider mightily, but d____n me if I like your game." At that I left him. "How did you come out, Bill?"— "I had her up to 195, was playing for the 200—she went—such a deal you never saw—three double cards and the cat hop all won.—The *Gos* seven—Mulberry eight, and *Spanker* nine, all lost their cases. D____n old asy's soul, I'll never bet another dollar agin him as long as I live."

"Oh, Miss Sa-l-l-y, you cant guess what I have got in my pocket, and it is in my jacket pocket too?" "Cake?"—"no." "Candy?"— "no." "Oh, it is a knife?"—"no, it aint a knife neither, it is a rac____" "Come, Pete, let us go"—"agreed," says I, for the "Fly brand" was dying in me and I begin to feel like a wet day so home I went, and right to bed. Such dreams, oh, lordy; I thought I was a fighting an old *he*, and that he smashed my dogs right and left—but no more.

Ever yours, PETE WHETSTONE.

[22] PETE WHETSTONE'S LAST

Race between the "Worm-Eater" and "Apple Sas."

DEVIL'S FORK OF LITTLE RED, (Arkansas)
Jan. 28, 1838.

MY DEAR MR. EDITOR—So you have been all the way to the Big Orleans and woulden't pay us chaps on the Devil's Fork a visit.[1] I reckon, may be, you haden't time. Well, we will be glad to

Text: *Spirit*, 8 (10 March 1838), 29.

1. William T. Porter had taken a lengthy tour of the racing circuit. The trip began in November 1837 and required three months to complete. He visited such cities as Baltimore, Wheeling, Cincinnati, Louisville, Vicksburg, Natchez, St. Francisville, New Orleans, Mobile, Montgomery, Columbus, Augusta, Columbia, Charleston, and Washington; see "The Editor 'at Home,'" *Spirit*, 8 (17 February 1838), 4.

see you, come when you will.

The way there has been all sorts of fighting over on *Cravat-Stuffing Creek,* is a sin to Crockett. Here is just about the way it was: Dan Looney bet a feller two chunks of second rate cows and calves, that the *Worm-Eater* could beat Bill Stones' pony, *Apple-Sas,* one quarter of a mile, with put up and put on both.

Well, Jim Cole, Bill Spence, and me, went over the day of the race. Going along, says I, "boys, *they* will be hell here to-day." Bill Spence asked me what made me think so: "why," says I, "*Rube Honey* is going to turn *Apple-Sas*."—"Is he," said Jim; "well, just let me turn the *Worm-Eater* and I'll show him sights, for since Giles Scroggins died I can out turn any man on the face of the earth, and I would bet more money on it than I would on 4 aces." [2] "Well now," says I, "Jim, don't you have any thing to do with it, for I believe *Apple-Sas* can slam him." "Why Pete, you are crazy," says he, "for I can prove by Bill Spence that *Worm-Eater* aint more than 17 feet behind *Old Swayback* in a quarter." "Well," says I, "are you sure of that?" They said they were.—"Well, then," says I, "we can knock the fur off Rube, and you know he is a monstrous thief"—so on we went. Well, when we got to the *paths,* there was a heap of people gathered, so I slips in the crowd and shook hands with first this one and then that one. "Well, Col. Whetstone, how do you think the race is gwine?" said one fellow. I knew he was on *Apple-Sas,* so says I "*Apple-Sas* is the horse for my money"—"Good as hell," says he, "and I lay my pile on him."

Up comes Dan Looney. Well, Dan and me aint been mighty friendly since I had the big fight with him—so says he, "good morning, Col. Whetstone," "good morning, *Mister* Looney," says I. "How are you going on the race," says he; "I haven't bet yet," says I, "but if the *Worm-Eater* is in good fix, and Hiram rides him, I'll go a forty dollar horse on him." "Good as the thing you set on!" said *Zacky Stones*—"done, and done," was the word. At that

---

2. Since most horse races run on the frontier occurred over simple straight cleared tracks which had no starting gates, "turning" was necessary to insure a fair start. Horses were headed in a direction opposite that of the finish line; when the "word" was given the turner headed the horse toward the finish line and released him. Speed in turning, therefore, was of vital importance.

Dan winked to me, and out we went. "Now, Pete," says he, "without talking the thing over, let us just wipe out that fight we had, and be good friends:" "agreed," says I: "well," says he, "it is going to be a foul race—I see the thing working, and *Rube has wrung* in *Piney-woods Smith*." "Who judges for you?" says I—"why, I aint picked my judges yet," says he. "Well, you pick Sam Jones and Bill Spence—put Bill at the start, and let Jim Cole turn the *Worm-Eater*, and if you win the word and get the *bulge,* it will be twenty feet clear day light." At that up comes Bill Stones. "Are you ready, Dan?" says he; "I will be as soon as my horse is cupped," says Dan:—"here let us fling up for the track; toss, and I'll call," says Dan. *"I have nothing but shin plasters,"* says *Stones:* "spit on a chip and fling it up," says I. Up went the chip. "Wet or dry?" says Stones—"wet," says Dan. It was dry, and Stones won the path—he took the left hand path. "Toss her up for the word"—up she went again. Dan cried wet: she came down dry side up, and Stones had the word. By this time the crowd was thick; I looked up the track and saw Jim Cole leading the *Worm-Eater*. Jim was stripped to his pantaloons and shirt—his sleeves were rolled above his elbows, and his *red head* was tied up in a striped *cotting handkerchief.—Worm-Eater* looked slick, I tell you: he is a strawberry roan, about 14 hands 3 inches high, with heavy muscles and big bony legs. Jim stopped, and Looney's friends gathered round him. "There is a hind leg for you," said one—"that shoulder beats them all," said another: "give him hell, Hiram, and pay him down," said a third; while a fourth continued, "Jim against Rube." Presently up they led *Apple-Sas.* He is a light sorrel, with white face and legs, and one glass eye, great back and shoulders. Stones' friends gathered round. "There is a *picter*," says one: "made little *Old Vol*," said another: "*Champion's* shoulder," said a third: "a *panther's* hind parts," said a fourth. "A likely cow and calf on *Apple-Sas*," cried a fifth—"Dick Wilson knows the cow, and she runs on the Corny Fork." "I'll bet you my spotted steer that runs over on the Dry *Fork*, if you'll give me 10 feet," cried a lame fellow from the Raccoon Fork. "Give you what you can git." "No harm done," said the lame fellow. The fellow with the cow and calf begin to cavort. "*Apple-Sas* can make a perfect smash of all your d____d ticky tail horses: you daresn't bet; Dan Looney nor Dan Looney's horse haint no friends." "You darsen't give me 10 feet, any how," said the lame fellow. "D____n my soul, if I don't give you ten, and risk it, as Paddy did his soul." "Good," said the lame fellow, and called up the witnesses. "Let us drink," said *Apple-Sas's* friend, and over he went to a little old cart standing under a tree, with a barrel of whiskey in it. "Give us half a pint," says he, "and damn the difference— come up fellows and take a horn." "Well, I don't care, High-tower, if I do take a slug with you," said a long, crane-built, fellow. "Well, they say you bet *dot-and-carry-one, Nelson,* a cow and calf on *Apple-Sas,* and give 10 feet." "Yes, I did." "Well, I'm afear'd you are picked up." "What? why Rube turns, and Piney-woods Smith judges at the start." "You don't say so?" "It is a fact." "Then you are in town,—yes, it is just as good as the thing you set on."

"The riders are up," was the cry. I went up to the head of the paths; Piney-woods Smith, and Bill Spencer were judging the start, Tom Brown and Sam Jones were at the out come. The Worm-eater was quiet as a lamb, while the way Apple-sas fretted was agreeable to Dan and his friends. "Come up," says Rube, "and let us git a fair start, I know I don't want the advantage of you, and you look like a man that wouldn't take advantage of me." But Jim was wide awake, and never asked the word unless he had the advantage. Rube saw that Jim was no fool at turning a horse, and after about forty minutes spent in trying, let go when Jim asked. Away they went; the timber was poured on Apple-sas with a perfect looseness. I saw the Worm-eater had him at the out come, and the start was about a foot in his favor, for I stood right behind Piney-woods Smith. Well, down I went. I meets Hiram.—"How was it, Hiram?" "I beat him out about three lengths," said Hiram. I raised the shout. Dan Looney's friends roared. "Wait for the judges," says one fellow. "No use of judging," says I. "Why, the Worm-eater got twenty feet start," said Bill Hightower. *"Fight! fight!"*

I looked up the track. Rube and Jim Cole had yoked. The crowd gathered round them.—"Go it, Jim!"—"Go it, Rube!—

stand back and don't crowd them." "Hurrah, Jim!"—"Hurrah, Rube!" broke from fifty voices. I knew there would be hell to pay. "Close on him, Jim," says I; and Jim grabbed him and flung him. At that I saw Stones grab Jim's leg; I pitched right into him. "Give them hell!" shouted Dan Looney, and the fight became general.

"I am stabbed!" was shouted by Bill Spencer. I rushed to him and found him cut down. I saw who did it, for he still had the knife in his hand.

"You d___d coward, set to me," says I, as I drew my knife. The first lick I made slashed him right across the face, cutting his nose in two. I fended off his lick, and the next moment Dan Looney was betwixt us.

"Come, men, this won't do—put up your knives." "I'll have his heart's blood for his killing Bill Spencer," says I. "Oh, he aint hurt much," says Dan. Well, I agreed to drop it. By this time the fight was over; we had licked them from *a-b—ab* to *crucifix*.

"What do the judges say?" says I. "They can't agree," says Dan. "Why not?" says I. "Piney-woods Smith holds out for a *draw*," says Dan. "Swear them," says I.

Well, it was agreed we should all go up to Squire Burns and have the judges sworn. Up we went; when we got there, Piney-woods Smith said he wouldn't swear. That made me mad, sure enough. Says I—"Piney, you are, prehaps, the d___dest rascal unhung." "You are a liar, Whetstone," says he. Cherow I took him: he staggered, and Dan Looney jumped between us; he rared and pitched. Rube came up and talked with him and that quieted him. "Well," says Rube, "inasmuch as the judges can't agree, we are willing to *give up half the bet* and drop the thing, or else run it right over." Dan agreed to take half.

Well, then, they begin to drink; I had a quart set out, and told the crowd to come up. By this time I had got over my passion, and begin to look around and notice the boys; such a banged-up set I never saw before; but they soaked the liquor and commenced cavorting. Rube and Piney-woods gathered their friends and soon put out, not before they had flung out some mighty big bouters. Jim told Rube he wasn't cut the right way of the leather, and that he couldn't shine among gentlemen. Rube looked mighty mad, but said nothing, for Jim had used him up in their fight.

It began to get late, and we gathered our horses and started home with Dan Looney. On the way we talked it all over. Says Dan—"What chance would a stranger have in that crowd?" "None," says I. "Well, after all, we came out pretty well," says Jim. "I reckon I did," says *Dot-and-carry-one,* who was tolerable tight with liquor, I tell you. "A cow and a calf aint made every day," says he, and at that he broke out in a sorter hiccupping laugh. "Sing, Dot," says Bill. "I can't," says Dot. "I know better," says Bill; "give us raccoon on a rail." "Well, I'll try:"—
          "Oh raccoon on a rail, raccoon on a rail—
Ladies and gentlemen, I wish I may be squeezed to death in a cider press if here wasn't the same identical raccoon—
          "A setting on a rail, a setting on a rail."
"Oh, I can't think of it." "No wonder, Dot, for you are as full as a tick," said Dan. Well, we staid all night at Dan's, and next morning Jim and me went home.

I start back to the Rock next week. More legislating, though that are small pox will run them off agin, I reckon.

Ever yours, PETE WHETSTONE.

[23] PETE WHETSTONE ALIVE AND KICKING

LITTLE ROCK, (Arkansas)
Feb. 9, 1838.

MY DEAR MR. EDITOR—Pete is here again, tho' the weather has most froze him. Well, I reckon that Mr. *Broadfoot* thought he

---

Text: *Spirit,* 8 (24 March 1838), 44.

had used Pete plum up: why he is as fierce as a crippled wild cat in a green briar thicket.[1] Now, if he don't bite his own nose off some of these times, I am deceived. Well, arter all, Pete diden't mean to say that Mr. Broadfoot had "wrung in beef bones for the pure ivory," neither did he *insinivate* that Mr. Broadfoot wasen't the *ginivine* owner of the Mammoth Elephant Columbus' tusks carved into round pieces; all Pete said, was that Mr. Broadfoot brought on a sorry lot of cattle: the proof of the pudding is in chewing the bag, and Mr. Broadfoot's horses have had a good chance, and cant shine. As to Pete's abusing Old Bertrand, that won't do, Mr. Broadfoot—he is all horse—and Pete has always stood up for him, and that is just why he thought it strange that out of so many Bertrands none could run.

Look here, Mr. Editor, Pete aint easily scared, by a ripping-snorting-routing-roaring-studhorsical preacher, or a roller of Mammoth Elephant bones. Pete writes what he thinks, and if anybodies' toes are mashed, all he can do is to give them the jackass' advice when he heeled and toed it among the chickens. Pete has hearn tell of *horse heaven*, but he reckons them two chaps only ask to go to Martin Van Buring's *buzzum* when they die. Now, Mr. Broadfoot, if you can save your distance in a race with old *Old Vol*, with any cattle you brought on, you can make more money than you can do in a year by rolling the Mammoth Elephant Columbus' bones.

I wonder if Mr. Broadfoot ever hearn tell of the *Patent Cravat Stiffners invented by Tom Benton?* well, the way the "*Whetstones*" are given to use them up is a caution. Well, now, I reckon "this stone of Arkansas" has rather mashed your *toe*, Mr. Broadfoot—so just take this piece of advice: *don't raise Pete's dander.*

Ever yours, PETE WHETSTONE.

1. The controversy between Pete and James H. Bradfute of Franklin, Tennessee, began with Pete's letter number 13.

[24 UNTITLED]

DEVIL'S FORK OF THE LITTLE RED,
March 17, 1838.

My Dear Mr. Editor.—I have only time to say Pete's glad you have got back safe without being blown up in a steamboat, or mashed to death on a rail road.[1]—The new *"Spirit"* is a sweet critter.[2] Pete's compliments to Mr. *"Expedition,"* and will be glad to see him next Fall, tho' if *"spun truck"* don't suit him, he needent come to the Devil's Fork, unless he will stand *Flax in the Bundle*.[3] Pete is much obliged to him for his advice about politics, and the more so bekase "Expedition" believes strong in the *Cravat stuffer*.[4] Pete don't boast how much he believes in the Spirit, but I

Text: *Spirit*, 8 (14 April 1838), 69.

1. For details of Porter's trip, see letter 22, fn. 1.

2. With the first number of vol. 8 (17 February 1838), Porter resumed his duties as editor of the *Spirit*, which appeared in a larger format with clearer type. These features prompt Pete's compliment.

3. A letter complaining about the weight which horses carried in races appeared over the name "Expedition" in the 17 February 1838, issue of the *Spirit*. In it "Expedition" writes, ". . . the rage for *light weights* and *heavy sweepstakes,* like the 'paper and credit system,' is likely to make a nation of gamblers of us. And as long as these rages burn, we shall never have *heavy weights* on our horses, or heavy money in our pockets. (Here, by way of an offset to Pete Whetstone, I might introduce 'a right smart chance' of politics; but having a fear of injuring your paper *before my eyes,* and a good feeling for you *in my heart,* I will not give you even 'a small sprinkling.' Tell Pete if such are his feelings for you and yours to do likewise. Also tell Pete that next Fall, 'the Lord willing,' as the preachers say, I shall be at the 'Rock,'—that I will not run against the *Bussing Coon,* for I don't deal in that 'sort of spun truck,' but the way I will make the conqueror of *Sir William* 'see sights,' as the Kentuckians say, 'will be queer.')" No other information concerning the identity of "Expedition" is given except that he is from Illinois.

4. Thomas Hart Benton, with whom Noland associates cravats (see letters 7 and 23). Benton was a strong supporter of specie or heavy money, thus drawing the bitter attacks of the residents of the frontier where specie was scarce. To say that "Expedition," who advocates heavy money, is an apostle of Benton is, for Noland, a genuine insult.

reckon he is about good for 14 subscribers to her.—Does "Expedition" believe that strong? [5]

Ever yours, PETE WHETSTONE.

[25] A WORD FROM PETE WHETSTONE

DEVIL'S FORK OF LITTLE RED (Arks),
July 17, 1838.

MY DEAR MR. EDITOR,—Well, I reckon as how you are thinking Pete's dead—killed off, or married. The truth is, he is been monstrous busy, one way and another, for a long time, and 'twixt legislating, frolicking, and the crop, he aint more nor had time to read the *Spirit* and pick his teeth. Besides that, he has sorter been about half in love; but this here aint to be told to everybody; all he will say is, that the gal is a *sprinkling past common*.

They say they are going to have lots of fun over at Fort Smith this Fall, for DAVY THOMPSON and JOHN DILLON have bought the best nags that could be found in Tennessee and Old Virginy.[1] They are just going to mash up all the Arkansas nags. The way

---

5. Beneath Pete's letter, Porter appends the following: "*Nota Bene* by *the Editor.*—In a postscript of a private letter PETE says 'Expedition thinks I injure you by Politics—'tis all my eye! I think if he feels as much zeal as he professes in your welfare, he will at least outdo Pete in getting you subscribers; *God* knows how well I wish you, and "Expedition" may *think* as he pleases.' Our excellent and facetious friend 'has him there,' just as clear as mud; you can see it sticking out. Pete's letter containing the postscript we have quoted, covered $50, and we don't know how many more subscribers, after counting a baker's dozen, we stopped. We should like to catch 'Expedition' or any body else playing that game." For additional details concerning the importance of this letter in evaluating the impact of the Whetstone letters on the subscription list of the *Spirit*, see Williams, "Charles F. M. Noland: One Aspect of His Career," pp. 52-58.

Text: *Spirit*, 8 (25 August 1838), 220.
1. In "Sporting Epistle from 'N.,' " *Spirit*, 8 (10 March 1838), 30, Noland speaks of these horses: "Maj. David Thompson, of Van Buren, I learn has purchased $20,000 worth of horse flesh in the Old Dominion, among them some *screamers*." Later racing reports in the *Spirit* indicate that, while these horses did well, they did not prove as outstanding as Pete predicts.

them fellers up there will bet is sinful to a christian. Jist let the *Sister to Lady Nashville* and *Experiment* come together, and the way the fur will fly, will be amusing to a hatter. Well, I was reading about Experiment to Jim Cole, and lawyer McCampbell over-heard me: says he,—"That horse won't win." Says I,—"Why?"—Says he,—"His name won't do, for the *last Experiment* has failed."—"Good," says I.—"Right tight," says Jim.[2]

[26] PETE WHETSTONE AGAIN IN THE FIELD!

DEVIL'S FORK OF LITTLE RED (Arks.),
Nov. 8, 1838.

MY DEAR MR. EDITOR,—Aint you thinking what the devil has become of PETE? Why, he has been sick. Such shaking and burning;—but the way Dr. SAPPINGTON's pills can make a mash of all such small matters as chills and fevers, is agreeable.

Well, we had a warm time in our election; lawyer McCAMPBELL got in by the skin of his teeth; they started a report on him that he was a *"Koalitioner."* He said it was as hard packing as a sack of salt; but I won't say another word about politics, for fear some-body will get mad.

---

2. Pete's letter suddenly ends at this point, with the following note appended by Porter: "We are obliged here to break off abruptly at the bottom of the first page of Pete's letter. He 'writes with fury and corrects with phlegm,' we take it, for having neglected to *sand* the 2d and 3d pages of his letter, one page looks so much like both, you cannot tell the other from which! We consider ourselves 'a Philadelphia lawyer' at deciphering cramped pieces of penmanship, and can make out pretty much everything in Pete's letter as clear as mud, except the proper names, but these occur in every line, and we must incontinently 'barst in ignorance' until the advent of Col. Whetstone himself, which, thank heaven, is likely to occur next winter.—" The letter was never rewritten and published.

Text: *Spirit,* 8 (15 December 1838), 348.

The way there has been all sorts of fun at Fort Smith and Van Buren—and the way a looker into a week might have made a pile, was a sin; every day the crowd guessed wrong;—such odds, and it a-begging, I never saw. Then there was a little old wheel grinding all the time—"Eagle by chance," says the roller.— "Well," says a fellow who had lost his last quarter, "things come by chance mighty often here." The way they piled it up on *faro* was a sin—two and three hundred dollars on a card;—such cursing and swearing when they lost. Well, now, it does seem to me curious how people will bet their money that way—I can't see the fun of the thing. When a feller gits stuck, his last ninepence goes, and I believe he would mortgage his body for a stake. The way they will swear off, and all such stuff, and then like "the sow to her wallowing in the mire," as the good book says.[1] It aint Pete's business no how, and he will say no more about it.

Well, they had some beautiful races at Fort Smith.[2] *Charline* and *Widow Cheerly* were well matched, and the Widow was put up to her best lick to get the money.[3] Well, they runs in *Jim Townley* in a mile race, but the biter was bit, and Rube Honey's *Peter Simple* slaughtered him. There was a pretty race 'twixt Proof-Sheet, Kelarup, and Swob-tail—jist one round. Proof-Sheet had a little nigger rider, weighing about 45 pounds, that looked jist like a toad on a russock. Kelarup had little George, who weighs about 40, and Swob carried about 55 pounds. Proof-Sheet was in training, the others saddle nags—everybody won on her. Says one feller—"Kurnel, by _____, you owe me three dollars and thirty-seven and a half cents for beef: say six dollars and six bits, or nothing." "Good," says the Kurnel, and he took the field against Proof-Sheet. The beef cost him six dollars and six bits.

"Now look here, Mister Sims, how come you to let that bill pass

---

1. The reference is to II Peter 2:22 and deals with dogs, sows, and people reverting to their old ways.
2. Noland's official report of the Fort Smith races appeared in the *Spirit*, 8 (15 December 1838), 349. Many of the circumstances mentioned here are also included in that report.
3. Widow Cheerly was the winner of the race.

without saying something?"—"Now war'nt I *preposterous* on the occasion?"—"Yes, but why didn't you spunk up to the fellows?"—"Why didn't I? I guess I was *pusillanimous.*"—"But, Mr. Sims, you are wet; and come, go home with me."—"I thank you, I feel *absurd,* and am very *reluctant* to see my wife." I reckon that is what they call grammar. Oh Lordy! What a thing eloquence is; if you jist could have heard the big Washington County lawyer t'other day;—oh, he made the jury cry. Says he—"Gentlemen of the jury, it is a principle *congenial* with man from the creation of the world—*it has been handed down from posterity to posterity*—that in case of murder, drunkenness always goes in *commiseration* of damages."

Ever yours, PETE WHETSTONE.

[27] "MONSIEUR TONSON COME AGIN!"

DRY FORK OF BEAR CREEK,
Nov. 23, 1838.

MY DEAR MR. EDITOR,—Don't get ashy bekase Pete hasent been heerd of lately—here he is, way up on the Dry Fork of Bear Creek. Mighty curious looking varmints up here: but the way they can "rack back Davy," is a caution to the *tune*-maker.[1]

Text: *Spirit,* 8 (29 December 1838), 364. Used in the title, the name of the famous horse is applied to Pete as a compliment. Monsieur Tonson once traveled 1,200 miles through wilderness and over mountains, often having to swim or wade across rivers in the process, without interrupting his string of victories. See William H. P. Robertson, *The History of Thoroughbred Racing in America* (New York: Bonanza, 1964), pp. 44-46. For Porter to draw the comparison between Pete and Monsieur Tonson should have genuinely flattered Noland.

1. Evidently "Rack Back Davy" was a popular contemporary song. Noland, in "Bulletin from the Far West," *Spirit,* 7 (10 June 1837), 132, quotes the following verse:

Rack back, Davy, Daddy shot a bear,
Shot him in the tail, and never *toch* a hair.

There was a big gathering at Squire JONES' t'other day. Now, Squire Jones is like the nigger who said he *"warnt above drinking with a millisha osifer,"*—he aint proud. Well, we had all sorts of fun, and then the candidates treated and made speeches. Well, arter they all got pretty well through, up jumped old DICK SMIDT, and declared himself; says he, "Boys, I'se a candidate for de 'Sembly, and if you'll take promises, I'll promise so good as any man. I'll change de dog days from July and August to Janivary and Febivary, but dat would be very bad—it would be onmarkable hot, and snakes would be onpossible bad in de vinter." Well, old Smidt is a jewel. He was out buffalo hunting once, and staid *eighteen months* from his old lady; when he got back and saw her, she had altered so much that he jumped back and said *"Umph!"* Says she—"Why didn't you stay at home and *umph* yourself?"

Well, I have had some bully Bear fights here; but I heard from JIM COLE today, and the way he is walking into them high up on the Devil's Fork, is a sin to Moses. Talking of bears, maybe you never hearn tell the tight place HEDGE TRIPLETT got in. Well, here it is. Hedge was out hunting in the cane; he got on a log to cross a deep sloo, and just as he got well on to it, he heard the dogs coming, and the next thing he saw was a big old *he*, on the other end, coming towards him. Says Hedge—"Now look here, you don't look like a varmint that is going to give the road;—*I will.*" And down he dropped, in twenty feet water, gun and all.

Well, I've been down to the Rock; the way they have dressed up the State House is awful: sich plastering and kirly cues I never saw before.[2] Says lawyer McCAMPBELL—"Whetstone." Says I—"What?" Says he—"Look up."—Says I—"I see." Says he—"That is a sprinkling above the Devil's Fork."—"I reckon it is," says I.—"Well," says he, "there is no democracy in that: it looks just like a palace."—"A what?" says I.—"Palace!" says he. Says I—"Lawyer, *I pass!*"

---

2. The state capitol building, begun in 1836, had only recently been completed. It is an excellent example of Greek Revival architecture, which McCampbell evidently thinks is too ornate for a democracy.

Well, there has been all sorts of racing; but that *Grey Eagle* in old Kentuck takes bush, rag, and all—

"An Eagle's flight is out of sight." [3]

And *Omega* at Washington City didn't let the dirt stick to her feet. I hearn a fellow say t'other day that it didn't take some watches as long to go round as it did others. I don't know what he was arter. There was an awful howling on the heath when the Waxy filly got beat at Fort Smith.

Well, they fought the *tiger* manfully at the races here. Lights, liquors, and *rent for a little back room*, is the only thing that will draw claws out of the tiger. In the long run, unless he is a strong varmint, he is bound to fall a victim.

Ever yours, PETE WHETSTONE.

[28] PETE WHETSTONE'S LAST

DEVIL'S FORK OF LITTLE RED RIVER (Arks.),
Dec. 26, 1838.

MY DEAR MR. EDITOR.—*Krismis gift.*—Well, it has been a long time since I nibbed a quill on your account; it aint been because I havent been thinking of you, or wishing you well, but I have been mighty busy one way or another. I have been to the Rock, and was at the races; I saw some brisk nags; one mare, they call Eudora, took my eye; she is just about as fast as an *old she* in summer time. The Marmion filly, too, is all sorts of a crowder;— the way she can hold on is sinful.[1]

---

3. Used here to apply to the remarkable speed and ability of the horse Grey Eagle, this line is the verse for the letter "E" in the *New England Primer* of 1727.

Text: *Spirit*, 8 (2 February 1839), 406.

1. The *Spirit*, 9 (20 April 1839), 81, in its list of winning horses for 1838, lists an unnamed filly by Marmion (dam not listed) which was owned by T. T. Tunstall. It is probably this filly to which Pete refers.

Well, I saw some *pure sweetners* at the Rock, among them was a chap called the *"Gobler."* "Give us the Piny Woods, Mart," said one fellow. At that, old Martin broke loose with all sorts of a gobble; then he give the *"Lowlands,"* and finally wound up with a roaring stave, commencing—

"The old sow rose in the morning," &c.

Old Mart has been in the Legislature, but his talents don't lie in that way;—he is mighty severe at a short race, and has the honor of having raised the "Hessian Fly." I heard him and *old Ben* cavorting and bantering against each other. Says old Ben—"Oh, yes, oh yes, I ask your attention a few minits. You are all thieves, and liars, and cowards, and darsn't bet; you raise a little cotton, and a poor lousy colt, and sell it for 20 dollars, and after you pay your store account, you have only a little piece of meat in the smoke-house; but breed to Volcano, and *your children will come with clothes on!"*

Well, I went to the play; I believe they call it a the-a-ter.[2] It was mighty funny, I tell you. They were piled up as thick as pigs in cold weather, and such a hollering, "down in front,"—"hats off"—"out counties are privileged"—"music!" and all such noises. I didn't git the swing of the thing right off, for there sat four fellers on a platform, one going it on a little fife about as thick as a spike buck's-horn, one on a big thing sorter like a blowing horn, and it wasn't a blowing horn either, and then two fellers 'on fiddles. They didn't play "Old Zip Coon on a rail," or sich like, but they were going it on the high faluting order. I heered one slick-cheeked chap, what was sitting behind me, singing as they were playing. It was awfully mournful; the two first lines went somehow so—

"The last link is broking that bound you to I,

---

2. The Little Rock Theatre opened Monday, 3 December 1838, in a warehouse located on an alley between Main and Louisiana Streets in downtown Little Rock; see Pope, *Early Days in Arkansas: Being for the Most Part the Personal Recollections of an Old Settler* (Little Rock: Frederick W. Allsopp, 1895), p. 226. This theatre was the home of a company managed by Sam Waters, who regularly performed comic songs. Waters' wife was the star performer during the first season. For additional details, see D. Allen Stokes, "The First Theatrical Season in Arkansas: Little Rock, 1838-1839," *Arkansas Historical Quarterly*, 23 (1964), 166-183.

The words you have spoking are very sor-r-y." [3]
Well, presently a little bell jingled, and up went a green apron—
and out came the queerest looking chap I ever see—they said his
name was SAM WATERS. Well I tell you he made us all laugh. He
commenced singing "Butter and cheese and I,"—well, when he
got through, the crowd went it with a perfect looseness—even
old Mart had wrung himself in, and gave the "Piny Woods" in his
best style—*on kore, on kore.*—*"On what,"* says I—"that's French for
him to do it again," said a nice looking chap that was sitting by
me. Well, he came out and sung it over. Then began the play—it
was *Virginius*—and they call it tragedy.[4] Tragedy or what, it aint
suited to that are sort of a crowd—they want fun and
laughing—no crying—and as to killing people, why there is
enough of that done in public, without paying a dollar to see it. I
reckon they are pretty slick fellows, for once or twice I found my
veins rising, and I felt jist like making a smash of Mister App-
ious Klaw-dious.[5] My paper has gin out—so no more at present.

Ever yours, PETE WHETSTONE.

---

3. "The Last Link Is Broken" was composed by William Clifton. Masterson, pp.
323-324, reprints the lyrics:

> The last link is broken, that bound me to thee,
> And the words thou hast spoken, have render'd me free;
> That bright glance misleading on others may shine;
> Those eyes smil'd unheeding, when tears burst from mine.

> Chorus:
> If my love was deemed boldless that error is o'er
> I've witness'd thy coldness and prize thee no more.
> I have not lov'd lightly, I'll think on thee yet,
> I'll pray for thee nightly, till life's sun has set.

> The heart thou hast broken, once doated on thee,
> And the words I have spoken, proves sorrow to me;
> Oh! hads't thou then treasur'd, my thoughts spoken free;
> Thou coulds't not have measur'd thine own love to me.

4. *Virginius,* a five-act tragedy by James Sheridan Knowles (1784-1862), was performed by Waters' company on 10 December 1838, and 2 and 6 February 1839, In the
16 March 1839, issue of the *Spirit,* p. 18, Noland mentions having seen *Virginius*: "SAM
WATERS has fitted up a room in handsome style, and nightly plays to crowded houses. I
saw *Virginius* played by a Mr. DOUGLAS, the other night, in most splendid style. I think
his personation of Virginius would do credit to FORREST."

5. On 6 February 1839, the role of Appius Claudius, the tyrant-king in *Virginius,* was
acted by a Mr. Wolfe; see *Arkansas Times and Advocate,* 11 February 1839. Probably
Wolfe also portrayed the role in the 10 December 1838 performance.

[29] PETE WHETSTONE'S LAST FROLIC

DEVIL'S FORK OF LITTLE RED,
Jan. 9, 1839.

MY DEAR MR. EDITOR,—Since the last time I writ you, I have had all sorts of times; I took a trip away out South. Well, when I got to the Rock, I was in a big hurry to keep on, so I walked up early in the morning to Goodrich and Loomis,[1] thinking I would rig out in a suit of their best, but they hadn't opened their store; so I steps into another, and bought me a pair of red broadcloth britches. The fellow measured me, and put up a pair that he said would fit me to a shaving. So I stuffs them into my saddle-bags, and put out South. Well, when I gets out, I was asked to a party, and I rigged myself up; but oh, lordy! my britches were big enough for the fat man what was blowed up in the steamboat. I had my gallowses up to the last notch, but it wouldn't all do, for I could have carried a grist of corn in them without stretching the cloth. I hardly knew what to do; my old britches couldn't do at all, and my new ones hung like a shirt on a bean-pole. Thinks I, there is no frolic for Pete; but just right at this time in pops Major Greene. "Well," says he, "Kurnel, aint you ready to go?" Says I, "I am thinking I won't go."—"Why?" says he.—"Look at my britches," says I. Well, he commenced laughing; says he, "Them britches were made for Daniel Lambert."[2]—"Well," says I,

---

Text: *Spirit,* 9 (16 March 1839), 20.

1. Goodrich and Loomis operated a retail clothing store in Little Rock as early as 1835. The *Arkansas Gazette,* 8 December 1835, carried an announcement of Loomis, Goodrich, and Company which was located in the east end of an area of Little Rock known as Ashley's Brick Row. The firm sold clothing and hats. By 1842, the firm had become Goodrich and Boardman, Merchants, Tailors; see *Arkansas State Gazette,* 17 August 1842, p.n.n.

2. In Noland's day, the name Daniel Lambert was synonymous with hugeness. At that time, Lambert, an Englishman, was the most corpulent man on record, weighing 739 lbs. at his death in 1809. See *Dictionary of National Biography,* 32:7. As late as 1857, a James Mansfield, who weighed 450 lbs., was referred to as "a second Daniel Lambert." See *Arkansas State Gazette and Democrat,* 10 January 1857.

"Daniel Lambert is a stranger to me, but I know they are a pretty loose fit."—"Oh, never mind them," says he; "come, go, and nobody will notice them." So I went. I found lots of people, and an abundance of pretty gals. Well, there was no dancing, and the folks were all sitting round the room; so I slips in a corner, thinking I would hide my britches. Presently some gentleman asked a lady to sing; so up she gits, and he leads her to something in the corner, that looked like the nicest kind of a chest. Well, she opened the lid, and it was right chuck full of horse-teeth; she just run her hand across them, and I never heard such a noise in all my life. I whispered to the next fellow to me, and asked what sort of a varmint that was? "Why, Kurnel," says he, "that is a pe-anny." Well, the young lady commenced, and I never heard such singing. I forgot my britches, and started to walk close up to the pe-anny, when I heard them tittering. "Daniel Lambert," says one—then I knew they were laughing at my britches. So I feels my dander rising, and began to get mad; I walked right up, bold as a sheep. There was a sort of a dandy looking genius standing by the pe-anny.—Says he "Now do, Miss, favor us with that de-lightful little ditty—my favorite—you know it." Then she com-menced,

"When the Belly-aker is hearn over the sea,
I'll dance the Ronny-aker by moonlight with thee."

That is all I recollect. When she got through, up steps Maj. Green, and introduces me to her. Says she, (and I tell you she looked pretty,) "Col. Whetstone, what is your favorite?" Says I, "Suit yourself, and you suit me." And that made her laugh. Well, right at that, up steps a fellow that looked as if he had been sent for and couldn't go. Says he, "Miss, will you give me 'the last link is broken?' "—"Why," says she, "indeed, sir, I have the most wretched cold in the world."—"Why, Miss," says I, "you wouldn't call yours a bad cold if you had seen Jim Cole arter he lay out in the swamp and catched cold." "Why," says she, (and lord, but she looked killing) "how bad was his cold?" "Why, Miss," says I, "he didn't quit spitting ice till the middle of August." That made her laugh. "Well," says she, "Kurnel Whetstone, that cures my cold." So she commenced—

"The last link is broking that binds you to me,
The words you have spoken is sorry to I."
Well, arter the lady was over, they all went into supper; lots of
good things. I sat next to a young lady, and I heard them saying,
"Miss, with your permission, I'll take a piece of the turkey," and
so on. I sees a plate of nice little pickles.—"Miss, with your permission, I'll take a pickle," and she said I might do so. I reached
over and dipped up one on my fork—it was small, and I put the
whole of it in my mouth. Oh, lordy! but it burnt;—well, the more
I chawed the worse it was. Thinks I, if I swallow, I am a burnt
koon. Well, it got too hot for human nater to stand; so says I,
"Miss, with your permission, I'll lay this pickle back," and I spit it
out. Oh, lordy! what laughing. "Excuse me, ladies, if I have done
wrong," says I, "but that pickle is too hot for the Devil's fork."
Everybody seemed to take the thing in good part, but one chap;
says he, "I never seed such rude behavior in all my life." At that I
turns round to him; says I, "Look here, Mister, if you don't like
the smell of fresh bread, you had better quit the bakery." Well, I
tell you, that shot up his fly-trap quicker. Arter supper the party
broke up. Oh, confound the britches! I wish the fellow that made
them could be fed on cloth for twelve months. Even the little
boys make fun of them, for I heard one singing—
"Mister, Mister, who made your britches?
Daddy cut them out, and mammy sowed the stitches."

Ever yours, PETE WHETSTONE.

[30] PETE WHETSTONE ON HIS TRAVELS

STEAMBOAT ROBERT FULTON,
mighty close to Old Virginny,
April 20, 1839.

MY DEAR MR. EDITOR,—Well, Pete's coming, and the way
his head is just chock full of strange doings, things and men, is a

Text: *Spirit*, 9 (4 May 1839), 102.

caution.[1] The world is twice as big as ever Pete thought it was; so many putty gals—don't say a word—why sister Sal, in her best day, aint a beginning to them. Sich riggins I never seed! why there aint as much finery in the biggest store at Little Rock, as one of these little varmints (God bless them) totes about her at one load.

But I'll sorter begin at the mouth of White River, and tell you how I got here: Well, the *William French* came puffing by—so I shoulders my wallet and walks on to her—jist like a big brick house, with more lookin' glasses than there are 'twixt the Raccoon and Devil's Fork. What a heap of people! some high flouting and some low flouting, just a sprinklin' of all sorts, from quality and bad-quality, to commonality, rubbish, and trash.[2] But, what took my eye, was a mighty putty gal—she was killing, I tell you; well, it want long before I spied out, that one feller had a mighty hankering arter her. He was a sort of crane built feller, with red whiskers and a striped cravat; he seemed in a mighty good humor with himself, for every now and then he peeped into a looking-glass. He always managed to get close to her at eating time, but I don't think she fancied him, and once in a while I could catch a killing smile coming over towards me. It made me pull up my shirt-collar, and brush the fuzz off my long-tail blue. Well, I didnt know how to get to speak to her, for that chap was always close to her side; so I give it up as a bad job, and all I could do was to look at her when eating time come about. She left the boat at Smithland, and striped cravat looked sorter like a *burnt offering*.

I got up to Louisville. Maybe it aint a big place—why Little Rock wouldnt be missed out of it.[3] Well, I went to the theatre, and it was right chock full; they played what they said was the

---

1. In "Tour of 'N. of Arkansas,' " *Spirit*, 9 (27 April 1839), 91, Noland writes, "Pete is along, his eyes are nearly popped in gazing at curiosities. He keeps a journal for lawyer McCampbell. I will try and *steal* it for you."

2. Noland first used this five-fold classification of humanity in "Life in the Far West," *Spirit*, 6 (31 December 1836), 365. Later it appears in letter 63.

3. The 1840 census places Louisville's population at 21,210.

Rival Pages.[4] Sich a play, oh, lordy!—two women dressed in men's clothes—(I reckon that is what's called wearing the britches!)—and one great big overgrown fellow playing the King. Why Jim Cole looks more like a king than that fellow did. Some body called him the *Ge-rof,* but he looked to me like a hard baked loaf of bread, that had got cold, because nobody had teeth sharp enough to bite the crust. When they got through, out come Madame Augusta;[5] I knew she was a sprinkling past common, from the way they shouted—why Sam Waters, in the old *cane house,* when he sung "Butter, and cheese, and all," never got half such loud hurraing.[6] Oh! but she is a beauty, and then she looks jist about as innocent as a turtle dove; the way she flings her legs is cruel—why a bounce ball, made out of a sturgeon's nose, dont begin to hop like her. She stood on one toe and put her other foot as high as her head, and then she would come something like a double shuffle—and it warnt a double shuffle neither. All the men, and the old looking ones in particular, were down in the pit, and when she raised her foot it made me feel mighty comical, I tell you. It was worse than sister Sal's riding old Barebones a-straddle, without a saddle; but they say there is no harm in this sorter thing, it is the hight of quality, as the newcomer said on the Devil's Fork, when his wife handed round segars and smoked one herself.

Well, I looked up to the boxes, and saw more pretty gals than I could count in a day. One box took my eye—there sot an interesting and all sorts of a pretty lady, that they said had just been married; just behind her was a fine looking man, with a

---

4. *Rival Pages: A Petite Comedy in One Act,* by Charles Shelby (1802-1863). The play was most likely performed at the City Theatre, built in 1828 and located on Jefferson between Third and Fourth Streets. For a more detailed description of the theatre, see *The Louisville Directory for the Year 1832: To Which Is Annexed, Lists of the Municipal, County and State Officers; with a List of Various Societies, and their Officers; also An Advertiser* (Louisville: Richard W. Otis, 1832), p. 139.

5. Noland, in a letter dated Louisville, Kentucky, 17 April 1839, and published in the *Spirit,* 9 (27 April 1839), 91, says of Madame Augusta, "I visited the theatre last evening, and saw the beautiful AUGUSTA; she looks like 'an angel just come down from the skies,' and is decidedly a small sprinkling past any thing I have ever dreamed of—there is a simplicity and modesty about her that is most bewitching—her dancing is splendid, but her acting is inferior to that of Madame CELESTE."

6. Pete gives details of Sam Waters' theatre in letter 28.

grey head, (it is no sign of age to have grey heads in this country, why boys they told me had them when 14 year old and had white heads sometimes); next was a queenly looking woman, then another pretty girl, and another just behind her; and then come the one what struck my fancy—she looked so amiable—jist like as if she was too good natured to say *no* to any sort of a clever feller. Her hair fell in curls and sorter hid her face, but, if she wan't beautiful, she was jist as pretty as Pete would want a wife to be.

My paper is about to give out, so I'll wait till next time before I tell you about my being axed out to tea, and what I saw. This here boat shakes my pot-hooks into hangers, and vice versa.

Ever yours, PETE WHETSTONE.

[31] PETE WHETSTONE IN THE OLD DOMINION

ALDIE, Loudon County, Virginny,
April 29th, 1839.

MY DEAR MR. EDITOR,—Pete is in old Virginny, and he has seen so many things he dont know hardly where to begin to tell. Well, when I got to Baltimore, and, oh lordy! but it is a terrible big place, why Louisville aint no more to it, than Little Rock is to Louisville, sich a big tavern. I reckon I ought to say hotel, that's quality,—now who do you think came to the hotel, the very same identical hotel I put up at? you can't guess, so I'll tell you;—Mr. Van Buring and all the Government, except Amos Kindle and Franky Blair. I sorter hitched up my collar, and give the long-tail blue a shake, and walks up into the crowd. Says I, "Mister barkeeper;" says he, "sir;" "can I see Mr. Van Buring and the government;" "certingly," says he; "whereabouts" says I; "No. 127" says he. Up I goes; well, I found the room very full, and first this

---

Text: *Spirit*, 9 (11 May 1839), 115.

fellow walking up and then that one,—"Mr. Snodgrass, Mr. Van Buring; Mr. Van Buring, Mr. Snodgrass." I found nobody was going to introduce me, so I steps up,—"Col. Whetstone, Mr. Van Buring; Mr. Van Buring, Col. Whetstone." "What, Pete Whetstone of the Devil's Fork?" "adzactly;" "well Col. Whetstone when did you arrive," says he; "last night" says I; and then he reached over and whispered, "I must see you privately, at present our griefs are too heavy to allow us to attend to ordinary business." "Griefs," thinks I, "well it aint New York city that makes you grieve, but maybe old Connecticut sets sour on your stomach;" [1] "but," says he, and he did it slick and easy, "let me introduce you to the government;" and then he whispered again, says he "they are all here but Amos and Blair, and the truth is, they are so perfectly ugly we darsent show them about." I liked Forsyth and Poinsett better than the balance of the government. Lordy, but it is no wonder them chaps went off with their hands full, seeing as how Levi is so fat; fat men have no business in office, they are good natered and never suspect any body. "Well" thinks I, "I'll be sloping;" so says I, "Mr. Van Buring I'll bid you good bye;" "I wish you well Col. Whetstone," says he, "and be sure and call and see me when you go to Washington;" "well I'll do it," says I, and we parted. When I went down I sees a feller and asks him what was grieving Mister Van Buring; "oh," says he, "why don't you know;" "I don't," says I, "or I wouldn't have asked you;" "It is the death of Gen. Smith," says he, "one of our oldest and best citizens;" "when did he die," says I; "yesterday," says he; "well" says I, "if a good man dies on the Devil's Fork we don't grieve for him in this here sorter way, when the 4th of July comes then we go it this way;" "oh but," says he, "this is fashionable grief;" "yes horse, I take," says I.

---

1. An untitled note from Noland in *The Batesville News,* 2 May 1839, speaks of recent elections in these two states: "You will be pleased to learn that Connecticut has gone the good way, and the Whig banner floats in every nook and corner of that once tory state. In New York, however, the Whigs have not done their duty—they have allowed bullies to frighten them from the polls, and have suffered a defeat, where a bold and independent course would have insured a victory."

I hardly know how to tell you all I have to say—the Capital and all I saw there—the great race we had in the stage—and then I saw Lord Admiral Reesides, and the lord knows who else—but I'm in a hurry, so good bye.

Ever yours, PETE WHETSTONE.

[32] A LETTER FROM PETE WHETSTONE

ALDIE, Virginia,
May 11th, 1839.

MY DEAR MR. EDITOR.—Well, I have seen the big races at Washington, and dident see much when I saw them. Boston and Portsmouth made such a mash of the other nags that there was no fun, but I reckon the *"devil and Tom Walker,"* give Boston his dose for the first three miles any how,—I tell you they don't fix things right some how—the big bugs are kept apart, and just fix things so that it is, no use to do nothing, as the feller said when his sick horse showed the whites of his eyes—and then them chaps what have so much money bet 20 to 1 and pick up the country boys cruelly.

After the first day's race was over, a very nice looking gentleman says to me, "Col. Whetstone, wont you ride up and see a cock fight." "I reckon I will," says I, and up we went—well now the way I had fun was about right—sich hurraing and shouting—"25 cents on the high comb," "50 cents on the low comb," "20 dollars on the white," "5 dollars on the red." Well at it they went—"hurrah for the white, hurrah for the red,"—"that is the time we saved him; stand back and don't crowd the pit,"—"Turn him out, turn him out," "Hurrah for Tague Orengan," and the way they did go it was funny—the white cocks were too

Text: *Spirit*, 9 (18 May 1839), 123.

much for the others.[1]

I saw a right good chunk of a fight, one fellow knocked up—but arter all, give me a race on the Devil's Fork for fun before any thing I have seen here.

I am going on next week to the Baltimore races, for there is to be fun there. Mr. Kendle, what owns the course, says to me, "Col. Whetstone be sure and come to my house and I'll show you fun,—they shall run for money there, and you will find Boston has his hands full," and then he gine me a sorter of a sly wink, and says he, "Watch Balie Peyton and Master Henry," [2] at that I sorter pulled up my eye lid—"Gad," says he, "a word of the sort is enough among gentlemen."

I jist want to see Boston and Portsmouth come together; when they do Pete drops a few on the *Black Ram.* They seem to be shying round each other sorter like Jim Cole and Dan Looney, the time they had a fuss on Cravat-Stuffing Creek—but I reckon before they go the rounds it will be hard dodging, as the louse said when the gal raked her head cross ways with a fine tooth comb.

Well, talking of gals, I reckon it is about time Pete was looking out for a wife; some how or other they don't fancy the Devil's Fork, for I sorter hitched up long side of one and commenced singing,

"Purty Polly, Purty Polly, your dad-dy is rich,
And I have not a fortune to trouble me much,
Will you leave your old mam-my—your dad-dy also
And round the wide world with your darling boy go."

Don't you think the little critter said *no*—and she did it so slick,

---

1. In the official account of the races run at the Kendall Course in Baltimore, 13-16 May 1839, the unnamed writer says, "Among other distinguished gentlemen in attendance, we were happy to meet our facetious correspondent *Col. Pete Whetstone,* who lately 'got a hard fall' on 'a chicken fight' in the Old Dominion, but who to-day 'dug out' again by 'going his pile" on the Argyle filly [Wade Hampton's Kate Seaton]. He may be expected to 'rise and shine' on the Island [Long Island] at the Second Meeting." See Spirit, 9 (18 May 1839), 126.

2. Master Henry, bred by Balie Peyton, won his race at the Kendall track in Baltimore on 16 May 1839. The purse was $500.

jist laying her thumb on her nose, says she "you can't come it Pete," and then she laughed and jumped off like a fawn, leaving me a good likeness of a rough specimen of the fine arts. In haste ever yours,

PETE WHETSTONE.

[33] PETE'S LAST

WASHINGTON CITY,
May 5, 1839.

MY DEAR MR. EDITOR,—I hardly know where I'll begin. I have been to Baltimore agin; the way they keep soldiering there all the time is malicious, I tell you; why, it was a string long as a mile track; the way they were nice looking fellers was about right; I reckon they could do a cash business in Florida.[1] But oh lordy! if you want to see strange varmints, just look at them high-faluting chaps—sich ear-locks—why the *head-bug* what swam the Devil's Fork to get to Wiley's upper story, would die with grieving if he could see such a *range*.[2] My patience, but they would make nice wimen; they are the slickest, nicest little critturs, I never did see, and then they think so well of themselves that it makes no sort of difference what the world thinks of them. Home is home arter all, and give me the Devil's Fork. Why nobody talks to you in a steamboat or a stage—they jist draw in

Text: *Spirit,* 9 (18 May 1839), 123.
1. The United States was, at the time of this letter, engaged in a second war against the Seminoles in Florida. This conflict was said to have been the fiercest of all wars waged against the American Indians.
2. This unique feature of Wiley's hair and the efforts of lice to get into it are reported in letter 16.

their heads like mud-turtles. Now in the West, a fellow will chat away at an awful rate, and will try to make the world get on smoothly. But one syllable is all I can squeeze out of these fellers. The Capitol is a heap bigger than I ever thought houses got to be.[3] Well, I reckon some fellers up on the raccoon fork of the War Eagle would stare if they were here—sich pritty trees and ponds, and the keenest little red fish, and then there is a thing that turns round of its own accord, and spouts water worse nor a water-pot—they call it a *ged-dow*.

I aint been up to see Mr. Van Buring—I reckon he don't know I'm here, or he would send his carriage; but I shan't stand on ceremony, as deaf Smith, the tailor said, when he knocked down a feller, because his mouth went like as if it said liar. I aint been out to the race-course yet, but I am going next week. I want to see how Bosting looks 'longside of the Warping-bars, or the Bussing-coon. I am in a hurry, so good bye.

Ever yours, PETE WHETSTONE.

[34] PETE WHETSTONE IN NEW YORK

NEW YORK,
May 20.

Dear Jim [Cole].—You musent grumble because I havent writ to you before—the truth is, I have been going so all the time, that some how or other I aint had no time—well I reckon if you

---

3. Although the Capitol was large in 1839, it was not as large as it is today. The House wing was not occupied until 1857; the Senate wing was not completed until 1858. The central portion of the building "was capped with a low wooden dome covered with copper." For additional details, see U. S., Congress, Senate, *Our Capitol,* S. Doc. 50, 87th Cong., 1st sess. (Washington: Government Printing Office, 1961), pp. 3, 5.

Text: *Spirit,* 9 (25 May 1839), 138.

were here you would think all the world had come here on a visit—why the Astor house (it is a *tavern,* but that aint genteel,) is bigger nor the State House at Little Rock—they are mighty kind polite people and treat me very well—all the waiters are white and nice looking fellers at that. I havent seen many niggers here, but then the way them I have seen *do dress,* would astonish the natives—well, would you believe it, every spoon and fork is the pure stuff, purer nor a spanish dollar—and as to forks they all have *four prongs,* and sarn me to the sarned if they aint the most inconvenientest things I ever come across.[1]

Broadway is the big brag street of the city—and such a grist of folks as are going on it all the time you never did see—and then there are some of the tarnationest purty gals twixt heaven and yearth—lord but they do look nice—the height of the fashion is to wear a slick little apurn behind.[2] You would soon tire out here—it aint like *the devil's fork,* any way you can fix it, you cant git fresh air—there is a place called the Park, what comes nearer it than any thing I can find, it is shaped sorter like a triangle and has only about three big houses in it, the balance is trees and grass; it is about as big as a 40 acre lot.

The finest looking house I have seen is the Custom House, but it aint finished—it belongs to Uncle Sam and they have been building it these 6 years, and it will be a long time before they finish it yet. The Exchange is most finished, it is a sprinkling past common, and is situated in what they call the burnt district.[3] Then there are three great big theatres, that hold twenty times as many folks as Sam Water's theatre[4]—I aint been but once, and

1. Most forks available on the frontier had only three tines.
2. Probably Pete is simply describing flounces which hung from the waist. The style increased in popularity until well after the Civil War. See Francois Boucher, *20,000 Years of Fashion: The History of Costume and Personal Adornment* (New York: Abrams, n.d.), pp. 378-381.
3. A disastrous fire on 16-17 December 1835 destroyed $20 million worth of property. The fire began in a store on Merchant Street and spread through 19 city blocks. It destroyed 674 buildings.
4. The three leading New York theatres of the age were the Bowery, the National, and the Park.

then I went to the one they call the *Bowery*—it is an awful nice looking house; I heard the Brass Band all the way from Bosting on their blowing horns—the way they can blow is about right— then there was a play called Nick of the Woods[5]—it warnt much—one feller was called *Captain Ralph Stackpole,* a ringtail roarer from Salt river—but if he had any fun or wit about him, he kept it to himself while I was there. Why, Old Ben from Spring river, or Old Martin from the Piney Woods, could out *cavort* him to death.[6]

I reckon you want to hear something about horse racing—well I have seen some monstrous fast horses. Boston is rather the best race-horse I ever saw—then there are Portsmouth, Vashti, Wonder, Steele, Master Henry, and Old Argyle, that are fast enough for most any thing in this world. There is great racing this week at Camden and I am going there. You cant guess who I saw here? why Daniel Webster—the man who is among men like Boston among horses. He has gone to England—every body said "God bless him" when he went.[7]

Well, as I was walking up town last night, I heard a fellow spouting away, so I jist stopt and listens—says he, "oh yes, I went to Bosting, and there I saw some little boys a rolling marbles—a little ring with five marbles in it—one little boy he rolled his marble, says he, 'if I aint *fat* I'm d___ d,' and he was the *leanest* little critter I ever did see—and then one little boy he plumped his marble, and another feller hollerd out, 'I'm *dead,* if I aint I'm d___d,' and he was the *livest* little critter I ever seen in my born

---

5. The *Spirit,* 9 (4 May 1839), 108, noted that the Bowery would open on Monday, 13 May, with "Nick of the Woods." On 25 May, the *Spirit* complimented an actor named Gates for his portrayal of Stackpole. An example of Stackpole's "roaring" is contained in *A Treasury of American Folklore: Stories, Ballads, and Traditions of the People,* ed. B. A. Botkin (New York: Crown, 1944), pp. 12-13, where it is reprinted from Robert Montgomery Bird, *Nick of the Woods, or The Jibbenainosay, A Tale of Kentucky* (Philadelphia: Carey, Lea and Blanchard, 1837).

6. Details of Old Martin and Old Ben cavorting are provided in letter 28. Additionally, Old Ben is used as the standard for measuring the bragging and cavorting of others in letter 51.

7. The *Spirit,* 9 (18 May 1839), 121, carried a brief note concerning Webster's trip: "By the steamer 'Liverpool,' which leaves this city this afternoon, Mr. WEBSTER departs for England, with his family, on an excursion for health and pleasure."

days." My paper is most give out so I must stop—give my love to sister Sal and the baby, to Bill Spence and Lawyer McCampbell.

Your friend till death, PETE WHETSTONE.

Jim Cole, Esq., care of Lawyer McCampbell, Kinderhook,[8] East Prong of the Devil's Fork.

[35] THE MILE RACE AT TRENTON

MY DEAR MR. EDITOR,—I reckon as how you would be obliged to me, if I would jist fulfil my promise about the *wring in* from *Old Kentuck,* at Trenton.[1] Well, the sooner I commence the sooner I'll get through. The Trenton course is the slickest and nicest in the world; it may rain and rain, and it still will be a good Course, and then the way Dr. BROWN is a liberal fellow is jist about right; as to eating, jist go to Snowden's, and the way you can git good things is nobody's business. But for *that* race;—well, it was a mile and repeat. A sorrel horse called *Stanhope,* entered by Van Mater, was the favorite. He is a great big, strong, animal, more like Boston in appearance than any horse I ever saw; then there was a Tonson, with Gil. on his back, and Dr. Poole's colt, a good 'un at that, and Old Shepherdess, and a bay mare; then last, but not least, came the *wring-in* from *Old Kentuck*; it was a bay colt, something like the *Warping Bars*, but not quite as big, and he hadn't as much muscle. He was kivered with an old saddle blanket, and his mane looked like as if it had never seen a

---

8. At one time a post office was maintained at Kinderhook in Van Buren County. See map. *The Batesville News,* 18 April 1839, carried a notice of its discontinuation.

Text: *Spirit,* 9 (8 June 1839), 163.

1. The official account of the spring races at Trenton, New Jersey, is contained in the *Spirit,* 9 (1 June 1839), 150-151. The meet was held from 28 through 31 May. The details of Pete's letter are borne out by that record.

curry-comb. The man that led him was only a dot behind Dan Looney. He entered him as *"the stolen colt,"* and there might have been more truth than poetry in the pedigree. His rider's dress, he said, was "yaller trousers, no hat, and black shirt." When the horn blew, and the riders mounted, the *wring in* looked chock full of wild oats and vinegar. The drum tapped, and off they went; *Wring-in's* rider, was dressed in a long-tail grey, and the way it spread and stuck out like the steering oar of a forked-tail hawk was sinful; for the first six hundred yards he was in the crowd, arter that he couldn't come it; Old Shepherdess won the heat. Some how or other, the judges forgot to drop the flag, and he wan't shut out. At it he went again, but he was worse off the next heat, and the flag left him on the wrong side, and he had to slope off. He bore his defeat like a man, the old saddle and blanket was again put over him, and the boy with the forked-tail coat mounted him, and the six footer led him off. The second heat was a dead one 'twixt Stanhope and the Tonson. The third heat was a dead one agin, the fourth Gil. won, the fifth and sixth Stanhope won, but it was most night before they got through.

I had a chill, and quit the field when the *Wring in* quitted the race. He told me to look out next Fall, and I'd see the big stars fall. Says he, "I was jist feeling them to-day; I have got a colt at home that can beat him thirty open yards in a quarter, and the further the worse; but look here, stranger," says he to me, "won't you light and take a little of the crittur? it will have an almighty good effect on that ar' shake you have got." "I don't care if I do," says I; and down I got. Well, in we went, and says he, "what will you drink, stranger?" "Name it yourself," says I. "Punch," says he. "Punch," says I. "Gentlemen, how will you have it" says the bar-keeper, "cut or squz?" "I'll take it *squz*," says I. "Ditto, peach," said the *Wring in,* and the liquor was mixed. I drank his health, and success to his *bite* in the Fall, bid him good bye, got into a Jarsey wagging, and cut out for Snowden's, where I had a rale tarnation shake.

Ever yours, PETE WHETSTONE.

[36] REMINISCENCES OF HIS VISIT TO THE EAST

By Kurnel Whetstone.

The fever and ague thick, and no Sappington's Pills—The Kurnel's new Rifle—Travelling at the North; Col. Johnson and his Stable—Old Reality—Arthur Taylor—Willis—Gil. Patrick—Craig—Mr. McCargo— Mr. Hare—Old Charles—Mr. Van Mater—Mr. Livingston—The Messrs. Stevens—The Kurnel's Movements—Lawyer McCampbell.

> *UP IN OLD VIRGINNY,*
> *July 2d, 1839.*

MY DEAR JIM,—I suppose you think it is time I was writing you, but the truth is, I have been tolerably flat on my back ever since I went to York, where I caught them confounded chills, and, would you think it, there aint the first box of Doctor Sappington's pills in that great big city. But, thank God, I am rising like smoke from a *tar-kill*, though I have nigh on to as bad a cough as you had arter you lay out in the swamps.[1]

I reckon your mouth will water when you see my rifle—fifty balls to the pound, and a little the slickest finished gun you ever did see.[2] I am going to New York agin before I start for the Devil's Fork, and maybe I'll shell out one for you.

You don't know how fast they travel here; it is the rise of two hundred miles from Washington to New York, and they go it in a day just like nothing.

Well, I suppose you want to hear something about the men I

Text: *Spirit*, 9 (13 July 1839), 223.

1. In letter 29 Pete relates in some detail the cold Jim Cole caught from spending the night in the swamps.

2. An early means of sizing a musket, rifle, or shotgun barrel was by the number of bullets a pound of lead would make for it. See Edwin Tunis, *Weapons: A Pictoral History* (New York: World, 1954), p. 127. Each bullet for this rifle would weigh about 1/3 ounce.

have seen; I'll jist begin at Col. JOHNSON's stable; he is the greatest man of them all. He out-generals them to death, and if he has anything like as good a horse as the balance, he is certain to *rake down the corn*. He is a middle-sized man, with a head as white as snow, with a very manly, handsome face, very much like that officer we saw arter the Black Hawk war (General ATKINSON), and then he is so kind and polite.—"Kurnel Whetstone," says he, "I won't forgive you if you don't come and see me and eat fried chickens, and take a glass of old rye with me." I told him I'd go, or bust a trace trying.

Says I, "Colonel, which was the best 4 mile nag you ever trained?" *"Old Reality,"* says he, and then he told me ARTHUR was the best rider he ever saw; for, says he, "Kurnel, he rode every horse in the race, and could always tell after a heat how the thing was going." Everything jist works like the wheel of a clock about the Colonel's stable. Arthur is a mighty quiet sort of a man, but he is as honest as the day is long, and as wide awake as the next. WILLIS is the chap what used to ride all the big races: he rode Bascombe the time the Southern chaps filled their pockets. He trains now, being most too big to ride, though he can ride 120 lbs. GIL. PATRICK is the rider of Boston, and sich a rider you don't often see; he sets like as if he was fastened to his horse with a sticking plaster. He is a Dutch boy, with a good-natured face, and is as quiet as old Arthur: and can ride a 4 yr. old and up, although he is about 22. He was raised on Long Island, and to show he *is cut the right way of the leather*, he supports his mother. The 3 yr. old rider is CRAIG. He is a broth of a boy, and will make a buster some of these times, *though he don't talk quite enough to suit Arthur*. The *tall man* ("York's tall son")[3] what prints the "Spirit" told me he was going to try and get a likeness of the OLD NAPO-

---

3. William T. Porter was six feet, four inches tall. See Yates, p. 8. The name "York's Tall Son" was given to him by his younger sister Sarah, who applied the name to him in a mock tragedy "Hophir" which she composed and sent to him with a letter dated 13 January 1837. See Brinley, pp. 48-53.

LEON, and have it engraved for his paper—he ought to do it.[4]

I liked BILLY McCARGO mighty well. He is the man what chased Boston so hard with Charles Carter and Duane. I reckon if he had chased him first with Duane, and then Charles Carter, maybe he would have caught him, though old Boston aint easy caught. Billy looks mightily like the backwoods, for he whiffs away out of an old cane pipe. He is a mighty friendly man.

OTWAY P. HARE is a crowder. He is a little feller, with the keenest black eye you ever did see; he is always full of fun, and no matter whether he is plaguing a body about the *tick-Doly-rue,* or laughing at "the Epsom rider" that was engaged for *Job,* he is the same Otway P. Hare. Old CHARLES trains for him, and I reckon with Willis and Job they will make the fur fly this Fall.

JOSEPH H. VAN MATER, or *"Old Joe H."* as they call him in the Jarseys, had a long way the best string of horses I saw. Why, at Trenton, he pulled in the truck seven times out of eight. He aint *nervy* enough to win much money, but then the Jersey boys piled up their 5's on him with a looseness, and I expect they made the biggest haul they ever made in their lives. If the *Blowing horn* starts, and "old Jo H." says he is right, why you may jist waggon off with the State.

The nicest man I saw was WALTER LIVINGSTON; he is always so kind and polite, "like a Fine Old English Gentleman all of the Olden Time," and jist looks like that gentleman that lawyer McCampbell told us about the night we killed the old *he* on the Dry Fork. Now, if you fancied a horse he had, and was to offer him $500 for him, and he thought the horse only worth a $100,

---

4. A note in the *Spirit,* 9 (14 September 1839), 330, contains the following remarks:
"*The Old Napoleon.*"—The suggestion of "N." to publish in our "American Turf Register and Sporting Magazine," a portrait of Col. [William Ransom] JOHNSON of Virginia, is echoed on all sides, and we are desired to give it of all things. It would doubtless be a very great curiosity to many, and we know of no picture that would give such general satisfaction. We beg to say to his "troops of friends," that all you have to do, gentlemen, is to get the Colonel's consent, and send us a good likeness of him, of which several have been painted. We will bring it out in the January number of the "Register," and if you will send the painting to us within six weeks, so that the artist shall not be hurried, we promise to have executed as beautiful and highly finished a portrait as has ever been engraved in the country.
The portrait was published as a broadside to accompany the *Turf Register.*

why you couldn't persuade him to take more than the $100. He raised Job, and everybody seemed glad that Job won, *excepting them what lost on Fordham.* The stuff he was made out of is gitting mighty scarce.

I saw Mr. JOHN C. STEVENS and Mr. ROBERT L. STEVENS, but I didn't get the swing of them somehow, as they were a little busier than a man buttoning up in a hurry; they employ in some way or other nearly 1500 men. The former is all the time fixing his sail boat—I believe they call it a *yot*; when it is done he is going to England, to sail against anything that swims the waters. When it comes to steamboats and locomotives, why Robert Stevens can take the corn.

Well, I'd best begin to tell you now about my own movements. In August I am going to *the* White Sulphur, and then to the Devil's Fork. I am gitting mighty anxious to be with you. I want to see lawyer McCampbell, and sister Sal and the boy. Tell the lawyer I bought the books for him, and I fixed his land for him; I can jist tell you that the Commissioner of the General Land Office is a rale chartered fellow; he is the cleverest democrat what holds office in the Federal city. Well, so the court giv it in favor of the old directory;[5] that is a great thing for Arkansas. I hear there was to be a little gunpowder burnt on the strength of it, but I hope not, for it is a heap better to burn it gin a bear than agin a human being.

I aint had the first letter from the lawyer; just tell him "he can take his own time, but I'll only give him till Friday," as Col. McCARTY said to the fellow what owed him a thousand.

My paper is most gin out, and I am weak as a fawn; so good bye; my love to the lawyer, sister Sal, and Jim Cole. Kiss the boy. What is Dan Looney driving at? Who runs for the Senate, Luke,

---

5. The Arkansas Supreme Court decided in favor of the directory of the Real Estate Bank of Arkansas in the matter of the method of electing bank officials. A contested election came to the court four times before a decision was finally given in favor of the "old directory" of the bank in May 1839.

or Johnny, or *Flax mane and tail?*

No more, but yours, PETE WHETSTONE.

To JIM COLE, Esq.,
Kinderhook, Devil's Fork, Arks.
P.S. I havn't seen "Boots," nor "Larkin," or the "Athletics."
P.W.

[37] INTERCEPTED LETTER FROM PETE WHETSTONE

ALDIE, Va.,
July 18, 1839.

DEAR JIM,—I was most tarnation glad to git your last letter, for I was afeard you chaps on the Devil's Fork had forgot Pete. Well, I hadent the smallest notion the old lawyer would ever fall in love, but there is no gitting round a widder, when one takes a hankering arter a feller he's a gone coon. And what is worse, it aint wice wersa, for the old song says,—
"I courted the widder,
Fifteen long years and couldn't git her."
Well, I'd jist like to be back to say a good word for the lawyer. Speaking of lawyers, I reckon I felt proud when I picked up a newspaper jist now, and saw where our friend ALBERT PIKE, of Little Rock, was taking the corn over the big waters.[1] Why the

---

Text: *Spirit,* 9 (27 July 1839), 217.
1. By 1839, Pike (1809-1891) had established quite a reputation as a poet. His "Hymns to the Gods," had appeared in the June 1839 issue of *Blackwoods'* with the following editorial comment: "These fine poems . . . entitle their author to take his place in the highest order of his country's poets."

way his poetry beats them all is a sin to Moses. He is the crack nag of "Blackwoods' Magazine," a book that never prints trash.

If any body is going down to the Rock jist git them to ask the Governor to offer a reward for *Coffee Vault,* the man what wrung in the beef bones for the pure ivory, and whose animal passions carried him beyond decency, and who perpetrated an outrageous murder. He is now as large as life and twice as natural in Indiana, in Vermillion county, and is figuring upon the honors that his democratic friends in Arkansas showered on him. Go it, my *Coffee Vault,* while you're young.

Well, I have had lots of fun in Old Virginny—maybe them chaps about Middlebury aint whole teams! They are the boys what are cut the right way of the leather. Sich barbacues you never *did* see—and I tell you good sheep meat aint easy to beat, and then they sling in the briled chicking, to say nothing of the liquors—punch with ice in it and the lemons *cut and squz* both. It is all done in the shade, and you can take off your coat and roll on the grass, some pitch, and then others go it with an old greasy "deck," sarn me to the sarneds if I dident see one feller so lucky, that he could float from Louisville to Orleans on a chip. And jist to make a long story short, I tell you a Virginny barbecue is next thing to a bear hunt.

I wish you could see the man what drives the stage here. His name is *Billy Whaley,* and I tell you he is a horse; every man, woman, and child on the road knows him. Says he to me, "Col. Whetstone, won't you ride outside,—do now, for I want to show you some of the keenest critturs you ever did see." "I dont care if I do," says I, and out I got and mounted long side of him. "These aint my bullies, Colonel; the road is heavy, and I must go slow awhile, but jist wait till I git to Fairfax Court House, and I'll show you perfect bounce balls!" Well, we got to the Court House—says I, "Billy, cant you lay something on your bosom?" and he said he would. So in we stepped, and there was a queer looking sort of a genius with nose and chin sorter like nut-crackers standing by the bar, so says I to him, "my friend, wont you jine us in taking a horn?" "I dont care if I do," says he. So the landlord set us out three julaps. Nut-crackers raised his glass, with "here is to you."

"The same to you and all your family," said Billy. "Well, look here, driver," said nut-crackers, "I'll tell you how a man should drink to enjoy it; when he first gits up in the morning, he should take an *eye-opener,* in about an hour, a *fleme cutter,* and jist as he sits down to breakfast, a *gall-buster.*" "Hah! hah! hah!" said Billy, and jist then the landlord asked us into breakfast. In we went, and I reckon there was all sorts of a good breakfast—presently the horn blew. "Stage waiting," shouted Billy. "Aye, aye," said nut-crackers, and in they got; I kept outside with Billy. Well, now I tell you he had a set of lively critturs. "All ready," shouted Billy, and drawing his reins well up he hollered "let go" to the boy what held his leader. She sprung like a wild cat, while Billy brought a keen crack with his whip and shouted "git out of the way *you money making dogs!*" I tell you *it* was the next thing to a steam car. After going about three miles, says Bill, "What do you think of them, Colonel?" "Think," says I, "why I think they are perfect race-horses, and how do you keep them so fat?" "Why," says he, "the secret is in favoring them over bad ground and up-hill." No more about Billy at present, only that when it comes to driving give me him.

Well, what has got into the people of Arkansas?—they are gitting jist as bad as they used to be before Mississippi and Texas took the corn. They must turn in and hang freely; that is the way to stop murders.[2]

My paper is about out, so I must close. My love to the lawyer and tell him I shall buy him a *plain gold ring*—to sister Sal and tell her I have bought her some of the slickest jewelry she ever did see. How does your boy come on? Give my love to him and tell him I have a heap of purtys for him. What sort of a paper is that

---

2. Many murders were committed in Arkansas during the early months of 1839. Probably the most noteworthy were the "Cane Hill Murders," famous in Arkansas history. William Wright and four of his children were brutally murdered on 15 June 1839, at Cane Hill in Washington County. The event was reported in the *Arkansas State Gazette,* 26 June 1839. John Richmond, James Barnes, and Jackson Turner were convicted of the crime and were executed on 29 July 1839; see *Arkansas State Gazette,* 18 September 1839; and Charles G. Williams, "The Cane Hill Murders of 1839 in History and Literature," *Arkansas Historical Quarterly,* 29 (1970), 209-214.

new paper at the Rock?[3] Tell the lawyer to subscribe for it for me.

Ever yours, PETE WHETSTONE.

To *Jim Cole, Esq.*, Devil's Fork, of Little Red, Arkansas.

[38] INTERCEPTED LETTER FROM PETE WHETSTONE

FLINT ISLAND, on the Ohio River,
Oct. 9th, 1839.

DEAR JIM,—I know you are grumbling because I havent writ, but the thing is jist so,—I have been expecting to start every day and thought it was no use. Well, I have had a heap of fun, and I do reckon saw jist about as great races at Louisville, as have ever been run since Adam was a yearling.[1] I tell you Wagner and Grey Eagle are mortal horses—they travel all the time, and as to picking it up, 'tis mighty like the lick the burnt-offering struck when Piney-wood Smith wrung him in on old Mart,—jist twenty-one and the breadth of the hoof, and clawing away like rats a fighting. Old Kentuck is a caution. The way her people stand up to her is about right,—a man darsent say turkey 'gin

---

3. *The Batesville News*, 28 December 1838, [p. 4], which probably would have been forwarded to Noland, carried a prospectus for *The Arkansas Star*, edited in Little Rock by David Lambert.

Text: *Spirit*, 9 (26 October 1839), 397.

1. By 1839 Louisville was already known for horse racing. The Oakland Course, located at the site of what is now the intersection of Seventh and Magnolia Streets, had been completed by May 1833, when regularly scheduled races were held. The race described here was the most famous one run during the fifteen-year history of the course. William T. Porter, who attended the race, describes this contest in detail in "The Louisville Races," *Spirit*, 9 (4 and 11 January 1840), 522-523 and 534-535.

Grey Eagle, or he was bound to catch it where Jim Spence shot the wild cat—right under the burr of the ear. You know what I writ about Old Boston,—well, I still stick to it, and say publicly and above board, that I think he can beat all the world, yet I rather reckon he couldent more nor make his bread corn off Wagner. Grey Eagle is all horse, and if he was well and sound to-day, and old Col. Johnson had the handling of him, and Gil. sat on his back, my money dident go agin him at dollar for dollar. He would have walked through the world, the tall horse of the western country, if he hadent have come across Old Wagner. He was hard to conquer,—for, like the fight 'twixt Dan Looney's sharp tooth and the panter on the lower fork, it was for a long time so good and so good. Wagner got him at last, but it was a tight fit and he won only by the skin of his teeth. Jist think of 7:48—7:44—on Monday, and on Saturday flinging it up in 7:51—7:43. The last mile was done in 1:48.

Ralph is a crowder—he belongs to Walker Thurston. Well, now, some how or other they talk hard about Walker, yet I hearn more nor twenty say they knew nothing wrong of him—only, "the people say so." He has nothing about his looks that seems wrong. I saw nothing foul in him, and I rather guess some people abuse him that aint as good as he is. They don't hardly give him a fair shake in some parts of Old Kentuck.

Cub is a jewel. She come to the stand, mouth open, and rider swinging, in 3:46—3:44, [I think]. *Telamon* is a caution. He is big and overgrown, but he has foot and game,—and sarn me to the sarneds, if I should be surprised to see him going low down into the 7:40's next year.—Old Billy McCargo was there. He had nothing but Old Missouri fit to run for sour cider. He says the climate is almighty hard on horses from abroad. He raked the corn down twice with Old *Missouri*,—she got down into 3:44. But that is a cruel fast track—it is a mile—a good fat mile, but then it is fixed so nice, and is sich good ground, that I almost think Old Boston and Wagner would fling it deep in the thirties.

Them Kentucky racers are cut the right way of the leather, and friendlier people aint to be found this side of the Devil's Fork. Most of them live close to the Forks of Elk-horn, and I reckon in four miles of Frankfort, they can start 50 race horses. Paddy Burns is a rare bird, and when he talks of the "Curry-kill-dare," all you have to do is to stand back and listen. He believes strong in "*Sydney,*" and when "Sydney's" nags fall "P. Burns" falls with them.

I went up to the Lexington races, but I was sick with chills and fevers and couldent enjoy myself much. But the way they are polite and kind to strangers is about right. They have a fine track and are improving it every year. The Louisville Jockey Club is very large and very respectable, and they do things on the very tallest scale. The President of it is one of the politest, most agreeable, and gentlemanly men ever I come across, and any thing over which he presides is bound to prosper.[2]

I suppose you want to hear something about the pretty gals. Well, Wagner beat Grey Eagle, but all creation can't beat Old Kentuck for nice and pretty women. Lord! but it would have done you good to hear them shout when Grey Eagle came out ahead the first heat. It was like soft thunder in the prairie. And then to see them when poor Grey Eagle let down. It was a sorrowful sight,—and if any man had jist got up and said, he wasent sorry, why he would have had to gone out of Old Kentuck to hunt for a wife. They go the *entire,* and with them, it is, "if you love me, you must love my horse, my dog, and every thing that is old Kentuck." Well, arter all, it is a noble trait, and though I think they "pile the agony a little too high" sometimes, yet I couldent help feeling that if I wasent a son of Old Virginny, I'd give all I had, to have been born in Old Kentuck.

Louisville is a nice place, and it is going ahead right smart, although money is so *skase.* They have built two splendid churches,[3]—and that makes me jist think about writing you that

---

2. The president of the Louisville Jockey Club for 1839 was Robert John Ward; see *Spirit,* 9 (4 January 1840), 522.

3. In describing Louisville, Noland writes, "The Presbyterian Church is the most beautiful thing I ever saw, and the new Episcopal church is said to be the very richest affair, that the eye ever beheld." See "'N.' upon His Return," *Spirit,* 9 (21 September 1839), 339. *The Louisville Directory* . . . 1832 . . . , p. 140, locates the First Presbyterian Church on Fourth Street between Market and Jefferson.

I have seen Maffit, and hearn him preach. He is a slick fellow; and I tell you he is awful flowery. He talks all about "putty gals," and "bright stars," and "gentle moon." He says some people are too ugly to be loved. Well, that is my way of thinking, but some how or other I dident think he ought to say it. I reckon maybe he was thinking of the gal on the "cony fork," whose eyes opened like window-shutters. He is mighty mad about Parsons going back to the theatre, and says "the devil will be sure to git him, but then he won't have him, for the devil's a gentleman,"—well, this is the first time I ever heard him called a gentleman. Maffit is a great man in his way, and he has a mighty way of making converts. The women carry him *nosegays,* and *great dobs of 'lasses candy.*[4]

Well, my paper is almost gin out and I must stop. I can't say when I'll git home, for here we are at the foot of Flint Island fast aground on the De Kalb.[5] The Col. Wood is ditto, at the head of the Island,—so with love to Sal and her child, and the rest on 'em, I am your friend,

PETE WHETSTONE.

Jim Cole, Esq., Devil's Fork, of Little Red, Arkansas.

---

4. Although Noland does not mention having heard Maffit during his trip, he does praise Parsons. ". . . I heard PARSONS—*Parson* Parsons, of the Methodist Church; I entered the church after he had commenced—he took no text—his subject, that of missionaries. His language was rich and his delivery fine; it was theatrical, but subdued and without rant; occasionally he was brilliant; always eloquent; his figures were simple and striking—one I recollect. He spoke of charity as the brightest of the Christian virtues—called on the rich and poor to exercise it in behalf of the noble cause in which Missionaries were engaged—'Fling your treasures,' said he, 'into the lap of the Lord,—draw on heaven, and you need have no fear that your draft will be protested.' He is destined to cut a tall figure in the profession he has chosen." ["'N.' upon His Return," *Spirit,* 9 (21 September 1839), 339.]

5. Noland, in the *Spirit,* 9 (9 November 1839), 226, provides a bit of detail concerning this adventure: "I left Louisville in the DeKalb, Capt. Lemon commanding, and was compelled to leave her at Wabash bar, as there was not water enough." He further relates that he boarded the *Gloster.* Flint Island was located on the Kentucky side of the Ohio River, approximately 80 miles downriver from Louisville, just above Derby, Indiana, and at the border of Meade and Breckenridge Counties, Kentucky. The Wabash Bar was at the intersection of the Wabash and Ohio Rivers. For additional detail, see Samuel Cummings, *The Western Pilot: Containing Charts of the Ohio River and of the Mississippi . . . Accompanied with Directions for Navigating the Same, and a Gazetteer* (Cincinnati: George Conclin, 1836), pp. 56, 58.

[39] PETE'S RETURN TO THE OLD "DIGGINS"

DEVIL'S FORK, of Little Red,
Nov. 21, 1839.

MY DEAR MR. EDITOR,—Well, after a long trip, Pete is once more at home, and when he says he feels happy and glad, you musent think he has already forgot the kind way you and others used him. No, it ain't so; Pete ain't got a short memory about friendships. But home is a sweet place to even an *Injun*, as them Seminolys in Florida have shown Uncle Sam.[1] You don't know how glad Jim Cole, Bill Spence, Dan Looney, and Sister Sal, and all the folks were to see me. They axed me a thousand questions; first about men, and then about horses. Jim wanted to know what sorter looking man you were, and Dan what sorter looking horse Boston was, and I hadn't time for the first three days to draw my breath, for answering them.

I went out and fotched a whoop, and, oh Lordy! but there was a noise. Old *Sharp-tooth* jumped with joy, and the rest on them fairly howled. Jim has a monstrous tall pack, and they can make an old *he* ache. I like to forgot to tell you—Poor Lawyer McCampbell is dead. He died while I was gone. He was a mighty good man, and the Devil's Fork will miss him a heap. But he is gone, and there is no use in crying over spilt milk.

I jist got to the Rock in time to see the races—lots of people and 'bundance of horses.[2] Capt. Tunstall and Jack Lafford walked right through—worse than old Joey H. at Trenton, for

---

Text: *Spirit*, 9 (21 December 1839), 498.

1. The United States had been at war since 1835 with the Seminoles because the tribe refused to cede its lands in Florida and submit to removal to Indian Territory. The war continued until 1842.

2. Noland, in "Arkansas Races," *Spirit*, 9 (7 December 1839), 475, provides the official report of the Little Rock racing meet, which took place 5-9 November 1839. That account confirms Pete's information. Of six races, Tunstall and Lafford's horses won five; they did not enter the sixth.

he left out one day; they took all,—sweeping the platter. Awful howling the first day—mortal nags came together—but Eudora is too fast for anything. I don't think *Cub* or Balie Peyton could catch her, Mile heats. Well, I reckon there were a heap of empty pockets that night that she won her race. There was no danger with some of them of being robbed. They could fling their britches in the middle of the floor and sleep sound. There was hard times on Sunday. The landlord's purse was hard to raise, and some of them had to live like Tyrse's mule, "on the vapors of a dungeon."

Well, the Vice President was at the Rock,[3] and they give him a big ball—all sorts attended; whigs and democrats—in office and out of office—every body, and Pete among them, went. Well, he is a mighty friendly man, and is as plain as an old shoe. They say he fit mighty hard, and killed a *big injun*,[4] and that he is a mighty good man; but, oh Lordy! he ain't smarter nor common people. But some how, in these times, *smart people* don't prosper. If you jist could see one man what the Gineral Government sent out with an office to these parts,—he is a bird! The way he *cuts on the scull* is awful! He has been indorsed, and passes current here.

Well, changing the subject, I saw Squire Gilfillan at the Rock; oh, I wish you could hear him tell his great story.—"And I spied a wee thing hanging to a bush, for all the world like unto a blather with a hole in the end of it. And I stepped up to it, and afore God, Charley Aderley, I had no more larm in my heart mon, than I have at this moment; and I jist brought it a wee kiff, gently like, with the back of my hand, jist so. And in the name of Jasus, what do you think come out of the hole in the end of the thing like a blather? Why, bum flies by the A____y C____t, and

---

3. Vice President Richard Mentor Johnson (1780-1850) arrived in Little Rock on 29 October 1839, on unidentified business. A ball was held in his honor, and Noland probably attended. He departed the city on 10 November. See *Arkansas State Gazette,* 6 November 1839, p.n.n.

4. Upon commencement of the War of 1812, Johnson raised a body of Kentucky mounted riflemen, whom he commanded on the Canadian frontier. The decisive charge of his mounted volunteers contributed greatly to the victory gained over the British and Indians at the battle of the Thames, 5 October 1813, and it was by his hand that the Indian leader Tecumseh is commonly supposed to have fallen.

they bit me, and they bat my wee bob tail pony, and they bat my brother-in-law, John Anderson's wee bob tail pony, and they bat my wife Janet, and all the bairns, till they had wabbles on their legs as big as the buttons on a huntsman's coat, and they bat the coulter of my plough that was made of the best Juniata iron, till it swelled up and burst the beam.

"One morning I rolled up my trousers, and was walking through the yard, when an old gander slipped up and nibbled my shin sorter behind like; and there was a wee gosling jist afore and in front of me, and I kicked him and I killed him, and my wife says, 'Squire Gilfillan, in the name of _____, what made you kill the goose's baby ?' 'D___n to his father's sowl, how came he to bite me!'"

There is to be a big corn race over in Jackson County—one hundred bushels of corn entrance, half forfeit—ten entered. Old uncle Tommy Wiseman's *Mobile* is gwine to take the *corn*. He offers to bet five hundred cool shiners he can run a mile in a minnit and a half by his clock, and as much more that he can out-pull any kivering horse this side of the hot place.

Ever yours, PETE WHETSTONE.

[40] DOINGS ON THE DEVIL'S FORK
By Pete Whetstone

To the Editor of the New Sporter Mag.

Devil's Fork of Little Red River,
Arkansas, August, 1840.

DEAR MISTER EDITOR,
I am glad to hear you git my first letter.[1] It is a right smart little

Text: *New Sporting Magazine*, NS 1 (January 1841), 8-9.
1. The story of Pete's first letter to the *New Sporting Magazine* is fairly complicated. In

walk from the "Devil's Fork" to the big city of "London," and I guess it aint every thing that starts from one place for tother that gits there. May be you have hearn tell of one Amos Kendall, that used to be Post Master General of all these diggins[2]—well, he has quit that business, and taken up another—his health was mortal bad, and by way of gittin what he calls *"relaxation,"* he has turned editor, and is publishing the "Truthful Organ," half a column of which, by particular request, is devoted to *"Irish Stories"*—well, I reckon when I was in York city, I saw what a sort of a life one editor led: it was the tall man which prints the "Spirit of the Times," and if that sort of life is the way to git "relaxation," why,

---

"Col. Whetstone again in the Field!" *Spirit,* 10 (11 April 1840), 63, Noland writes:
  Some time in the latter part of December I enclosed to your care a letter from my friend PETE WHETSTONE to the Editor of the "New Sporting Magazine," London. I suppose it has miscarried. This will anger Pete, for he had received rather a flattering letter from the Editor of the "New Sporting Magazine," and had given him out of pure gratitude a taste of the "Devil's Fork." I will endeavor to spur him to another epistle when I see him.
Beneath Noland's note, Porter appends a response:
  A recent number of the "London Sporting Mag." quoted Col. Whetstone's last letter in the "Spirit," [number 37] and after complimenting the writer in the highest terms, the Editor announces his expectation of importing an original "thriller" himself. The letter referred to has been forwarded to him, through this office.
The letter reprinted in the *New Sporting Magazine* to which Porter refers, appeared in its January 1840 number (pp. 65-66). It was headed by a brief editorial note:
  Colonel Pete Whetstone.—This original, wild, and amusing correspondent of the "New York Spirit of the Times," [(] a Journal that *will* "go a-head") has furnished another letter to its agreeable columns [referring to letter 37]. We calculate on importing an epistle from this real sportsman, direct for our pages,—before many moons are wasted.
In the July 1840 issue (vol. 19, p. 2), the editors offered an explanation of why no Whetstone letter had appeared as promised:
  The paper which we promised from *Peter Whetstone* of Arkansas, reached the hands of our friend, Mr. Porter, in New York, but required, as the latter has informed us, decyphering, even for the eyes of an English Editor. It was promised by a late packet, and will, we have no doubt, reach us in time for the August number.
No letter appeared; no mention of a Whetstone letter is made until the December 1840 issue, in which the editor acknowledged receipt of an N. of Ark. piece—evidently those published in the January 1841 issue. Exactly what happened to the letter cannot be determined. In all probability, it was lost between New York and London.
  2. Amos Kendall was appointed Postmaster General by Jackson in 1835; he was retained by Van Buren, retiring because of ill health in 1840. He cleared the Post Office Department of debt and corruption and instituted reforms which remained in effect long after his retirement. He had two unsuccessful publishing ventures, the first of which is noted in this letter.

I'll take to "the harvest field" in preference, when I have a calling that way.

Confound the whigs, they had no more manners than to fire off cannon right close to *Kindle's* house, and his children happened to be asleep, and were most frightened to death. This was cruel treatment, to a man who had done so much for his country; why, he has got our mails so regular and brisk, that Jim Cole darsent bet me 2 to 1 that his old bear dog Hell-fire, can beat the mail from this to Batesville. But I'm jist going to quit the Postmaster General, and tell you a little about the Devil's Fork.

Well, we are all going it for old Tippecanoe.[3] Oh! it would do your heart good to hear me, and sister Sal, and Jim Cole, and Bill Spence, and Dan Looney, just sing,

"Oh where, tell me where, was your buck-eye cabin made."[4]

I tell you it makes the tears stand in a tender-hearted man's eye, when we all git together with a little "hard cider," and sing that. But that aint here nor there. He is gwoine to be our next President—there is no two ways in it, burnt brandy carnt save the little Dutchman.[5]

Well, this is a mortal *mast*-year—white oaks, black oaks, scrub oaks, hickories, hazles, and in fact, all sorts of trees, are full of nuts and acorns. The way the bear meat, and hog meat will be fat this fall, will be "a sin to Crockett." And sich crops of corn, but it is mortal wet, jist about this time;—talking of rain, makes me

---

3. William Henry Harrison was, at the time of this letter, the Whig candidate for the presidency opposing Martin Van Buren. The name "Tippecanoe" came from Tippecanoe Creek where, on 7 November 1811, Harrison and his troops defeated Tecumseh, bringing to naught Tecumseh's plans for a powerful Indian confederation in the Northwest Territory. Harrison won the election, but he died after serving only a month, leaving John Tyler to serve as President. Noland was one of Harrison's ardent supporters; the *Arkansas State Gazette,* 1 April 1840, reports that at the state Whig Convention, "C.F.M. Noland was loudly called for. He arose and passed the compliment, saying the Devil's Fork would go for Harrison, and resumed his seat."

4. The reference is to a campaign song for Harrison who ran an exuberant campaign stressing his background of "log cabin and hard cider." For details of the campaign, see Robert Gray Gunderson, *The Log-Cabin Campaign* (Lexington: Univ. of Kentucky Press, 1957).

5. Martin Van Buren. During the campaign, Van Buren was given several derisive names, e.g., "Matty," "Martin Van Ruin." See Glyndon G. Van Deusen. *The Jacksonian Era, 1828-1848* (New York: Harper and Row, 1959), p. 147.

think of a dispute I had about this moon—she hung right on her horn, and I said *wet*—three or four said *dry,* I stuck to *wet.* They said, when she lay flat of her back it was sign of wet.[6] "Who told the truth," as old Ben Jimboden, said, when he laid out Billy Black tolerably limber drunk, I tell you.

Dan Looney, Jim Cole, and Bill Spence have got a mortal team of dogs; and the way they will have lots of fun this fall and winter, will be very amusing. Dan's old stout dog has got a bad place on his back, where a bear bit him last winter, but a travelling man has advised him to use Holloway's Ointment, which he says will heal it up, and hair it over, before you can say Jack Robinson.[7] May be it is like that medicine a fellow rung in on poor lawyer McCampbell, to kill fleas, bed bugs, and all sich small game; and made the lawyer believe it was so heavy that *three ounces* weighed a pound.

We had right smart sprinkling of fun tother day at Squire Woods' grocery—May be you never heard tell of the Squire. Well, he is what Judge Jones calls "a villanous compound of ignorance, stupidity, and vanity." The way the thing happened was just about so—a new comer got his skin right full and begin to cavort, swore he had a little the fastest piece of horse-flesh that ever made a track on that hill—that he could beat any mare or mare's colt, Morphradite, or Gilflint, that water wet or sun dried, one quarter of a mile, with his weight on each, for 100; cash up and no grumbling—Well, Dan happened to have "The burnt blanket" along, and says he, "It is a wedding, Stranger—I take all sich," and begins to draw his pocket-book. The stranger hadent the truck and commenced cider fisting. Well, Dan let him off and

---

6. Details of forecasting wet or dry conditions by the position of the new moon are given in John Quincy Wolf (p. 84): "Every spring some of our prophets foretold the approach of a disastrous drought because the new moon was standing on its point, thereby showing that the water had already run out of it and left it dry as powder. An opposing school of forecasters maintained that we could expect a rainy summer and fall—so wet in fact that the crops would mildew—because the new moon was standing on its point, showing that it was going to pour out great floods of water."

7. Dan Looney is apparently very susceptible to traveling salesmen who claim to be selling wonder drugs. In letter 11 he is said to have been duped into buying "Bengal Salve" from a pedlar who promised such results in twenty-four hours.

went about his business. The stranger got another drink in him, and then commenced cavorting on himself—swore he was a mortal man—a full team—a little the best piece of man-flesh that ever walked that hill; his weight with his shoes off was 180, and he neither gived nor asked a pound. He run on a while—but at last he give Dan the lie—Dan took him a lick side of the head and at it they went—it was awful fightin I tell you—the stranger was no small potatoes—down they went, and up they riz agin. "Hurrah for Dan! Go it my Dan!" Nobody hollered for the stranger. At last I saw Dan's finger working towards the stranger's eye. They fell, Dan on top. "Take him off. My eye's out." We dragged Dan off, and the stranger was decently whipped, I tell you. We all went to Dan Looney's, where we had fun in abundance. Dan and me yoked two new comers at Old Sledge, Six bits a game, and just as the chickens crowed for day—We had them for eight dollars and twenty-five cents. No more at present.

Ever your's, PETE WHETSTONE.

[41] A LETTER FROM JIM COLE TO PETE WHETSTONE

DEVILS FORK OF LITTLE RED,
Decr. 8th 1840.

DEAR PETE,—What in the name of the world keeps you so long at the Rock—Dan Looney says them chaps, what Tyree calls the "Koppras Dye" aint gwine to give up four dollar a day these

---

Text: *Spirit,* 10 (2 January 1841), 523.

hard times without a fuss—Now do try and get off—I reckon you never seed jist sich a mast as Bill Spence and me found out on the border fork—there is a mortal sign there, and we fout two old he's, but got only one of them—That black pup out of old *June*, is a leetle the best fighting animal I ever burnt powder over—old *Drive* got mightily chawed up—it was Bills fault, he blazed away jist as the bear turned round to fight, and at the crack old Drive closed in—If you had have been home last week, we could have won right smart of truck; but Bill Spence got drunk and played smash with all the arrangements. I'm afeard he aint going ever to be of much account—that gallon law what you writ to Jo Ginel about may save him.

Some of the racoon boys went over to White river to see the race between Tomsons horse and the bay mare—They got used up—He was laid out 30 feet—but Jim Smith wrung in "Old Shore" on a feller from Missouri, and waded right into him—I reckon he won two as likely mules as you ever see.

They say them fellers down on White river lost a mortal sight of truck betting on election. Tom Jones won a heap of plunder. He bet on one state and another, but he laid up most on Old Kentuck. Squire Looser, from the middle fork, went into Tennessee last summer and he come back and crowed awfully—He dared any man to face him, and got so rantankerous that he went over to Batesville—They do say they wooled him monstrously—He has lost nigh on to the rise of five hundred dollars in money, and some of the best sort of plunder.

The Squire says he reads the paper and he cant see what you are all doing—He says Governor Yells message is a first rate document, and if you all will follow his advice about "retrenchment and reform," our State will soon be well off.

Now be sure and be home by Christmas—bring me 2 pounds of good powder. Sal says you must bring the boy a cap and the baby some beads. Bill Spence wants a good skinning knife—them little butchers with black handles are the best.

Sals love to you.

Your friend, JIM COLE.

Kurnel Pete Whetstone, Little Rock, Arks.

[42] LETTER FROM PETE WHETSTONE

Devil's Fork of Little Red River,
Feb. 24, 1841.

MY DEAR MR. EDITOR,—You needn't think becase Pete has got into that paper way over yonder, he has forgot his old friends. When Pete fails to fork up for old and tried friends, there must be a harder run on him than there was on the United States Bank, and I guess six millions of the hard stuff is nigh on enough to make any thing come in.

We have had a tolerable tight winter—cold enough sometimes to make a goose stand on one leg. But Jim and Dan ain't been idle—they have made the deer see sights, and as to koons, the way they have used them up is sinful. Only think Peltry is worth thirty cents a pound, and coon skins three bits a piece. Jim says if they will only stay "riz," he can make his everlasting fortune, and Squire Woods says they are bound to be "rizzer," because we are going to war, and that the British dress their soldiers in buckskins, and that the *smooth beavers*, like the one I bought at Little Rock, is made out of coon skins.

Bill Spence is got to be well on to no account—he is mighty puny—ailing in his breast—sorter consumpty. Old Granny Moore says, that a sure cure for all sich is to go with the *varmints*. The sagacious elephant, the ferocious hiptoptaimus, and the untamable hyena. She says their smell will make a lean man fat. I reckon as how the first chance, Bill will stir up the monkeys.

Dan and Jim went away up to the Cony fork, to a quarter race—they don't look overly pleasing since they come back. I guess they dropped their kit on the "weeping willow," for the way the "Oxford filly" made a smash of her was a sin to Moses. Jim bears it better than Dan. I reckon he sorter waded out, on a soft snap at old sledge. There was some talk about foul riding,

---

Text: *Spirit,* 11 (27 March 1841), 42.

but then Squire McFudgins used to say, that he never saw a quarter race but what the losers said they had been robbed.

There has been a ventrilokist up here, and I tell you nigh on to half the old wimmin in these parts thinks he has something to do with the devil. Why he can talk way out of doors, and stand in the house. I reckon he has got a false stomach, some like a possum. He war auful at what he called "tricks of magic." Why he beat up some eggs into Sam Walker's Sunday hat, and brought them out fine pan-cakes, and never siled her. I guess when he began to break them it took two men to hold Sam off on him, for that ar hat cost Sam a mortal sight of Peltry, and the way he walks tall with her on his head is sinful. Sister Sal and all the folks often ax arter you. No more at present.

Ever yours, PETE WHETSTONE.

[43] A BOUNCE AMONG THE BEARS, AND QUARTER RACING ON THE BARREN FORK:
By Pete Whetstone

Devil's Fork of Little Red,
Feb. 25, 1841.

MY DEAR MR. EDITOR, WELL, would you believe it?— two numbers of that work you prints away yonder in London, has git to the Devil's Fork;[1] and now the way it makes sister Sal walk tall is a caution. When she spied Pete's name in it, I guess she hopped higher nor a bounce ball made of a sturgeon's nose;

Text: *New Sporting Magazine,* NS 1 (June 1841), 401-404.
1. One of the issues was that of January 1841, containing letter 40; see fn. 2.

and even Dan Looney cocks his old cap more to one side of his head nor he used to do.—Sal read that ar letter from the Devil's Fork more nor twenty times, and Jim Cole thumbed them ar picters till he nigh on to siled them. That ar dog takes Dan's eye.[2] He says he would be willing to lay right down and die, jist to git to fight an old he, with six sich.

Well Dan, and Jim, and me, went out week before last, to try and kill some bear—we had a right tight team of dogs—the best start dog was Dan's Sharptooth—we started three the second day and killed two—one was mortal fat—but the next day we had no luck—so we left them diggings, and struck over to the Brushy Fork and camped—Next morning about sunrise we put out— afore the sun was two hours high I do reckon we bounced a little the biggest old he that ever was rustled up in these parts.—It was awful scrimmage, I tell you—thirteen as good fighting dogs as ever powder was burnt over, stuck to him like brothers. Once in a while he hugged them a little tighter than ever Dan did his sweetheart, but they fairly kivered him.—He got a lick with his paw at Jim's pup, and I guess he set him a howling;—but that ar pup is a caution, and the way he went to his work agin was amusing to Jim. Well, I do reckon they had it over a piece of ground as big as a pertater patch, for it was no use to try to shoot—we stood jist as good a chance to kill a dog as the old he,—and then too, when a gun cracks, you must look out, for a good pack will light on him quicker nor an out-township constable on to a widow woman's cow. At last he grabbed old "Game"—this was more nor Dan could stand. He went to work with his old butcher.—It was an awful sight, but Dan is a horse— the way hair and blood did fly was nobody's business—once I thought Dan was gone—but Sharptooth and Lion nailed him before he got to Dan.—He didn't stand it long after he felt the knife twixt his ribs.—We skinned him and fixed up his fleece, and by this time it was nigh on to 12 o'clock;—arter we took something to eat, we struck for the head prong of the Rocky

---

2. At this point the *New Sporting Magazine* inserts a footnote: "We presume that our friend alludes to the picture of 'Marmion,' in our January number."

Fork, and got there about sun-down; when who should come up but Bill Davis, Sam Jones, and Dick Allen, from the Upper Fork.—They had had great luck,—so we all camped together right at the foot of the Pine Hill. After supper, Bill Davis and Sam Jones pulled out an old greasy pack, and bantered us for a game of double-handed seven up, and offered to bet bear skins.—Dan ran over the cards awhile and found out *their marks* and agreed that he and me would play them a bear skin a rub—so we all went and gathered pine knots and brought them to camp.—Dan and me straddled a log, and Bill and Sam tooled some chinks, and put them on both sides of it.—Jim had a little the cleanest hunting shirt—so he hawls her off, and we spread her and went to work. Jim and Dick Allen stood by and held the lights. Now it like to have been bad work for Dan and me—they had us one time down to the big bear skin, and it was six and six, and game and game, and Dan he dealt.—Bill sat right on his left, and held the ace of trumps,—so I guess you think we were gone; well now the way Dan did hustle up a Jack was a caution to old Jack Dyer—jist afore the break of day, one side had no bear skins—it wasent Dan Looney's! After this we all took a nap.

There has been a mortal sight of quarter racing at the Barren Fork,—some fellers came in here from Missouri with quarter horses, and thought they would pick up mighty soft snaps.— They went over to a house-raising that was at Squire Long's, in the middle settlement, on the Barren Fork. Now Squire Long aint one of them sort what goes in for the gallon law; so he warnt slow in bringing out a jug of a leetle the best truck that ever slipped down a thirsty man's gullet.—"Come men," says the squire, "walk up and take a horn." Well, he did'nt have to say so twice, before it was going down like suds in a sink hole; they foddered all round and went to work.—While they were putting up the house, there was some little bantering, but when they did get it up, and about the time the old jug had Moll Thompson's hand on it for a sixth time, there was slick doings, I tell you. One of the Missourians broke out like a bear in a cane brake; says he "If you have any sportsman among you, just lend an ear to a travelling man, while he tells you what he can do. He can slow all your horses, your mares, or mare's colts, one quarter of a mile, at four hundred and forty yards—for all sorts of money, and all sorts of truck!" Well, I looked round and spied Dan Looney, and I seed at once the rattlesnake rising in him.—So says he, "Look here, old Stranger, trot out your nag, and give us a peep at him." "Good as hell," said the old Missourian; and he tells one of his gang to bring out *"Old Bear Meat."*[3] Well, out they brought him; I tell you he was an awful muscled animal, and looked like as if rats a fighting was slow travelling to him. Dan walked around him, and eyed him close—At last, says Dan, "Stranger, how many feet will you give me?" "Give you! well that beats hell," said the old Missourian. "I heard you were sporting men, but you have no sportsman among you; you are all cowards, and darsent bet; you have no race horses among you."—"Look here, my old chap," says Dan, "I guess you had best neck your bullets." And at that up steps Jim Cole with the "Weeping Willow," a mortal fast filly, that had been sent up from White River, for Jim to wing on Piney Wood Smith's "Burnt Blanket." But Piney knew Cole: he had travelled, and it was K.K.—The old Missourian eyed the "Weeping Willow" a good while. At last, says he, "I can slash her

---

3. Although used fictionally here, a stallion named Bear Meat was owned in 1841 by Thomas T. Tunstall of Batesville. He was foaled in 1835, and was by Bertrand out of Black Kitty Clover by Eclipse. In 1844 Noland apparently owned the horse, for in the Batesville *North Arkansas,* 7 October 1844 [p. 2], he offered him for sale under unusual terms:

"A RARE CHANCE FOR POLK MEN.

I will sell my fine young Stallion *Bear-Meat* on the terms proposed below, taking a note well secured payable 1st Jan'y, 1845, with ten per cent. per annum. He is of the best native blood, having been got by old Bertrand, out of Black Kitty Clover by Eclipse, (she being half sister to the celebrated Sir Lovel). I paid the last year $300 in specie for him to a gentleman of Sumner Co., Tenn. where he was bred.

TERMS—I will take $250 for him. Nothing if Polk is elected next President.
$300 for him. Nothing if Polk gets 120 electoral votes.
$400 for him. Nothing if Polk gets 100 electoral votes.
$500 for him. Nothing if Polk gets 80 electoral votes.
$1000 for him. Nothing if Polk gets 61 electoral votes."

Polk was, of course, elected; however, no record of anyone accepting Noland's offer appears. It is quite possible that Noland's banter was wholly fictional. Tunstall had owned the stallion as early as 1841. Noland says he bought him in 1843 and that he was young. The several discrepancies in the two accounts of the horse suggest, at least, that Noland was perhaps enjoying a hoax.

from A, b, Ab.—to Crucifix." "But you darsent give me twenty feet no how," says Dan. "I dares to give you ten and the breadth of her hoof," says the old Missourian, "for a couple of hundred in money and three hundred in likely horses." "Pack a hundred to little Bill Allen," says Dan, "and it is a wedding." "When will you run?" says the Missourian. "Saturday," says Dan, "and over Joe Cohen's paths." "Give us your corn stealer," said the old Missourian, and they locked fists. They put up a hundred for forfeit, with Squire Long; and after a heap of loud talking, and clearing out the seventh jug for Squire Long, they all put out.

Well, Saturday came, and there was a mortal crowd; Piney Wood Smith and Old Moat judged for Dan, and Squint-eyed Jones and Sam Bradshaw judged for the Missourian. Bill Spence turned the "Weeping Willow," and the old Missourian turned "Bear Meat." When they came up, the judge weighed "Bear Meat's" rider, and he was a hundred to a half notch. Little Bill Allen looked as fierce as a wild cat in a briar thicket. The old Missourian's horse fretted awfully, while the "Willow" was as cool as a cowcumber. They flung up for tracks, and Dan won choice, but the old Missourian got the word. I knew Bill Spence was good at turning, but then Giles Scroggins in his best day warnt a match for that old Missourian. He tried all sorts of ways to make Bill mad and to fret his nag,—but Jim is all horse, I tell you. They worked nigh on to four hours starting, and twixt the time Bill Allen stroddled the "Weeping Willow" and the start, there was thirteen cows and calves and three horse brutes bet on the race. Well, at last the mare began to fret, and Bill to get mad; so when they came up, the Missourian had a little the advantage, and Bill asked him. "Go," says the Missourian, and away they went. It was awful lumbering—they stuck to each other like a tick to a dead nigger. I saw the start, and if anything, Bear Meat had it by a foot—so I hurried down to the out come. I meets Dan,—"How was it at the out come?" says I. "He beat me six feet," says Dan. "You have got him," says I. "Got him," says Dan. "Why I get all sich."—So the judges met, and after about half an hour they brought it in "Bear Meat" won by seven feet two inches; not quite enough to save the Missourian's truck.—Well, he give it up like a man, and Dan treated to three gallons and sugar.—They had all sorts of times.—The old Missourian got into a game of poker and was wading out of his losses. I heard him call a feller for twenty on three jacks, jist as I left,—the feller had three tens.—"I was close to your tail," said the feller.—"Yes and so was 'Bear Meat' to the 'Weeping Willow,' but it didn't save my truck," said the old Missourian.

Ever Your's, PETE WHETSTONE.

[44] LETTER FROM PETE WHETSTONE

DEVIL'S FORK OF LITTLE RED,
Sept. 12, 1841.

MY DEAR MR. EDITOR.—Well, it has been a long time since I writ you. The truth is, it has been a tight time on us here—crops burn't up and money scarce. The Govenor is death agin the Bank, and the Banks say they darsent lend any more; so twixt them and the Governor, it is hard times.[1] The way, too, they shave Arkansas money is sinful. But then we thought we were going to have better times, until the *veto* come.[2] I reckon I never

---

Text: *Spirit*, 11 (9 October 1841), 378.

1. The early years of the State Bank were filled with a succession of scandals. Finally, on 1 November 1839, the main branch at Little Rock was forced to suspend specie payments; the branches soon did the same. By 1840, it was virtually impossible for the Bank to collect debts, and it was well on the way toward insolvency. Governor Archibald Yell ordered an investigation even before he was elected in 1840; the legislature finally liquidated the State Bank in 1843. Prior to liquidation, Yell kept a critical eye upon the activities of the Bank.

2. After John Tyler succeeded to the presidency upon the death of William Henry Harrison on 4 April 1841, he immediately found himself in a conflict over the attempt to reestablish a national bank. Congress passed such a bill, but on 16 August 1841, Tyler vetoed it.

seed jist such a fuss. The dimicrats shouted for Tyler, and the whigs were wrathy. Sam Jones said he ought to have the *witch weed* used on him—Squire Long said he want to blame for his *conscience* would not let him sign it; but Mr. Thompson, the schoolmaster, said d____n his conscience, for he had read of one Sir Purty-nax Mac Siccofant, who had been in Parlyment nigh on thirty years, and never heard of such a word.

Never mind, they say the Land Bill will pass, and that is gwine to do us a heap of good,—and we have had late rains, and the way there will be a big mast is no boddy's business.

There have been lots of quarter races on the Barren Fork;— one party smashed right open. They say they bribed the other side, and then were flung off.—Where is old *Boston?* Aint he coming out to Kentucky? That is the place for him. If he can lay *Wagner,* the truck can be walked off with.

Bill Spencer and Dan Looney have a great team of Bar dogs. They expect tall fighting this Fall. We had a round t'other day with an old she panther—it want no fight—they waded right through her.

Jim Cole has gone over to the War Eagle to try to wring in a bite on Piney-wood Smith. Piney is not soft, but Jim has old *Bullet-neck,* and if he lumbers, the truck is his.

Bill Spence has quit drink, and taken to hard work.

Ever yours, PETE WHETSTONE.

[45] LETTER FROM PETE WHETSTONE

DEVIL'S FORK OF LITTLE RED,
October 4, 1841.

MY DEAR MR. EDITOR,—Since I last writ you, we have had an awful fuss on these diggings. That ar second veto set us all a

---

Text: *Spirit,* 11 (6 November 1841), 426.

snorting.[1] One kick in the stomach is as much as a common man can stand, and when it comes twice in so short a time, human nater will show itself. The whigs here stuffed a jacket and breeches with straw, and fixed a hat on it, which they called Tyler. They then raised a pole, and hung it up and set fire to it. As the blaze begun to raise up, I spied veto in two places, over the spots where they say the President's conscience lies, and the next moment, Bill Spencer, Dan Looney, and Jim Cole cracked their rifles, and I guess they made a smash of them papers. There was a mortal big crowd present, and all seemed to enjoy the thing. The chaps on the Devil's Fork can't stand shin-plasters any longer. Why, it is gitting so that it is no use to sell truck,—a cow and calf wont bring as much silver as would pay for a man's dinner in a big city. Squire Aken is awful wrathy; he says his next neighbor in Illinois was Judge Upshire, who used to live right smack in the fish-bone country; and he knowed all about them Virginia transendenters and abstractioners, and he says they are like his bull horse, great at the off-wheel, but mighty unsartain in the lead. Why he says two of them like to have fout once about the difference 'twixt sheep-meat and mutton. But I shant trouble you any more with polyticks, only to say John Tyler had better not put his foot on the Devil's Fork.

Well, there has been hot times on the Mississippi.[2] They jist tied fellows head and heels and threw them in the river. This was cutting the thing too fat,—law is law,—and the man that won't stand the law, aint much in a bear-fight.

---

1. On 15 August 1841, President Tyler vetoed a bill to reestablish a national bank. Congress then passed a second bill which they thought would more nearly conform to Tyler's wishes, but on 9 September he vetoed it. In protest his entire cabinet, save Webster, resigned. Considerable dislike for the President resulted from these two vetos. See Van Deusen, pp. 156-158; and Frederick Jackson Turner, *The United States, 1830-1850: The Nation and Its Sections* (New York: Holt, Rinehart and Winston, 1935), p. 497, n. 25. Pete's animosity toward Tyler reflects Noland's feelings; he wrote to a brother, "Pres. Tyler has knocked us into a cocked hat—I view him as a traitor to the party and have lost all confidence in him." [HLS, C.F.M. Noland to Callender Noland, 11 October 1841. Univ. of Virginia, Alderman Library, Berkeley Papers, 38-113-33.]

2. Although this event possibly occurred as Pete describes it, no mention of the execution is made in the Arkansas press.

I forgot to tell you that night they burnt the *veto,* there was a pedlar camped jist across the creek. He got there late, and before he stripped his horse, arter he unhitched him, he spied the light, and the straw man a blazing. He thought it was a sure enough man, and the way he hitched up and made tracks was awful. His old horse got the better of him, and tin cups, nutmegs, and clocks flew the right way. His outfit was knocked into a crackling, and such a report as he spread about the country was a sin to Moses. He got up as high as 20 men that he had seen hung up.

Well, there is a mortal mast. Bears will be fat, and Jim, Dan, and Bill have a crack team of dogs. They expect lots of fun.

There is a great quarter race to be run before long over the Yellville paths. Both sides spunky and sure. I aint time to write more.

Ever yours, PETE WHETSTONE.

[46] PETE WHETSTONE AGAIN IN THE FIELD!

DEVIL'S FORK OF LITTLE RED,
Jan. 25, 1842.

MY DEAR MR. EDITOR.—It is no use to try to git out of a thing when you aint got the possibles, but then if Pete aint had hard shakes enough to loosen a man's fore-teeth, it is no use to have the ager. I jist wonder what them tarnal shakes were made for? I guess jist to show man he aint no more in his Maker's hand than a snow-bird in an old *he's* clutches. I am rising agin like smoke from a new-laid improver of the airth.

Well, I aint writ you as much as I ought—but I tell you when corn gits to 20 cents, and big steers to 8 dollars, and Arkansas money shaved till there is none left, a man don't feel like shed-

Text: *Spirit,* 11 (26 February 1842), 615.

ding ink,—but then you are somehow or tother sich a kind oblig-
ing man, I can't git over flinging a quill once in a while.

Well, I see old Boston and that ar New Jersey filly are to come
together[1]—I guess it will be the lion and the panter in all their
ancient ways.

Aint that ar Reel a caution; why I do reckon old Bullet-neck
couldent gin her more nor 10 feet down the quarter-stretch. I
have bet Squire LONG two cows and calves old Boston slays Fashion, and JIM COLE staked up 20 head of likely young hogs with
Sam Jones, from Coney, the same way.

They talk of gitting up a track over on the Middle Prong—a
fellow has come in with an awful tall horse; here is one of his
handbills:[2]—

"THE SUPERIOR STABLE HORSE 'YOUNG GOURD-VINE'"

Will make the ensue-ing sesin at the house of sam Jones on the
middle prong and at the house of squire grubbs on the devil's
fork internally at the reduced price of two dollars the sesin and
three dollars to inshow a mare to be with fole—n.b. I'll take any
sort of truck from kune skins to bars-ile—

PEDIGREY.

Young Gourd-vine was got by *Old Sir Archibald* that great race
horse what Kirnel johnsin run against Eklipse for $100,000, and
his dam was the famous mare *ole speckel back* got by the *pisen shirt,*
g.d. the fastest nag that ever made a track, tu wit, *blue ruin* got by
the imp. *diomead* out of the imp. *taturs mare* and she out of the
flying pop gun and she out of the *godolphing arabin*—nothing could
be richer than gourd vine's pedigrey—

---

1. The race between the two great horses, Boston and Fashion, was contracted on 30
November 1841, and the sporting press, including the *Spirit,* wrote of the upcoming
race throughout the winter. It was held on 10 May 1842, at the Union Course on Long
Island before a crowd estimated at 70,000. Fashion was the winner. Details of the race
are given in Robertson, pp. 61-63.
2. Noland is parodying the pedigrees which regularly appeared in the Spirit, e.g.,
"Imported Whale," *Spirit,* 11 (13 March 1841), 23. Almost without exception, these
pedigrees claimed that their particular animal was the finest in the land. Though
fictional, Young Gourd-Vine's pedigree makes use of several names which were quite
similar to the names of actual horses, e.g., Sir Archy and Diomed.

PURFORMINCE

at 3 yr. old he was put in training for a match of 440 yards or one quarter of a mile agin Bill Allen's Old dish face for fifty dollars in truck, and the way Gourd vine laid him, was a kaution. Arter that he fell lame and aint been trained since—

DESKRIPSHION

Young gourd vine will be 13 years old next grass—he is a kreme color with a white mane and a black tale—the sise of sixteen hands high with all sorts of muscel and perhaps the gratest hind leg that ever was hung to a horse—I jist ax breeders of fine horses to come and look for themselves—my motto is 'roll your bones and fair play.'

his
Dick X Cobble"

Witness tom carnell J.P. mark

I reckon Reel, Bosting, and all sich must look out—Dick Cobble has the tall dog now—Bill Spence like to got a fight out of him by offering to breed his old blind mare mule on the shares.

Well, I see from your paper that the Mexicans have got that ar clever fellow what prints the "Picayune;"[3] I reckon if they know what is good for them they had best not hurt him. The way the Devil's Fork would turn out would be a caution. Them ar Spaniards aint half as good as wild ingens. They darsent hurt Kendall.

If every sort of truck want so low at Orleans, Bill Spence and me would start next month to the Massassappy with a flat boat, and git there to the races—I am told it is a mortal tall city, and I'd like to take a peep at it.

---

3. "Trebla" [Albert C. Ainsworth], "Sayings and Doings in New Orleans," *Spirit*, 11 (1 January 1842), 517, contains the information Pete read: "News came in town to-day [16 December 1841], direct from Yucatan, confirming the rumor that the *Santa Fe Expedition* (rendered sacred by the memory of poor, good, worthy, GEO. W. KENDALL) has been taken." Kendall, one of the founders of the New Orleans *Picayune*, had joined the expedition in 1841 to serve as a war correspondent. The *Picayune* became famous for its wide and speedy coverage of the war with Mexico. He was finally rescued from the Mexican government through the efforts of wealthy and influential friends and wrote of his experiences in his *Narrative of the Texan Santa Fe Expedition* (2 vols., 1844). The definitive biography is Fayette Copeland, *Kendall of the Picayune* (Norman: Univ. of Oklahoma Press, 1943).

There has been a smart sprinkling of game this season. Bill and Dan have killed 13 bears and 2 panters.

Koon skins aint worth as much as they were last year, and Dan floored a feller bekase he said the reason was Old Tip was dead.[4] Squire Smith says the new Xchecker aint democratic, bekase the circulation aint limited. He says no man aint competent to say how much meat and bread it will take to do other folks' families from one Christmas to another.

Ever yours, PETE WHETSTONE.

N.B. Col. Pete Whetstone's compliments to Mr. Trebla, and he may look out for him at Orleans in the last of February, on a broad horn—no preventing Providence, as our circuit rider says.

[47] PETE WHETSTONE'S TRIP TO NEW ORLEANS

DEVIL'S FORK OF THE LITTLE RED,
March 25, 1842.

MY DEAR MR. EDITOR,—I am home agin, thanks to the Lord. I had a tight time gitting to Orleans, and a harder one gitting back.[1] I went down on the soft end of the current, on a

---

4. The late President William Henry Harrison, who died 4 April 1841.

Text: *Spirit,* 12 (23 April 1842), 85.
1. Following one of Noland's letters in the *Spirit,* 12 (5 March 1842), 1, Porter appends a note evidently based upon information received in a private letter: "He [Noland] has arrived in N.O. accompanied by his friend [William F.] DENTON, of Batesville, and the celebrated Col. PETE WHETSTONE, the universally popular correspondent of the 'Spirit of the Times' and the London 'New Sporting Magazine,' etc. Col. Whetstone hailed the 'Pawnee' just as she was clearing the Devil's Fork of the Little Red, when she rounded to and took him on board, with his famous hunting jackass 'Levi Woodbury,' so famous as a racer on the Snakebite Prong. We shall address the Colonel to-day, a letter of congratulation upon his arrival at New Orleans, where he will be 'the big dog of tanyard.'" This letter is Pete's response.

broad horn. Jim, and Dan, and I, had a load of steers, two pet
bears, 100 venison hams, some bear skins, and "Levi Woodbury."
I tell you we trafficked the coast, having first touched at Vicksburg and Natchez; the venison hams were a brisk sale, but them
ar steers stuck to us like brothers; we got them off at last, being
able to hold our own. But Levi was no go.

Well, when we got to Orleans, I spruced up, and made strait
for the St. Charles—a nice house, I tell you. In I walks, and the
first man I spied behind the counter, was the identical man I saw
at the Astor[2]—"Col. WHETSTONE, as I live," said he, and at that
we forked.

"Col. Whetstone's baggage, No. 58!"—at that I guess the folks
began to look. I looked too, and who should I see but Captain A.
of the Army. I tell you he is all sorts of a feller, cut the right way
of the leather, and out of the right sort of leather. He had Mrs.
Tigertail, and little Tigertails, and a whole lot of Ingins, right out
of Florida, carrying them to the Arks.[3]

Well, Alick and I walked down into the cellar, and the way
there was a crowd, war a caution. I can't begin to tell all who I
saw—GARRISON, Uncle NED, Maj. DAVIE, and lots of them—and
then I saw JEF WELLS, the gemman what owns Reel. If he aint to
my notion, just let the ager walk into me once a day. Well, we
liquored, and arter a while the *gong* sounded, and sich a gitting
up stairs I never did see.

Well, if it didn't look funny jist to see that spread, arter eating
three weeks on a broad horn. I can't begin to tell what we did
have; soups, and meats, and game, and all sorts of nicknacks,
and wound up with a pudding puffing fire and brimstone like a
young earthquake.

Speaking of game, did I ever tell you how they wrung in a bird
on me at St. Louis. "Well," says the servant, handing the bill of

---

2. Pete's impressions of the Astor House are recorded in letter 34.

3. Tiger Tail (Thlocks-Tustenuggee) was a Tallahassee Indian, who, along with many
of his followers, was deported from Florida in 1842. The destination of the party was
Arkansas, but Tiger Tail died in a barracks at New Orleans. See Caroline Mays Brevard,
A History of Florida, ed. James Alexander Robertson (Deland, Florida, 1924), I, 171-172,
as cited in Masterson, p. 324.

fare, "what game, Col. Whetstone, to-day?"

"Give me this fellow," says I, "with the long French name."

Well, he brought it. The head was on, and as I live, it was no more nor less than an old-fashioned *fly-up-the-creek,* vulgarly called *a poke!*

"Well," says I, "look here, stranger! you can't wring in any sich on me. I know that ar varmint, if he is rigged out,"—and when I named him, I guess some of the game eaters begin to git sick about their stomachs.

Arter dinner wor over I wor introduced to the gemman what prints the "Bee,"[4]—if he don't git his share of the honey, there is no use in looks. Mr. TREBLA and Mr. PROFILE also came to see me, and they treated me mighty nice.[5] We went down into the cellar agin, and talked horse. They believe in Reel, and I do expect she is a caution. Her owner talks the right way. He don't banter, but he is open to the winner of the big match. That is the way to talk it.

I went to the Opera. Lord! if there aint more fools in this world than would fill the big bend on the Devil's Fork. There I was rammed and jammed worse nor fighting musketers, on a hot day, and sich nonsense and stuff!—Oh lordy!—"Nish ne," "nosh ne," "noosh ne," "nosh ni."—"Ingun to me," says I.

"Rich Italyon," says a dandy looking fellow.

"How vulgar," says another.

I knew it was me he meant—so says I, "Mister, if you don't like the smell of the apples, you had best quit the cider press."

At that he bristled up and raised a sorter looking spy glass, and begin to take sight at me—he eyed me awhile and lowered his glass.

"Well, how do you like me?" says I.

"Here is my card," says he.

---

4. Pete probably refers to Alexander Bullit, who, with John Magne, was the editor of the *Bee* from 1839 until 1844.

5. It was following this meeting that "Trebla" (Albert C. Ainsworth) wrote his long, affectionate tribute to Noland which appeared in "Sayings and Doings in New Orleans," *Spirit,* 12 (26 March 1842), 37.

"Where do you keep?" says I.

At that his dander raised and he begin to talk war-talk—but I guess I cooled him, for I told him at last "them ar cold sassinges he sold Jim, and Dan, and me when we first landed on the Levee on our flat boat had red flannel in them," and then I guess he sloped rapid.

I got away after the first act—now look here, is it sure-enough-fun or is it make-believe with them? Do them ar chaps that bellow bravo, *"hit him agin, his eye aint out!"* and the like, git the worth of their money, or do they go there because it is the hight of quality?—I wish Giles Scroggins was alive, I would ask him.[6]

Well, we got back to the St. Charles—talked horse and had lots of fun—I guess Rio Jinery JIM was in that crowd—if he wasn't it was somebody that is tolerable cute, I tell you.

Well, arter all, I couldn't stay to the races. I got sick the second day and I wanted to git home. I don't believe in going under the ground where there is as much water. It was like pulling eye-teeth to quit them ar fellers, but then them ar shakes; now don't talk—headache; why I had enough at one time to supply a regiment. I put out on the Pawnee—she is slow and sure, only 14 days to Batesville—but then we stuck on the bars, and that made a fellow mighty smart. He asked me why the Pawnee was like Dan Looney, and I gin it up, and he said she was a *bar*-hunter.

Well, I guess I brought *Levi* back; they couldn't git him for nothing, no way they could fix it. He is a mortal jackass, and travelling south, has holp him mightily. There was a fellow tried to swop me out of him with a he pig of the Berkshire breed; he couldn't quite come it—he said $20 in blue backs, I said $200 in the ordinary truck—so it was no go. I am going to show Levi alongside of the Young Gourd Vine.

I have shuck some since I got back, but am rising agin.

Ever yours, PETE WHETSTONE.

---

6. Recall that Giles Scroggins was the local authority on class distinctions.

[48] KURNEL PETE WHETSTONE ON HIS TRAVELS!

WAY UP IN OLD VIRGINNY,
July 15, 1842.

MY DEAR MR. EDITOR,—Well, I guess the next time I come over them ar' mountings I'll have my life insured. Why, they make no more of smashing a feller up than a Temperance man would of bolting a pint of cold water. I did have a *life preserver* along, but then she warnt blowed up.

I have been down to Washington. I saw the Senate and the House of Representatives. That ar' Senate is a nice body.—They are as still and solemn as Jim Cole at a prayer meeting. But that ar' House is rather inclined to be a little rip-roarious—there is too many of them in one room—they can't all keep quiet at one time—the thing is unpossible. I guess I hearn about the best of them speak, and I reckon the worst too, for there was an awful leaving once or twice. For a right slick speech, I believe I would put up my money on Dick Thompson, of Indiana, and for larning, on old Johnny Q.[1]

I guess I was at the White House, and the way I was treated was nice—a bottle of wine 407 years old—but it was only to look at. Some not quite as old did me, for I aint proud. Speaking of wine, makes me think of the Temptation Societies. I tell you they made a big to do on the 4th. They are working wonders, making a sober man out of a drunken one, and enough left for a small dog. If it lasts, they will have every bottle from Maine to Georgia uncorked. I wish them well, though I fear they are running the thing in the ground. If they would go only the whole hog there

---

Text: *Spirit*, 12 (23 July 1842), 242.

1. In 1830 John Quincy Adams was elected to the House of Representatives from Massachusetts. He served until his death in 1848 and was reputed to be one of the best educated men of his time.

wouldent be any danger, but that ar' snout and bristles may choke them.

I haint seen old *Bosting* yet, though I came pretty close, having met the old Colonel and LONG at the big city.[2] I tell you they aint whipped yet, and if *Fashion* don't keep out of the way this Fall, there will be more lumbering 'twixt her and the old horse.[3]

Blue Dick, they say, comes down the quarter stretch sorter at the lick that *Bullet-neck* struck when he beat *Burnt-blanket.* He and Sarah Washington will come together this Fall; if they do, jist hold your hat. She is jist about as slick a critter as is in these parts, and if he beats her, good bye to all the crop of Fairfax, from blackberries up.

I have hearn lately from Jim Cole; he says sich a mast never was seen, and the way he is counting on peltry is a sin to Moses. He writes me that *Levi* haint done much in the way of benefitting his country; but I guess Jim laid them out when Levi beat the *Young Gourd-vine.* It was tighting and tighting for the first thousand yards, but Levi was too *windy* for him. Jim sent me one of the spurs used by Bill Allen on the occasion, to be presented to you. It is a crowder—jist about as big a one as you'll see in a week's travel.

Dan Looney has found a lead mine on the *Dry Fork.*[4] He holds his head high, Jim writes. Old lawyer McCampbell always said there was lead there, and Squire Kulp said "It only needed a *bottynist* to tell what sorter *rocks* they had!"[5] No more at present.

Ever yours, PETE WHETSTONE.

---

2. "The old Colonel" was William Ransom Johnson, the manager of the horse Boston. "Long" was James Long of Washington, the owner of Boston.

3. There was much talk during 1842 of a rematch between Fashion and Boston (see letter 46).

4. In the late 1800s considerable lead was mined on Cura Creek in northeast Independence County. See *Biographical and Historical Memoirs of Northeast Arkansas* (Chicago: Goodspeed, 1889), p. 625.

5. In "Still Later," *Spirit,* 23 (14 May 1853), 147, Noland retells this anecdote: "I once travelled from Little Rock in a four-horse postchaise, where I had been playing the part of legislator, in the company with several Solons, among them old Father Culp, who, in the innocence of his heart, as we passed a cliff of rocks, said—'Well, I have often wished to travel by here with a *botanist,* to know what sort of *rocks* these are.'"

[49] LETTER FROM COL. PETE WHETSTONE

A Camp Meeting—Mr. Maffitt—Boston and Fashion—Cause of Jim Cole's getting his eye "squz"—Tom Marshall and the Teetotallers—Gen. Worth, the Florida War, and Lieut. McLaughlin—Election in Arkansas—Henry Clay the next President—Dan Looney, and the Prospects of Sport, etc.

WAY UP IN OLD VIRGINNY,
August, 30, 1842.

MY DEAR MISTER EDITOR.—I do guess they have had the biggest Camp Meeting in these parts—why that ar one on the Eagle Fork two years ago, didn't begin to be a priming to it. They had nigh on to the rise of 10,000 people on Sunday. Mr. MAF-FITT was expected; he didn't come, but I reckon that ar young ROZELL rolls his bones nigh on to as well as Maffitt. He is young 'tis true, but jist wait a few years and if he aint a caution I am deceived—why larning jist rolls out of him, like falling off a log. He is very much liked and Pete says "God speed him."

Well, where will Boston and Fashion come together? I think the proprietors are too liberal, for, as Bill Montgomery once said, gold may be bought at too high a price. I like the fellow what manages the Course at Alexandria, he seems inclined to do what is right. Speaking of Alexandria makes me think of the man that prints a paper there.[1] Now I do say, take it year in and

---

Text: *Spirit,* 12 (10 September 1842), 326.

1. Edgar Snowden succeeded his father Samuel as editor of the Alexandria *Gazette* in 1831. He held that position until about 1847, when his brother Harold took over.

year out, that is the best paper for infomation and politics, this side of the mountains.

But changing the subject I heard from JIM COLE. He has got into a terrible bad scrape. I guess Jim forgot them teetotal principles what I thought were instilled into him. He got drunk, I reckon; any how a big fellow from the Caney Fork like to have squz one of his eyes out; but I hope he will fall back on the good principles of temperance. They say the good cause is going ahead in Arkansas—I hope so—but then *there*, they don't expect because a man joins the temperance society he is to say his prayers three times a day; but they expected that from Tom Marshall, and jist because he fout a duel they tried to read him out of their ranks.

Well, the Florida War is over at last. That ar General WORTH is a great man, and I tell you that are Lieut. McLloughlin totes a mortal old head on young shoulders. He is some in a bear fight, I tell you.

Hot times in Arkansas—banks or no banks. The election comes on in October, 4 Loco Focos out for Congress, and no Whig.[2] The Whigs never trained the first horse this year. I guess the old member will get to the stand first.[3] He is a mighty clever man, and so is Dr. Chapman one of them that runs against him.

There is no telling, however, who is Governor till after the election, but if Henry Clay aint next President, any man can walk off with six likely cows and calves, and several chucks of horses, that I have got running on the Devil's Fork.[4]

DAN LOONEY writes me that the masts is great this year and he expects lots of fun.

Levi is fat and thriving, and expects next season to make the *Young Gourd-vine* squat out of these diggins.

Truly yours, PETE WHETSTONE.

---

2. Pete gives more details of the campaign in letter 50.

3. Edward Cross, who had held the office for several years, is the "old member." He was reelected. For details of the campaign, see Ross, pp. 181-185.

4. Henry Clay was, by 1842, actively campaigning for the presidency. He was defeated in 1844 by James Polk.

[50] SPORTING EPISTLE FROM THE DEVIL'S FORK
Letter from Jim Cole to Pete Whetstone.

DEVIL'S FORK OF LITTLE RED,
Sept. 1st., 1842.

DEAR PETE,—I ain't bin much at riten, bekase it is oncommon
hard work to me—I had rather split two hundred rales any time
than try to rite, and besides, if the truth must out, I got a most
tarnation using up not long ago. I was tight and yoked a big
feller from the Dry fork, and he was too much for me—he fout
fair, and guess it was my fault, that the fuss took place. I am
monstrous quarrelsome when my boat is loaded, as you well
know—but I am a teetotaler now, and so you see I'll be wide
awake the next fite I have. There has bin lots of fun in these
parts since you left us—we had two camp meetings—Bill Smith,
Jim Nedle, and Sam Marshall all jined—Jim sold his quarter
horse two days arter meeting broke up.

I was down to Marion t'other day—Brown C. is out for the
Legislater. He is agin the Banks, but goes his death for a big one,
to be managed by old Uncle Sam. He had some as nice mineral
as I ever seed, and thinks he has found a bully lead.

In this county we have nigh on to a dozen candidates—Dan
Looney has the best chance I think. Lawyer Evans is running for
Kongress, but he used to be States Feliciter and prosicuted too
many fellers in these parts, for his own good.[1] Doctor Chapman

---

Text: *Spirit,* 12 (24 September 1842), 349.

1. In all, five candidates entered the race. The incumbent Edward Cross, Lemuel D.
Evans, Dr. Daniel J. Chapman, and Euclid L. Johnson ran on the Democratic ticket.
William Cummins eventually declared his candidacy as a Whig. See Ross, pp. 182-185.

is also running—he was up here and made a speech—he is a dimmicrat, but goes his death for the improvement of White river, and I guess if no Whig comes out, he will git a rite good lift all about here. As to Lawyer Johnson he ain't known much in these parts.

They had a big quarter race down in Tolbert's Settlement— Old-Boon stands Ball agin the field yet, tho, they say his friends darsent turn him against Old-Bullet-neck—but I hearn John Darboy say publickly and above board, last Friday at Squire Smith's house raisin, that Old-Boon was the best nag that ever water wet or sun dried, and that if he was a fool his money wasent. He aint one of the back out sort, and I guess it will be a wedding, if they agree on the paths. Morg Carter trains Boon, and says he is the best horse to git off, and the surest horse arter he does, he ever handled; but Sam Jones says he always has had the advantage of his own paths.

I reckon twould do your hart good to see the mast—if bar ain't thick this season it is no use to make kalkilation—be sure and bring some good powder, and if you can git a cheap rifle about 32 to the pound, why tote her out.[2]

Old June's pups are the rite sort—they will make an old he see sites—Amos Robinson offered me a tolerable good chunk of a cow for the black pup with white ears, but I laffed at him. I tell you we will be broke up when that breed of dogs gives out. They say there is a mighty fine breed down about Batesville, that the Caldwells and Bean and Barnett used to have.

Levi is fat and I guess he will do a good business next season.

All our folks are about—Sal has been ailing some since you left, but two doses of Sappington cured her—you are often axed after.

Your friend, JIM COLE.

Kurnel PETE WHETSTONE, Aldie, Va.

---

2. See letter 36, fn. 2. Bullets for this rifle would weigh one-half ounce.

[51] SPORTING EPISTLE FROM
PETE WHETSTONE

DEVIL'S FORK OF LITTLE RED,
Feb. 6th, 1843.

DEAR MISTER EDITOR: It's no use to give an excuse for not writing; but I am doing better nor that; making up for lost time.

Well, there has been tall racing down on White River. *Old Sense* was there; he is some in any crowd. You jist ought to hear him lumber once. OLD BEN or GOBLER can't shine where he is. JIM MEALBAG was cavorting in awful style, daring any man to face him, when Old Sense come in contact with him. "You are my man," says Old Sense; "just let me look at your eye—you are a judge of human natur, *Mealbag;* you, like me, have only to look at the os-frontis of a man to read him!"

"Look at the what?" says Jim.

"At the os-frontis, you d____d fool; why you are a nice man to talk big and not know what the *os-frontis* is. You jist might as well look at another part of the body that I shant mention here."

"Don't talk that way, Mister, or I'll make a perfect smash of you!"

"A smash of me! why look here, Mealbag, I have rid down two chunks of ponies and three mortal race horses hunting for the man could do that. Do you know me? Why I am *Old Sense!* When *I* talk, fishes sink low and seek deep water; snakes and reptiles creep back to their dark corners; steamboats of a hundred horse power refuse to turn their wheels and float back into the channel—the mighty African lion as he roams over the burning

---

Text: *Spirit,* 13 (4 March 1843), 7.

sands of the great desert, shaking his mane and roaring out young thunder, stops, and then tucks his tail, and heels it like a scared dog; seas cease to ebb and flow; Etny, Vesuvius and other burning mountains refuse to belch forth their *larver*; the laughing hyena and the cunning jackall lose all relish for human flesh. And the deadly rattlesnake, the terror of bare-footed men in summer time, swallows his own pisen. When *Old Sense* speaks, the earth trembles, and Millerites think the day is coming.[1] Now, Mealbag have you the nerve to face sich a man?"

"I aint got nothing agin you, Old Sense."

"Then, Mealbag, jist call for a little of 'Nature's Grand Restorative or Vegetable Cordial;' or to speak to dull comprehensions, trot out a half pint of *Old Bald Face!*"

I tell you there was lots of fun there. One fellow from the South Fork talked tall. *He was lousy with money,* and dared any man to face him. Lame Sam Jones from Coney *set to him.* They cavorted a long time, when they laid up a three dollar shinplaster each. I guess what was made or lost 'twixt them would'nt hurt nobody, for both notes were the rankest sort of counterfeits.

There was a sort of Roll-the-bones at work, and the invitations to come up and sport a dollar or two, warnt slow. They gathered round it thick. One feller with a cap made out of the raw material, and I guess from "that same old coon," whenever he laid down a quarter and won, would hop up, sort of cut the double-trouble and sing

"Oh Jinny is your hoe cake done, my dear,

Oh, Jinny is your hoe cake done?"

The *roll-your-bones* took in a heap, but when they come to sort it, nigh on to the rise of half warnt fit to buy sour shucks with.

Old Sense closed a quarter race, and he thinks he has the feller by the wrist; but I guess he will earn all he makes, for if there is a keen one, 'twixt sunrise and dark he has woke him up this time.

---

1. The name "Millerite" was a popular expression applied to members of the Adventist Church, so called because of their founder William Miller (1782-1849). Miller predicted that the second coming of Christ and, hence, the end of the world would occur in 1843.

They have had all sorts of racing at the Rock. JIM COLE has been gone there nigh on to three months legislating. He has made a perfect smash of all the Banks but one, and that lets out its paper from a small silver box. We are to have plenty of silver now, and then we are to have a Stay Law, and who cares about owing money? I'll tell you the Devil's Fork is rising like smoke from a tar-kill.

Bars are fat, but not overly plenty—deer aint worth killing, as peltry is worth but 8 cents shaved.

No more, but just rest easy that I am ever yours,

PETE WHETSTONE.

[52] SPORTING EPISTLE FROM "N. OF ARKANSAS" [Excerpt]

The way the natives sometimes talk is amusing. The following dialogue occurred on the Dividing Ridge of the Devil's and Cony Forks. OLD SENSE met DAN LOONEY, and they were strangers to each other. Says "Old Sense," "Good morning, sir, are you well?"

"If you call a man well that has run twenty miles, I am *that*."

"Did you see any bear?"

"If you call a big black thing about the size of PETE WHETSTONE's black mar, or hoss, I did."

"Had you a gun?"

"Now you hit me."

"Did you draw blood?"

"Do you call my double, double handsfull of brains, *blood*?"

"Had you a dog?"

"Is *Old Bose* a dog?"

"Did you skin him?"

Text: *Spirit,* 13 (13 May 1843), 127.

"Well, if you call a man in his shirt sleeves, with a knife 17 inches in the blade among ribs and meat, *skinning*, I was *thar!*"

"Was he fat?"

"Do you call cutting 18 inches on the ribs, *fat?*"

"Did you pack him in?"

"If you call four poney loads *packing*, why I packed some!"

"Light loads, I reckon."

"If *four hundred pounds* to a poney is a light load, they were light."

"Did you eat any of it?"

"Do you call drinking *a quart of bars ile*, eating?"

"You must have meat."

"If you call *two thousand seven hundred pounds* of clean meat, without a bone, safe inside of a smoke house, *meat*, we have got *some!*"

"They must be fat at your house?"

"Do you call a *candle* fat?"

Here OLD SENSE brought a perfect squeal, and swore he had found the very man he had been looking for.

P.S. They had closed a quarter race up the last accounts.

[53] A NEW ARKANSAS CORRESPONDENT
"Sam Grindstone," An Acquaintance of
"Pete Whetstone"

BATESVILLE,
Dec. 26, 1843.

MR. EDITOR.—Times are in a bad fix here, and no mistake. We don't know what to do. There is no such thing as doing without

---

Text: *Spirit,* 13 (20 January 1844), 553. Undoubtedly Noland composed this letter; see Masterson, p. 322, fn. 1.

the change, and there is no such thing as getting any, and so you
see we are gone coons. We did hope to get rid of these shinplas-
ters, but all hopes are abandoned—they will last forever, "and a
day longer." It is now "Christmas times," and a fellow can't raise
enough stuff to get toddy on, and consequently there are a few
sober among us.

Notwithstanding these hard times, however, there is some
sport afloat. They have had several races lately in Jackson
County, and are going to have a regular meeting soon, of the
new Jockey Club—but there is no telling whether they will do
much—one thing is sure, they have no money to bet, and a
fellow would be doing a poor business to bet with them on a
credit.

There have been but few bar hunts in these diggins this winter; the fact is there is not much mast near abouts. I heard some
one say there were lots up about the *"Devil's Fork,"* but I 'spose
there is nothing in it or we should have heard *Pete* lumbering;
but then he has quit writing *funny* pieces, and has set his head to
politics—I am sure his articles were more interesting when he
used to send to the "Spirit," and tell big yarns about OLD SENSE
and Bar Hunts.

Since I mentioned Old Sense, I'll tell you what has lately happened to him—he got a most dreadful flogging. He let his pony
into young SHOULDERSTRAP's old stud, and they had a fight, and
the pony was about to lay it on to the old stud, when up slipped
Shoulderstrap, and gathered a may-pole and had well nigh
made a finish of poor Old Sense—who left these diggins on the
strength of it, and God knows where he is now, I don't. I saw his
partner 'tother day. He is a great big tall fellow, about half Injun;
they call him *Doctor,* but he don't practice any except in certain
cases of necessity. Last summer he kept a stud for old MEALBAG,
and stood him part of his time at old Squire CHINEY's. The horse
made a pretty good stand, and, from all accounts, the doctor
made another; at any rate, him and the old Squire had a monstrous falling out about the time the season expired; and had not
the Squire given his better half an awful flogging, one would
have been at a loss to know what the falling out was about, but

since it is a fact that he did, "then and there, with malice aforethought, both expressed and implied," most wantonly and brutishly "pouncd" his old wife, the natural supposition is that her and old Sense's partner had been too thick—perhaps as thick as "two in a bed." But that does not justify old Chiney in beating the poor old critter till the blood run, as he most certainly did, and sent her forth in the world to "shift for herself," almost without a "shift."

As I said above, *Pete* has lately devoted his talents to politics. He is now engaged in writing a series of letters to the "North Arkansas," which I think quite inferior to those he used to write for the "Spirit."[1] They are entirely political. But then *Pete* is a first rate fellow, and a mighty strong politician, and he must be excused. I heard him say 'tother day that he was going up on the head waters of Spring River to look up "sign;" and if he happens to find a nest of old *hes,* and gets himself engaged in skinning them, we may look out for some tall epistles from the Devil's Fork.

Yours, SAM GRINDSTONE.

[54] LETTER FROM COL. PETE WHETSTONE

DEVIL'S FORK of Little Red, Arkansas,
Dec. 4, 1844.

MY DEAR MR. EDITOR.—Well, who would have believed it?—we are knocked into fits![1] D____n it, but I am mad, but

1. If Noland actually contributed Pete Whetstone letters to the *North Arkansas,* they are lost. Only four issues survive from 1843: 2 August, 6 September, 13 September, and 25 October. None contains a Whetstone letter. If they were reprinted in other Whig newspapers, none has surfaced.

Text: *Spirit,* 14 (28 December 1844), 522.

1. Pete's consternation is brought about by the news that James K. Polk had defeated Henry Clay in the presidential election of 1844.

there is no use in crying over spilt milk. Jim Cole has had misgivings ever since he kotched a big coon in his steel trap. Well, don't it beat all natur? why, it is worse than when that Tennessee feller from Calf-killer beat the Warping Bars with a lousy looking two year old! They have *skum us some,* and if they had had the *narve* could have made the fur fly cruelly. We waded out smartly on old Tennessee, God bless her! and 7,000 on Kentucky, who is too good even to need a blessing.

When the news first come, I tell you, there was tall gobbling! Dan Looney won a likely horse off of Pat Flanigan—Pat swore that Polk was a son of the ould hero, and that his name was Poke Jackson, and that he knew him when he wasn't knee high to a Muscovy duck. Dan told him he was a fool, and knew nothing. At that, like a Virginia gentleman, Pat backed his statement with his horse. Dennis O Conner swore he knew Jake *Jones*[2] in the old States, and he was a broth of a boy, and, "be Jasus," he should have his vote all the time. Jim opened him for a cow and calf, on his knowledge of men and measures.

Well, we boys of the Devil's Fork are so used to such beatings, that we bear it like men—but jist to think of such a man as Henry Clay being beaten! I tell you he is a head and shoulders taller than any man but old General Washington that ever *did* live.

"Darn me to the Darneds," if I aint gitting a worse opinion of people every day—like that most oncommon nigger that I saw at the White Sulphur, I am thinking but few are to be trusted. You have hearn of that Charley, I reckon?[3] Well, if you aint, I can tell you: he is as black as the ace of spades, but is jist allowed to do as he pleases—he buys everything for the Springs, and trades all over the country. He stepped up to Col. SINGLETON, and slapping him on the back, said, "Col. Singleton, I know the carcumstances of nearly every man in the two counties, pecoonietily

2. Porter inserts an explanatory note at this point indicating that he could not decipher the name in Pete's letter and has merely provided the name Jones.

3. In "Race at the Salt Sulphur Springs, Va.," *Spirit,* 9 (7 September 1839), 319, Noland speaks of Charley: "The greatest man in these diggings is black *Charles,* of the White Sulphur. He talks like a book, and says he knows the situation of every man, pecuniary and political, in the country. I heard him boasting of having 'meat, meal, and money without limit.'"

and perlitically, and I can tell you, there is d____d few to be trusted." If old Charley aint "some" in a bear fight you can take my hat!

Well, there is to be tall limping at New Orleans this month, and I do guess the big stake is over before now. Blue Dick will have to bow his neck if he gits the track, though, I would not mind going a chunk of a horse on him at a venter.

Racing is most used up on the Fork, but they say a man that can travel to Fort Gibson and beat John Ross, can come away with more of the hard stuff than would set up two Massassippi Banks. Them ar Cherokees are oncommon friendly, and nobody that has the horses and truck, need be afraid of their *hair* among them. I guess they have got two schools to our one, and you can't sling a dog through the cracks of their houses.

Well, there is an oncommon mast this year, and lots of bear. Jim fit an old she 'tother day, but he didn't git her—I guess she was lean, for the dogs never got up to her but once, and then he thinks none but June's youngest pup and "Little Spot" even did that.

Deer are plenty and fat, but wild turkies scarce, I tell you. I guess the big freshets last spring drowned them out. I forgot to tell you the Legislater is in Session. Bill Plumpie was elected from this county. He ran as the poor man's friend, and it is an oncommon popular ticket to run on. Old Billy Sims says you may start any sort of a man, and he has no chance agin a real giddy-giddy-gout, barefooted at that, who claims to be the poor man's friend. He says that people are oncommon curus critters. They take mighty little to satisfy them sometimes—and then up and tells how, at a big "revival" at Huntsville, when Maffit was there, and it seemed a good time to build a church, so round went the subscription, after meeting. Sister Smith went $50, sister Jones $40, sister Carter $100. They come to a Miss Bassett—mighty smart lady, but not in the church—says she, give me the paper, and after she got it she wrote, "Miss Bassett, her blessing"—well, now, says old Sims, these barefooted friends of the poor man can do as much for him, as Miss Bassett's blessing did towards building the church.

Ever yours, PETE WHETSTONE.

[55 UNTITLED]

"Old Sense" was in to see us a day or two before we received the Advocate, and told us that he expected to enter *"a nag"* at the next races at Fort Smith, that would *take them all.* A friend who read the piece in the Advocate, and who thought it correct, met *Jim* a short time afterwards, and thus accosted him:

"Hallo, Jim; is that you?"

"This is what's left of me."

"Well, Jim, I heard you had been murdered by the Indians?"

"So did I," replied Jim; "but *I* knew it was a lie, as soon as I heard it; 'Old Sense' is too smart for that. You'll be over to the races, at the Fort?—Good bye."

Text: *Spirit,* 16 (18 April 1846), 85. No author's name appears with this brief item. Porter's introduction states that it was taken from the Van Buren *Arkansas Intelligencer;* however, research has not uncovered any such item in that paper. Possibly Porter put the piece together from private correspondence from Noland. The point of view is that of the editor. Porter introduces the anecdote with the following note:

"Old Sense," *of Arkansas,* an original character immortalized by 'N.' of that ilk, was reported as having been killed off lately, but the "Intelligencer," published at Van Buren, relieves us from any anxiety on the subject, by the annexed characteristic paragraph:—

The Cherokee Advocate, of the 19th inst., unintentionally, *kills off* Mr. *"Jim Mussett,"* the original "Old Sense." We are happy that we can inform the editor that it is a mistake; the person who was killed, was named Reynolds, and was in the employ of Mr. Tyree Mussett.

[56] 'COL. PETE WHETSTONE' AGAIN 'ABOUT'

Devil's Fork of Little Red,
Jan. 5, 1850.

MY DEAR MISTER EDITOR.—I reckon you had begun to think Pete was dead, or else he had gone to Kalliforny—well, he ain't neither. Jim Cole was fool enough to think he could make his everlasting fortin, by going way out yonder to dig gold, but I guess, from the way he writ us a short spell back, he'd rather be at home, under his grand mammy's bed, eating dried apples.[1] The way they have had hard times, is a sin to Crockett; raw mule more nor once, and glad to get it, at that. Then the Inguns were feeling mighty close for their hair. Some mighty good people have gone from these diggings, and they will git gold, if it is to be had. If they had spent half the time, and trouble, and truck, close at home, they might have done better. Why, just across the country in Marion County, they are shovelling up the very best of lead ore; and now that the folks there have got sort of tired of killing one another, there is no telling what they will get out of the bowels of the yearth.

The Devil's Fork in particular, and Arkansas in general, is filling up monstrous fast; more nor four come in for every one that goes out. Young Lawyer McCampbell—and he is a right

---

Text: *Spirit,* 19 (19 January 1850), 570.
1. Between 1848 and 1852, when the gold rush saw its peak, the population of California increased from approximately 15,000 to 250,000. Jim Cole's failure, spoken of here, represents the failure of thousands of others. No mention is made of Jim finding gold nor the date of his return to the Devil's Fork. The next reference to him is in letter 61, when he is back in the area.

smart chunk of a lawyer, I tell you—calcilates that at the next sensus we shall git as high as three members of Kongress. There has been more nor one of the big bugs among us lately. They talk slick, I tell you. Why, the Devil's Fork is gwine to be the port of navigation, and that big rail road to the Pacific is to go right by every man's door in ten miles of us. Old To-nail has riz two dollars a head on his big cattle since he heard them talk. McCampbell says the Tiligraph is the greatest thing discovered since the day they found out how to make whiskey from nubbins of corn.[2] He gits a St. Louey paper once a week, and says he is now not more nor two hundred miles from Washington city.

Last Friday there was a corn shucking over at Squire Looney's—lots of people. Arter we had eat dinner, McCampbell pulled out his paper, and read us the news. It had an account in it of the way one Billy Brown was smashed up.[3] I guess them Southerners won't be fooled next time. I tell you, Jim McKonett, who came in here two years ago, from the Spartan District South Carolina, like to biled right over; swore he would take fifty men off the Devil's Fork, and go right strait on, and thrash every abolitioner there was. But old Uncle Billy Sims told him that wouldn't begin to do. "Boys," says he, "it is a poor way to cure a sore finger by cutting off the hand; this union ain't going to be broke up, no way you can fix it!" Here he began to get warm. "Boys, our forefathers fit too hard to make it, and it is good enough for any body; if you destroy it, my word for it, you will repent it the longest day you live. And what is more, giving the devil his due, them abolitioners ain't all the ones to be blamed; them hot headed chaps do nigh as much mischief. A tuck tail dog won't begin to do in a bar fight, but a pup that is barking at every thing in the woods, is well nigh as bad. If I had my way," continued old Uncle Billy, "I would just lay out three hundred feet square in Washington, for Giddings and his gang, and then

---

2. By 1850 telegraphy (invented in 1835 by Samuel F.B. Morse) linked most of the country in a rapid communications network.

3. Throughout the 1850s, George William Brown was active in opposing the mob rule methods of the Know-Nothing Party in Maryland.

build a shanty, half on his resarve and half off of it, for Billy Brown."

Just here the conversation was broken off, by the Squire's gals coming out to tell us old Peter Chiney had come with his fiddle, and everything was ready for a dance. Well, the way we went it, was a sin to Moses—kept it up all night.

Game is mighty scarce on the Fork this year; there was no mast. I hear there is a power of bear over on the War Eagle. Tom Spence has a fine team of dogs, and we think of going there to try our luck.

Ever yours, PETE WHETSTONE.

[57] COL. PETE WHETSTONE TURNED UP AGAIN

DEVIL'S FORK OF LITTLE RED RIVER,
January 11, 1853.

MY DEAR MISTER EDITOR,—I reckon you think I have forgotten you, but it ain't so—Pete ain't one of them sort that forgets his friends. Well, it has been so long since I writ, that I hardly know where to begin. Here is young 1853, and he has crowded out old 1852. Well, 1852 has been some, and I guess will be remembered about as long as any other year, for in *it* Clay and Webster died.[1] Old Uncle Bill Spence, and he is a man amongst men, said to me the other day, when we were talking about them, and what a loss they were, says he, "Whetstone, I jist tell you, the death of Clay and Webster, happening so close together, made me feel like I did that time on the dry fork, when

---

Text: *Spirit,* 22 (12 February 1853), 615.
1. Henry Clay died on 29 June 1852; Daniel Webster died on 24 October 1852.

right at the beginning of the best bear season I ever seed, I had, right in my fust fight, *Old Sharptooth* and *Ginral Jackson,* my only stout dogs, killed. It is true, I had some mortal good young dogs, and old *June* was a pup, but they had to larn."[2]

Well, General Cass is alive yet, and in the Senate.[3] He is one of the old safe sort—and then Old Bullion, I hear, is elected to tother House of Congress.[4] Now, arter all, he is a mortal tall gobler—'tis true, he is some at blowing his own trumpet, but he is full of larning and full of pluck; why, even last summer, when I used to read the "Republican," printed at St. Louis, and seed how he wos fout by friends and foes, and how he fout back, I tell you my heart naterally warmed to the old fellow—I felt sorter like Dan Looney did when we had two bully teams of dogs down on the Red Fork, fighting an *old he,* at one time. I tell you, the fellow made them see sights, but they fairly kivered him; every now and then he would choke them off; at last Dan couldn't stand it, and he sung right out, "hurah, bear!"

Well, it won't be long till the new President comes in.[5] The Devil Fork boys think a power of Mr. Fillmore, I tell you. The way they would spread bar meat, and the best they have, if he was to come along, would be a sin to Crockett. They, however, think well of the new President, and are willing to give him a fair trial. The fact is, Mister Editor, twixt you and me, they have got what they call measures and principles so mixed up, that if it wasn't for the label, whig or democrat, it would take an uncommon man to tell tother from which. Indeed, there ain't very much said about Pollyticks jist now—of course it is expected old office-holders are to go out and new ones to come in. Pete has a very *near relation* that he expects will have to walk chalk.

Mr. Editor, ain't you a bachelor? I know you used to be. How in the name of mercy do you find it? Why, Pete has had to be

---

2. In Pete's early letters, all three dogs belong to him. No mention is made of their having been given or sold to Bill Spence.

3. Lewis Cass was a Senator from Michigan.

4. Thomas Hart Benton had recently been elected as a Representative from Missouri.

5. President-elect Franklin Pierce was to be inaugurated on 4 March 1853.

separated from his wife not quite two months, and he feels now as lonesome as a stray orfing two year old. I think of them chaps what go to Callifornia for two or three years, and occasionally for ever, and that gives me some comfort.

Well, our Legislature has been in session a little longer than it takes a goose to make two hatchings of eggs. I expect they have done lots of good things for us, and no mistake. Slow and sure is the good old way, they say, to make laws; they made a law called the Homestead Act; now it is making a wonderful talk, I tell you—some swear they will kill it at the next Legislature, or faint trying. Now, jist set down Pete as one of the boys that stands up to it, through thick and thin—if it ain't a good law, anybody can have my hat; a great many abuse it, and say it is jist like the Bankrupt Law—that won't do; one cleared out all, behind and before, old scores and everything, and set a man right up new in the world. The Homestead Law compels all scores to be wiped out before you can get any good out of it; 160 acres of land is most too much, but then land ain't much in this wooden country. You can't limit a house and lot, I guess—for if the law said $500, and the house was worth a $1000, how would you git it out of it. Some want to say it takes advantage of a merchant when he credits a customer. He has no right to credit him on the homestead, because he knows it is exempt; then, my dear Mister Editor, old batchelor as you are, you knows that the wimmin and children ought to have some show in the bear fight.

Some people put me in mind of an old gambler who was travelling on a steamboat. He sat down to play with a green one—the game was poker; well, the young fellow showed two one hundred dollar bills on the table. The old fellow sorter held back for a while, but before many hours, had got one of the bills; the young fellow had sense enough to see he was in a bad place, took up his remaining bill, and observed he was satisfied with the game.

"Why," says the old fellow, "you ain't going to jump the game—ain't you going to give me a chance?"

"A chance at what," said the young man; "have you not got one of my bills?"

"Oh, yes," said the old gambler, "but then I want a chance at the other." So with some of the opponents of the bill.

We have got two congressional districts now, and I tell you we will have lots of candidates. Eight dollars a day is equal to a full ounce a day in Callifornia.

Well, sich a winter I never did see—abundance of rain, and sich changes in the weather! I tell you it has been hard on Pete's constitution, and made him spit blood right sharp here of late. He thought Ayre's Cherry Pectoral was going to make his cut at least the 1000th part of a inch on the rib, but somehow or other he ain't picking up quite as fast as Squire Woods' *Bald Hornet* did, when he "jumped twenty-three feet and the breadth of his hoof, and picked it up, like rat fighting." I am bound if ever I git down in Louisyanna, and git a chance, to try one of them sugar-houses—I believe strong in such things. Well, good bye, and may '53 never pass away till you get you a good wife,

Prays your old friend, PETE WHETSTONE.

[58] PETE WHETSTONE AND THE MAIL BOY

Pete Whetstone, of Arkansas, was once travelling on horse-back through the interior of the State, and called one evening to stay all night at a little log house near the road where entertainment and a post-office were kept.[1] Two other strangers were

Text: *Spirit*, 23 (26 February 1853), 17. No author's name appears with this tale, which is credited as having appeared in the *Southern Watch-Tower*. Research has uncovered no trace of that publication.

1. A somewhat similar tale appears in the *Spirit*, 17 (23 January 1847), 508. In that version the trickster is a Louisiana Creole who claims to have lice. A version of this Whetstone piece, with Noland rather than Pete as the victim, is given as having occurred when Noland and W. Fontaine Pope were traveling to Texas to fight their duel in 1831. See Pope, pp. 119-120; and John Gould Fletcher, *Arkansas* (Chapel Hill: Univ. of North Carolina Press, 1947), p. 96.

there, and the mail rider rode up about dark. Supper being over, the mail carrier and the three gentlemen were invited into a small room furnished with a good fire and two beds, which were to accommodate the four persons for the night. The mail carrier was a little shabby, dirty, lousy-looking wretch, with whom none of the gentlemen liked the idea of sleeping. Pete Whetstone eyed him closely as he asked:

"Where do you sleep to-night, my lad?"

"I'll thleep with *you*, I reckon," lisped the youth, "or with one o' them other fellars, I don't care which."

The other two gentlemen took the hint and occupied one of the beds together immediately, leaving the other bed and the confab to be enjoyed by Pete and the mail boy together as best they could. Pete and the boy both commenced hauling off their duds, and Pete getting in bed first, and wishing to get rid of sleeping with the boy, remarked very earnestly—"my friend, I'll tell you before hand, *I've got the Itch,* and you'd better not get in here with me, for the disease is *catching.*"

The boy, who was just getting in bed too, drawled out very coolly, "wal I reckon that don't make a bit o' difference,—I've had it now for nearly these theven years," and into bed he pitched along with Pete, who pitched out in as great a hurry as if he had waked up a hornet's nest in the bed. The other two gentlemen roared, and the mail boy, who had got peaceable possession of a bed to himself, drawled out—"why you must be a thet o' darned fules,—mam and dad's got the eatch a heap wurth than I is, and they thlept in that bed last night when they was here at the quilting."

The other two strangers were now in a worse predicament than Pete had been, and bouncing from their nest like the house had been on fire, stripped, shook their clothes, put them on again, ordered their horses, and, though it was nearly ten o'clock, they all three left, and rode several miles to the next town before they slept, leaving the imperturbable mail carrier to the bliss of scratching and sleeping alone.

[59] COL. PETE WHETSTONE "ABOUT"

DEVIL'S FORK OF LITTLE RED RIVER,
May 2, 1853.

My Dear Mr. Editor.—Well, I do reckon Gineral Pierce has knocked one of the Whetstone family plum from taw—mighty mean—mighty country he is got the overseeing of. The Dimecrats stuck to Pete like a brother, but then the Legislater they tacked a fellow, and out went Pete.[1] The fun of the thing, if there is any fun in it, is, that there is an oncommon snarl about the new man. He ain't good at figures, and, some how or other, ain't much at cyphering, and he will have to git some one to attend to the thing for him, and that is gwine to raise an awful hornet's nest around his ears. But—there is no use crying over spilt milk—Jim Looney, and Dan, and lots of the boys, let out right sharp when they first heard it, but old Squire Sims spoke right out—says he, "Boys, it is the greatest thing ever happened—we will git up an indignation meeting and run Pete for Congress." "Hurrah for Pete," shouted all the boys. But jist then in come Bill Spencer, and when they told him, I tell you he got mad. "No, boys, it won't begin to do; I know Pete; he won't run on the sympathetics." "D____n your sympathetics," said Dan, and if it haden't bin for the old Squire they would have yoked. Jist right then in I popped. "Here he is, and let him say it himself." "Well, look here, boys, it won't begin to do to fuss over this matter. I can't run—ain't got the time to go out—got to be making something for the little Whetstone. I tell you what we can do,

---

Text: *Spirit,* 23 (4 June 1853), 182.
1. Just what office Pete (or Noland) lost is not recorded.

we can go with a rush for old To-nail. I tell you, boys, I have had a chance to heft a heap of them big men in our diggings, and take To-nail up one side and down the tother he is pretty nigh as smart as any of them, and he lives right among us, and if he don't do something for the Devil's Fork, I don't know who will." "Good as tater," said Dan, "and I guess the Devil's Fork will roll up a right heavy vote for old To-nail."

Had a mighty dry spell—had to stop the plows—but the way it is raining now is some. Looks like a good show for *meat* this Fall. I guess the bear ain't gwine ever to be as thick in the Dry Fork as they used to be—too many people coming in.

They begin to talk of a railroad coming over in these parts.[2] I guess it will run all the game out of the Range—but laws, here in our country it is so much talk and no cider.

Ever yours, PETE WHETSTONE.

[60] STILL LATER

DEVIL'S FORK OF LITTLE RED RIVER, *May 9, 1853.*

MY DEAR MISTER EDITOR.—We have had all sorts of high water.[1] They say it never rains but it pours; well I guess it has poured down some in these parts. Lots of cows and calves drowned on the Dry Fork. Jim Rossy like to have been drowned. He had been over to Clinton, and was tight as a drum head, and

---

2. During the spring and summer of 1853, the *Arkansas State Gazette and Democrat* reprinted from the St. Louis *Missouri Republican* a number of articles dealing with proposed railroads. See, for example, *Gazette,* 12 August 1853. Local meetings to launch campaigns to get railroads through particular areas were also held throughout the state.

Text: *Spirit,* 23 (4 June 1853), 182.
1. In a letter in the same issue of the *Spirit* (p. 183), Noland speaks of heavy rains. His letter is dated 2 May.

when he come to the Devil's Fork it was looming, but in he went, and like to have seen his coffin nails, sure. Rossy is some punkins. He gets wolfish sometimes, and fairly spiles for a fight. About two weeks ago he went over to where Bill Owens was plowing; well, Bill is a mighty stout man, I tell you—peaceable as a lamb, but when you do raise him he's *thar,* certain. Rossy had about a strained pint in him, and was chock full of fight. He and Bill were always friendly, but that was neither here nor there. Says Rossy—

"Now, Bill, I have come for something, and I must have it."

"Well, what is it, Rossy?"

"Well," says Rossy, "it is a fight—must have it."

"Oh, go way, Rossy," says Bill, "and don't be a fool."

"It won't do, Bill," says Rossy, "you just as well might stop that horse—a fight I must have. Why, Bill, I am spiling for a fight—begin to smell bad."

"Well, Rossy," says Bill, "if nothing else will do you but a fight, you shall have it," and at that he began to strip. "Now, Rossy," says Bill, "I am gwine to give you the best I have, and unless you are pretty much of a man you will catch hell."

"Well, now, jist hold on, Bill," said Rossy; "I don't begin to see any use of our fighting. Why, Bill, didn't I set up all night with your old daddy, drinking whiskey together, and ain't he and me been on a spree together, for a week at a time. Bill, it won't begin to do for us to fight," and so off he rode.

Well, I had a letter from Mr. Pierce. Here it is:—

WHITE HOUSE, Washington City, April 12, 1853.
Dear Col.—Had to lift you out of your boots. Sorry for it, but could not resist the outside press; betwixt you and me, Pete, this thing of being President is not what it is cracked up to be—have not time even to sling a cat in. Would like a few quiet days on the Fork; could you get me up a bear hunt this Fall? Hard work to slip away from the New York fellows that are after office.

In great haste,
Your old friend, FRANK PIERCE.
To Col. Pete Whetstone, of the Devil's Fork.

Here is my reply:—

DEVIL'S FORK OF LITTLE RED RIVER, April 30, 1853.
Dear Gineral.—Glad you did it—corns on my toes every
hour. You are a trump; most sorry I went for old Fuss and
Feathers.[2] Office ain't much, after all. Glad to see you on the
Fork this Fall—*mast* going to be fine. Got the best pack this side
of sundown. Bring Jeff. and Young America with you[3]—them
Old Fogies could not follow June pups through the cane. I can
keep off them New York fellers.

Always yours, PETE WHETSTONE.
Gineral Frank Pierce, President of U. States.

[61 UNTITLED]

*DEVIL'S FORK OF LITTLE RED,
January 3, 1855.*

MY DEAR MISTER EDITOR—It has been so long since I have
heard from my old friend, the Editor of the Spirit of the Times,
and the mails, old uncle Johnny Sims says, are as uncertain as the
females, so I have concluded to git you to print this.

Mighty hard times on the Fork this year—truck oncommon

---

2. Winfield Scott (1786-1866) was the Whig candidate for the presidency in 1852; he
was overwhelmingly defeated by Pierce.

3. "Jeff" was Jefferson Davis, who at the time was the Secretary of War. Noland's
acquaintance with Davis probably began when the two were cadets at West Point.
"Young America" was probably George Nicholas Sanders, who was associated with the
Democratic Review and was quite vocal on national politics. The term was also applied to
a faction of the Democratic Party, headed by Sanders, which advocated "free trade,
foreign markets, a subsidized merchant marine, annexation southward and the encouragement of republican movements abroad." See S.F. Riepma, "Young America,"
Dictionary of American History, V, ed. James Truslow Adams and R.V. Coleman (New
York: Scribner's, 1940), 509-510.

Text: *Arkansas State Gazette and Democrat,* 12 January 1855, [p. 3].

scarce, and if it warnt for the *mast* I do guess, there would be a monstrous chance of empty stomachs—but the bars is wonderful plenty. Dan Looney, Jim Cole and me have made a smash of twenty-three—among them, three of the rousenest *old he's,* that ever made a track on the Devil's Fork. Well we have had lots of talk about rail roads, and until the Legislature met, why every neighborhood was gwine to have one—but some how or other the tune is changed, and we find it takes a powerful sight of money to build them, and old Squire Pruett, nigh on to the smartest man we have got among us, says the show is a bad one jist now to build any thing. He says them wars going on in Europe and the balance of the world, is going to make a smash of every thing.[1] He says old Nick has got the allies sure, and that unless Gineral Pierce sends old Churubusco, to help them, the dog will be dead with them.

Well there is monstrous fuss here about some fellows they call the Know Nothings, but no body seems to be able to find them.[2]

There is a new comer among us named Barney O'Spriggins, who is looking for a little place to enter under the *graduation* bill.[3] He is a broth of a fellow, and the other night we had a time of it, at Bill Spence's grocery. Says the old Squire to him, "Mr. O'Spriggins, will you be kind enough to give us a history of your travels since you left your own country." "With all my heart," says O'Spriggins and after clearing his throat with a glass of about half and half, he gave us the following history: "My name is Barney O'Spriggins—it will be three years come next St. Anthony's day, since with a heavy heart, and a couple of pounds sterling in my pocket, that after tenderly embracing Mrs. Judy

---

1. The Crimean War, which had begun in the fall of 1854, was well underway. This war, said to be one of the worst managed, most badly led, ill supplied, and unnecessarily wasteful of life of all modern wars, lasted until the signing of the Treaty of Paris on 30 March 1856. Pete is one of many Americans who felt the United States should join the Allies in battle.

2. Officially named the American Party, the Know Nothing Party sprang up in 1854. It was a secret organization "solidly committed to nativism, its main thesis being that immigrants and Catholics should not be permitted to take an active part in government." (Ross, p. 314) The party was never an important voice in Arkansas politics.

3. Graduation bills were topics of discussion several times during the period covered by Pete's letters. Essentially, such bills provided that the longer public lands remained unsold, the cheaper they would become. See Van Deusen, pp. 129-130.

O'Spriggins, and the two little O'Spriggins, that I bid adieu to swate Ireland—after a long and tedious voyage, I landed at New York—the second day after I got there, as I was walking up one of their narrow streets, who should I espy just ahead of me, but Terence O'Flaherty. I followed on, and he entered into a little doggery—stepping up to him and slapping him on the back, says I 'good luck to you Terence,' 'the same to you Mr. Barney, and all your family, but how in the devil came you here man?' 'It was my heels Terence, that brought me from the landing,' says I. 'Well Barney, my boy,' says he, 'is it any word you bring me from Mrs. O'Flaherty, and the four little darlints I left behind'—and here gintleman, I would mention, that the rogue of a fellow had slipped off from the lake of Ballinahan, leaving his wife and four children, with but little to go on. 'It is but little comfort, on that score, I can give you Terence,' says I. 'The divil take the priest,' says he, 'and all my wife's thaving relations, for was it not a good cotton plantation and sixty likely nagers I left them in ould Ireland—bad luck to the day I ever left them; but Barney, my boy, tell me something of Mrs. O'Spriggins' father, and how he comes on—by the sowl of me, but he was an illigant gintleman, and did he not own an illigant carriage, with but *one wheel,* and himself the horse?' Well, Terence and I had a time of it. My head next morning felt like a hornet's nest, and when I waked up, Terence was gone, and my money was gone, and I was in a mighty bad fix—'may the curse of St. Patrick rest on your head, Terence,' says I, 'you thaving spalpeen—you are a disgrace to ould Ireland.' But gintlemen, Barney O'Spriggins was niver the boy to give up, so to work I set and I was not long getting into a good sitiation. I laid up some money, and my employer tould me, there was a gradiation law, and if I would come to Arkansas, I could get a little farm for myself and the ould woman, almost for a song, and pitch the tune myself—so to this State I came, and to the land office I went. 'Good morning to your honor,' says I—'the same to you,' says he. 'If your worship plazes,' says I, 'its a little farm I would be after gitting, for Mrs. O'Spriggins and the little ones, under what they call the gradiation bill.' 'What are your numbers,' says he? 'Bad luck to the numbers, for it is none, I have your honor.' So he told me how I should go to one

Thomas Carter, who could tell me all about it. 'It is obliged to your honor, I am'—'you are welcome,' says he, 'but Mr. O'Spriggins, let me guard you against the Know Nothings.' 'The Know Nothings,' says I, 'why your honor had better believe but I have seen lots of them since I put my foot on your free and happy country.' 'It is a secret society, I mean.' 'A secret society, your honor. Well, barring your honor's presence, may his cloven-footed majesty catch all secret societies—and could your honor be after explaining the principles of this hideous monster.' 'Well then,' says he, 'they are against all foreigners holding office.' 'Forninst fuireigners did you say, may the giant of Bally-na-hole swallow them alive,' says I. 'Against all Catholics holding office,' says he. 'May Pope Pius the IX, with book, candle and bell, send the whole of them to purgatory,' says I. 'They are for making everything purely American,' says he. 'The ghost of old Lafayette swallow them,' says I. Jist then up stepped a couple of nice gentleman—one he called Squire Sneeves, and the other Squire Nick, and may be we didn't give it to that secret society about right. Squire Nick said, if he could get them all together, and could raise the powder, he would blow them to hell and no mistake, while Squire Sneeves was kind enough to explain a great deal of their rascality to me—says he, 'Mr. O'Spriggins, they commit murder, they burn houses, they stale nagers, and you can do nothing with them. They are always ready to sware each other out of any scrape.' 'Squire Sneeves,' says I, 'if I may be so bold as to ax, what are the flesh-marks of these animals?' Says he, 'Mr. O'Spriggins, the way to find them out, is to rise early, and watch close for chalk-marks. They hould their meetings in the lofts of stables and out-houses, and have no lights, their deeds being evil, but each one carries a big lump of chalk in his mouth.' 'It is thankful I am to your honor,' says I, 'and it is a good day I bid you'—so I put out for Mr. Carter's. He tould me to come over to the Devil's Fork, and I would find some choice bits of land, so gintleman, here I am." Old Squire Sims carried him home, and it is hoping we may have Mrs. O'Spriggins for a neighbor.

Excuse this long letter, and believe me, my dear mister Editor,
Your friend, truly, PETE WHETSTONE.

[62] PETER WHETSTONE'S RECEPTION OF THE SPIRIT

DEVIL'S FORK OF LITTLE RED RIVER,
October 6th, 1856.

DEAR MR. EDITOR—Jim Cole went down to Clinton, last Saturday, and they give him a paper at the post office, all wrapped up so nice, and directed to "Col. Whetstone, Devil's Fork,"—Jim allowed it was one of them 'lectioneering dociments, so he never fetched it over till Sunday evening. There wos lots of fellows at the Devil's Fork when he come over—well, I reckon when I tore the kiver off that paper and seen it was a "Spirit of the Times," with a new skin on it, and the same old hoss at the head of it, the boys did go on.[1] Jim wondered if that Picter was like you[2]—Sister Sal laughed, and said you was as hairy as the man she read of in the Bible,[3] while old Squire Sims donned his specs and inspected it close. Now Squire Sims is give up to be the smartest man in our settlement, since old To-nail moved to White River. The Squire tuck a long look at your picter, and then, says he, "boys, if there is anything I'm a judge of it is fizzyognomies." "Fizzy what?" said Bill Spence's oldest boy.

Text: *Porter's Spirit of the Times,* 1 (1 November 1856), 140.

1. According to Francis Brinley, Porter abruptly left the *Spirit* late in the summer of 1856 and began *Porter's Spirit of the Times;* he inaccurately notes that the first issue of the new publication appeared 26 September 1856. The correct date was 6 September. See Brinley, p. 266.

2. The front page of the first issue of *Porter's Spirit* carried a portrait of Porter drawn by Charles Barry from a photograph taken by Meade Brothers of New York. His hair is long, reaching well onto his collar; he also wears a full beard which easily reaches his second shirt button.

3. Sister Sal is probably thinking of Samson, whose long hair was associated with strength; see Judges 16:15-20.

"Hush up, you loon, you haint half sense, no how. Fizzyognomy, boys, is the art of telling what sort of a man you meet by looking at his face; now boys, if Squire Sims aint a natral fool, there is a face will do to lie to." Jist then, Dan Looney rid up and lit, and when he got a sight of "Porter's Spirit," he fairly shouted, and drawing a bottle out of his *saddle riders,* says he, "boys, here is to the old Spirit and the new Spirit, but especially to the new Spirit." Well, Dan is been way up in the State of Ohio, and I reckon he thinks he has seen about as much as the next man. I'll tell you how it was: Old Uncle Johnny Price, that lives on the head of the Dry Fork, has hunted a heap with Dan, and is mighty partial to him; well now, Uncle Johnny is a mighty good man, and got a nice set of children—lors, but he's got one oncommon modest boy. One night he was out coon hunting, and when he come home he had no coons; so Uncle Johnny asked him what was the reason: "well now, daddy," says he, "I lost the *rooster* off the lock of my gun." Now, old Uncle Johnny had a sister up in the State of Ohio, and she tuck it into her head last winter to make a die of it, and left Uncle Johnny a ligacy, so he rid over one day and told Dan about it, and that it was the rise of four hundred dollars, and if he would go and get it, he might have half of it. Dan agreed; and as soon as he laid by his crop, he saddled the Weeping Willow and cut out for Madrid, where he tuck a steamboat. He had no difficulty in getting the money, but the way he talks of his travels is amusing. I tell you he is bound to go to the Legislature next term. He says he saw the nicest steamboat called "Pete Whetstone," up there at Louisville, so he went aboard;[4] sich carpets, sich looking glasses, and slick furniter, he says it beats all creation, and when the Captain found out where he was from, why, Dan says he treated him like he had been a member of Congress. Says he, "*Major* Looney, I hope you like

---

4. The *Pete Whetstone* was built in 1856 at the Howard Shipyards in Jeffersonville, Indiana. She was a combined freight and passenger packet, and her home port was Louisville. She had a wooden hull, and her dimensions were 225.0 feet x 38.0 feet x 7.5 feet. See Charles Preston Fishbaugh, *From Paddlewheels to Propellers: The Howard Shipyards in the Story of Steam Navigation on the Western Rivers* (Indianapolis: Indiana Historical Society, 1970), p. 195.

our looks." "Well, I guess I do, Capting," said Dan, "for she is a leetle ahead of anything I ever seed before." "Well, *Major* Looney, I shall always be glad to see any of you Devil Fork chaps on my boat, and I will take your truck, from a sucking-pig to a six year old steer, at half price." Says Dan, "Cap. Growler, you are a gentleman and a scholar;" so the Captain asked Dan up to the bar to take a drink. Dan says jist as nice fixins as at the bar of the big hotel, at Cincinnati![5] "What do you drink, pray?" "Not per-ticular, Capting," says Dan; "whatever you take is good enough for me." "Well," says the Captain, "I will take an ice punch;" "the same for me," says Dan; and at that, Dan said, the nicest, slickest looking fellow inside of the bar turned to him and said, "Major Looney, do you take your lemon cut or squz?" "Squz," said Dan. After drinking, Dan bid the Captain good bye, and swears now he would walk barefooted, of a frosty morning, ten miles, jist to git to travel on that boat.

Dan brought home two of the finest *black tans* you ever laid your eyes on. He calls them Fillmore and Donelson.[6] They got him into a bully fight, of which I'll try and write you some time. 'Bundance of mast, and the way we are going to walk into the bears is awful. Dan has the finest team of bear dogs on the top of the ground.

Ever yours, PETE WHETSTONE.

---

5. Probably the Exchange Hotel, located between Main and Sycamore Streets, is the one to which Dan refers. For years the Exchange was considered one of the finest in the area.

6. These hounds are named in honor of the former President Millard Fillmore and Andrew Jackson Donelson, the nephew and aide of Andrew Jackson and the 1856 vice-presidential candidate.

[63] DAN LOONEY'S BIG FIGHT IN ILLINOIS

Written for
"Porter's Spirit of the Times"

DEVIL'S FORK OF LITTLE RED RIVER,
October 10, 1856.

MY DEAR MISTER EDITOR:—I writ you a few days since, and I told you I would try and send you an account of Dan Looney's big fight in Illinois. Well, it is a sorter of a dull day; and here goes, in Dan's own words:

I tuck a steam-boat at Louisville—one of your real jam-up boats. Lots of passengers; and as I had old Uncle Tommy Price's ligacy, and felt rich, and as old Bill Montgomery used to say, I cared no more for a silver dollar than a Pennsylvanian would for a yoke of steers, so I told them to book me for the cabin. I tied the pups way up on top of the boat, and agreed with one of the servants to pay him for feeding them. We started out jist before dark; and when supper came on, I tell you, there was nicer doings than there was at Squire Sims' Infar. After supper I went forward to take a smoke, and soon made two acquaintances; one of 'em a great big raw-boned fellow from old Kentuck, with about 20 head of the likeliest mules I ever did see, that he was carrying to New Orleans; the other a monstrous pale-looking little fellow, that had the chills so long that he had an ager-coke nigh on to as big as a small-size sifter—he was from old Virginny—from what, he said, they called the *Pan-handle*. He

---

Text: *Porter's Spirit of the Times*, 1 (8 November 1856), 159.

was little, and sickly, but had a craw chock full of sand, as I afterwards found out. I tuck a mighty liking to them, and we three kept mighty close together. When all the supper fixings was cleared away, in we went to the cabin and tuck our seats. Pan-handle was full of fun, and oncommon smart. Says he, "Mr. Looney, if you will jist skin your eye close, you can see all sorts of people, on a big boat like this." Well, I did look round; for I had heard old Giles Scroggins say, mankind was divided into five sorts—viz., quality, bob-quality, commonality, rubbish, and trash.[1] Says I, "There is three sorts of people here, but two kinds are missing—I can see quality, bob-quality, and commonality, but no rubbish and trash." "Ah, Mr. Looney," said Old Kentuck, who was a mighty plain matter-of-fact man, "when you have traded mules to Orleans seventeen seasons in succession, you will be a better judge of rubbish and trash than you are now; for I would be willing to take $200 for the best pair of mules I have got on this boat, if them hairy-lip fellows over there, cutting up such shines, ain't trash, and the meanest sort." Well, there was a pe-anny on board, and some of the nicest ladies; but I tell you, Pete, if you was buying them by weight, unless you put the stilyards to them, you would be a ruined man. Why, there was one standing up by the pe-anny, and I heard one feller say, "Well, if these hoop-dresses don't alter a gal faster than anything I ever seed— for there stands Miss Sally Spinel, that I have seen every day, for weeks and months at a time, and I hardly know her." "An oncommon hearty and robust gal," said a big Yankee, that was standing by the fellow who knowed her, "what do you think she would weigh?" said he to the Yankee. "Well," said the Yankee, without hefting her, "at a rough guess, I would say, not less than 215 pounds." At this, the first fellow broke out laughing; "Why, she don't weigh 115 without her rigging."

Bime-by they be gone to play on the pe-anny and sing songs, some of 'em mighty high falutin; but there was one young gal, I

---

1. This same five-fold classification of humanity is made in Letter 30. Noland also uses this classification in his own "Life in the Far West," *Spirit,* 6 (31 December 1836), 365. In all three cases it is attributed to Giles Scroggins.

tell you, could make a mocking-bird ashamed of himself; she sung "Old Folks at Home" and "Master is in the cold, cold Ground;" and I tell you, I found the tears coming down my face.[2] "Well," says Pan-handle, "I'd rather hear her sing, than go to the Circus—there." "My sentiments," said Old Kentuck; "and, gentlemen, let us take a drink and go to bed." "Agreed," says I. But Pan-handle left mighty unwilling. I tell you, that gal had charmed him.

Next day, about two hours before sun-down, the boat landed at a little town on the Illinois side; and as the captain said he would be kept there till dark, I thought I would take the pups ashore, and give them a little chance to stretch themselves. So I told Kentuck, and he said he would go; but Pan-handle was listening to that gal singing, and knowed it was no use to ax him. Well, we went out, and the pups seemed to enjoy it mightily. We walked up towards the town; and jist at the edge of it, we spied a little flag flying, with only 16 stars. Soon as Old Kentuck spied it, I seed his neck-veins swell. Says he, "Mr. Looney, that is what I call a bad sight." "What does it mean?" says I. "It means," says he, "*disunion:* free States against slave States."

Right then, up stepped a good-sized, square-built fellow, that seemed to have about three drinks aboard. "Smart-looking dogs, them of your's, stranger," said he. "Clever pups," said I. "What do you call 'em?" said he. "Fillmore and Donelson," said I. "What might your name be, stranger," said he. "Dan Looney," said I. Says he, "I knew the Looneys in Ireland, in the county of Cork; and, saving your presence, stranger, they were no great shakes." "No apologies necessary," says I, "for I was born in the State of Tennessee, three miles from the head-waters of the Calf-Killer. My father and two uncles fout in Jackson's war, and I am an out-and-out American." "Where do you live?" said he, and he

---

2. "Old Folks at Home," which is actually entitled "Sewanee River," was composed by Stephen Foster in 1851 and was immediately popular. "Massa's in de Cold, Cold Ground" was composed by Foster in 1852. See John Tasker Howard, *Our American Music: A Comprehensive History from 1620 to the Present* (New York: Thomas Y. Crowell, 1965), pp. 184-185. Both songs were introduced and performed by Edwin P. Christy and his minstrels.

begin to talk sassy. "On the Devil's Fork of Little Red River, in the State of Arkansaw," said I. "Why, you are one of them nigger-drivers," said he. "I reckon not," said I, "for niggers is rather scase on the Devil's Fork; but stranger, if you have anything to say agin the South, spit it out." Said he, "Look at that flag." "I have looked," said I. "Well, we are going to split this Union wide open." "Stop," said I; "when I left home, stranger, to go to the State of Ohio, my wife Sally said to me, said she, 'Dan, you are going among strangers, and you can't be too careful. Don't get in a fight on any account.' Said I, 'Sally, my darling, I am a great man to hold in on big occasions, and unless one of them abolitioners talks too sassy, I'll be meek as a lamb; but if they talk about dividin' these United States, I'm bound to fight.' 'In such a case,' said she, 'fight;' and I said I would; and stranger, I never did tell Sally a lie." So I told Kentuck to hurry the pups on board the boat, and come back. I began to examine the chap. He was about five feet ten inches, and put up like a jack-screw. Said I, "My good fellow, you may as well shed your rags, for I'm gwine to whip you, or try hard." At that he broke out in the biggest kind of a laugh. "Why, spooney, I can tan yer dog skin, and never draw my coat." By this time old Kentuck had got back, and with him Pan-handle. The latter's face was lighted up, and he didn't look like the same man. I handed my coat to Kentuck, and stepping up to the stranger, who had buttoned his, and was standing with his arms sorter crossed. Said I, "Are you ready?" Said he, "Nobody's afraid, if you aint." At that I aimed to hit him about the bur of the ear; when Whetstone, just as true as you are sitting there, he fended it off with his left hand, as easy as ever you seed on. Oh! he ripped out a young dog, and with his left hand he hit me a jo-reefer right under the left eye. I tell you, I thought a bumblebee's nest had bursted in my head; but I pitched in, and we clinched. We divided the under holts, but I tell you, he was some at rastling. It wan't long before he got the back-lock on me, and it was no use—he flung me. Just then Pan-handle sung out, "Hurrah for Looney!" Well, I riz with him, and we had it round and round. I tried to come the hip-lock on him, but he was too quick, and he come the back-lock on me, and flung me again. "Stand up to him, Looney!" hollered Kentuck and Pan-handle, and I riz again with him. By this time there was a big crowd round us. "Why," says one, "that feller from Arkansaw is wasting his time; he don't know he is fighting Dick McCormick, that whipped the one-thumb bully from Kentucky." I heard it all, but kept in good heart, for little Ager-Coke encouraged me all the time. This time we had it around and about for a good while. I got so that I could keep clear of his back-lock, but never was able to get the Piney-woods hip-lock on him. At last he shifted his game, and tried me on the in-turn. I found out what he was after, but he sorter got it, and we came down a perfect dog fall—side and side—and we riz again. I tell you, Ager-Coke and old Kentucky shouted, while one feller, that was on McCormick's side, said, "I tell you, Arkansaw is some punkins in a fight." "You'd better believe it," said Pan-handle; "why, Looney is just coming to himself!" Well, we had it round and about again—he made lots of passes at me, but I had learned his locks, so he tried the in-turn, but I was quick, and come Piney-woods onter him. I flung him an oncommon hard fall, but he riz again. I knew now I had him—felt as sure he was my meat as Sam Adkins did of the widow Poolet, when he touched her on the naked neck with the thigh bone of a tree frog. We had it round and about, but it didn't last long. I had out-winded him—too much whiskey, I reckon—and this time I flung him an old fashioned Sam Hinton fall, and he did not rise; but I played my thumbs into his eyes, and he sung out; but before they got me off, I reckon my right thumb got mighty near to the fust jint. You ought to have seen old Kentuck and Pan-handle. The way they did shout! Said Dick McCormick, after he got up and washed his face, "Well, gentlemen, I have been fighting all my life, and this is the first time I ever got whipped." "Why," said I, "that is what Davy Gibbs said when Sam Beard whipped him, and Sam said, in reply, that he had fout, man and boy, through thirteen of the old States and some of the new ones, and that Davy Gibbs was the first man he had ever found he could whip." Just then the whistle blew, and Kentucky and Pan-handle and me went aboard. I let on I wan't hurt, but I tell you I was sore enough. It was an accident I whipped him. I got out at Madison. Kentuck all but shed a tear at parting, and offered me the best mule he had to go all the way to Orleans. Pan-handle said if he could he would come up and see me. I told him with bear meat and sulphur water I could knock that ager-coke all to pieces.

But I am getting tired, and must close Dan's fight and trip.

Ever yours, PETE WHETSTONE.

APPENDIX 1
An Imitation of the Whetstone Letters

Sporting Epistle From "The Swamp."

ROLLING FORK OF DEER CREEK, in Old Mistysippy,
Nov. 7th, 1842.

MISTER EDITOR.—JIM LONG has just got up from Vicksburg, where he went to help BERRY MARSHALL down with a raft. He reports the Yazoo very low—three feet water and fifteen mud. I sent down the skin of an old *he* by him to trade for powder, and I told him to get it from Old Daddy Swett—he keeps the right kind. Well, he fotcht it, tied up in a *newspaper;* it is first rate. I filled my horn, and put the rest in my gourd. Jim and me then set down to read the news. The first thing we saw was the name of the man that prints it—Porter! We first thought it was our old friend Pat Porter, but we all know that Pat is nothing, except in a bear fight, or on a raft. Jim said he heard some fellow say, at Vicksburg, you was a very long made man; we then concluded that it was *Long Jim Porter;* but OAT BROWN come down two weeks ago a deck passenger on a coal-boat from Pittsburg, and says he saw Jim Porter at Shippingport, and that he is high sherriff there, so we concluded that we didn't know or care a d____n who you were, and went on with our spelling.

Well, the next thing we saw, was a letter from that eternal cuss, BILL COLE, from Rackinsaw, to one of the *Whetstone family.* It's the first time I have heard of Bill this three years. If you see him will you just enquire what had become of my kir dog *Grab?* They left here about the same time. I will tell you what made Bill leave; he was laughed out of the Swamp. He was hunting, and lit up an old *she*. He made a bad shot, and

---

Text: *Spirit,* 12 (3 December 1842), 476.

they went at it. Bill, instead of reaching over and popping his knife in her back, attempted to stab her in front; the way she knocked the knife out of his hand was a caution to all greenhorns. He would have been most eternally chawed up, but RALF COONY was poking about in the cane with his old killdevil, and heard the racket. Ralf at first would not interfear, but he said the bear did not fite fare, she would take foul holt; so he put a half ounce of lead through the old she, which let Bill out of the scrape. Mind I don't say he *stole* my dog; but I do not think he would have followed such a *poor* hunter if he had not have been tied.

Old BELCHER floated along here in his dug-out, yesterday. Do you know Belcher? If you dont you never was up Sunflower. When that river was *discovered* he was *thar*! He does not look any older now than when he was first discovered! He is sometimes missing for two or three months at a time, and they do say, that he crawls in the mud like the alligators, and comes out as good as new. About one thing there is no mistake—he is a battallion in a bar-fight! I will tell you how he paid a barbill on one of the Yazoo steamers. He was coming up from Vicksburg, where he has been to sell his skins; every few minutes he would treat all hands; he would wink at the barkeeper, and tell him "When I go to git off, I will settle it all up"—he shewed him that he had plenty of cash. Well, about two miles below the mouth of Sunflower, where he had left his dug-out, he pretended to be mighty drunk and tumbled overboard. He took care to fall over behind the wheel, hollering "save me! save me!" The boat was rounded to, but Belcher was gone! About an hour after that he was paddling his dug-out up Sunflower, with two cur dogs he had left to mind it setting in the bow, and his rifle, that he had left in a holler log, by his side.

But I forgot to tell you what old Belcher tole me yesterday; he says about the mouth of Coony and the drift of Sunflower, the *bar* is plenty as hogs. We are fixing our dug-outs, and in a few days there will be tribulation amongst the varmint at the foot of the drift. Bill Cole says the mast is fine in Rackinsaw; here it is awful.

You go TOM OWEN'S woodcock story blind! You certainly do not gainsay Uncle JACK'S feat with the cotton bark. Woodcock are not in these parts in the summer; it was last January I made my successful hunt. I shot with a broad brimmed panama on my head, but I stood between the light. I will try it again and keep behind the light. There is a bird called the *rale* in the Louisiana swamps; they fly badly. Tom does not mistake the rale for woodcock, I hope. I can go the niggers and sticks—on a *rale*.

Sister SAL has got a setting of alligator eggs; she puts them in the sun in the day time, and in bed with her at nights. She says if they hatch well and look promising, she will send them to you.

Your friend, Here In the Swamp.

APPENDIX 2
Glossary of Proper Names

A., Captain [Captain A of the Army]. Probably Thomas Ludwell Alexander of Virginia. Alexander entered West Point in 1826. He was a captain at the time of Pete's letter. He died 11 March 1881.

Aderley, Charley. Fictional.

Adkins, Sam. Fictional.

Aken, Squire. Fictional.

Aldie, Virginia. The small town in Loudon County where Noland was born. His family lived in Aldie, which is 39 miles west of Washington, throughout Noland's life.

Alexandria. The Virginia city, a suburb of Washington.

Alicum Guiacum. Possibly a patent medicine of the age. Guaiacum is a genus of American tropical trees. Guiacol occurs in the distillation of sap from these trees and was once used as a medication for respiratory ailments.

Alick. Probably Thomas Ludwell Alexander of Virginia; see A., Captain.

Allen, Bill. A fictional jockey of the Devil's Fork area.

Allen, Dick. Fictional.

Anderson, John. Fictional.

Apple-Sas. A fictional horse.

Archy, Squire. Fictional.

Argyle. A horse, by Monsieur Tonson out of Thistle by Ogle's Oscar. Owned by W. R. Smith of South Carolina.

Arthur. See Taylor, Arthur.

Asa. See Thompson, Asa.

Ashley, Chester. (1791-1848) In the early days of Arkansas' statehood, Ashley was a prominent lawyer, land speculator, and political manipulator. He was Director of the State Bank and, by association,

216

frequently thought of as barely less than criminal. During the period of time prior to about 1845, he and Noland were political enemies. After Ashley was elected to the U.S. Senate in 1844 (for a time he was chairman of the Judiciary Committee), he and Noland found themselves increasingly more in agreement. Noland wrote a capsule biography in "Early Arkansas Settlers—No. 3," *Spirit,* 19 (29 December 1849), 529.

Astor [House, the]. The leading New York hotel of the era.

Asy. Probably Asa Thompson.

Atkinson, General [Henry]. (1782-1842) General commander of the troops in the Black Hawk War of 1832.

Augusta, Madame. An extremely popular *danseuse* of the day. Born in Munich, she danced for kings prior to her coming to the United States in 1836. Her first U.S. appearance was 18 September 1836. See *Spirit,* 9 (30 March 1837), 37-39.

Ayre's Cherry Pectoral. A popular patent medicine for chest ailments.

B.B. Roswell Beebe, a wealthy Little Rock land speculator and owner of the Little Rock Foundry and Smithery. Beebe was a political and business associate of both Woodruff and Ashley.

Bald Hornet. A fictional horse.

Balie Peyton. A horse; unknown.

Ball. A fictional horse.

Ballinahan. No lake by this name appears on modern maps of Ireland, although several towns with similar names are located in north-central Ireland.

Bally-na-hole. Probably a dialect rendering of Ballinahan.

Barebones. A fictional horse.

Barnett. Probably an actual resident of Batesville, though now unidentifiable.

Barren Fork. One of the tributaries of White River approximately twenty miles upstream from Batesville. See map.

Bascombe. See John Bascombe.

Bassett, Miss. Fictional.

Batesville. One of Arkansas' oldest towns, located approximately seventy-five miles north-northeast of Little Rock on the White River. Batesville was Noland's home throughout his adult life. See map.

Bean [Jesse]. An early settler of Batesville. His knowledge of the Southwest was extensive enough that he was selected to accompany Washington Irving on his famous tour of the prairies.

Beard, Sam. Fictional.

Bear Meat. A fictional horse.

Ben. Fictional.

Ben Desha. A horse; unknown.

Bengal Salve. A patent medicine; probably fictional.

Benton, Tom [Thomas Hart]. (1782-1858) Elected U.S. Senator from Missouri in 1820, Benton was a strong Van Buren supporter. He led the congressional floor fight in opposing the establishment of a national bank. He was the champion of "hard money," and for many years was one of Washington's most powerful voices.

Benton County. The county located in the northwest corner of Arkansas. Bentonville is the county seat.

Bertrand. A horse; unknown.

Bess. Probably the name of Pete's gun.

Biddle, Nick [Nicholas]. (1786-1844) Appointed by President Monroe as one of five directors of the Bank of the United States, Biddle became the Bank's president in 1822. The success of the United States Bank, under Jackson's administration, in creating a sound and uniform currency was largely due to Biddle's efforts.

Big Lick. Not identified on maps of the Devil's Fork area.

Biling Pot. A fictional horse.

Bill [loser at Faro]. Fictional.

Bill [horse]. See Sir William.

Black, Billy. Fictional.

Blackjack, Tom. Fictional.

Black Ram. See Boston.

Blair, Frank [Francis Preston]. (1791-1876) Founder and editor of the Washington *Globe.* Blair used his newspaper as an administration mouthpiece during the presidencies of Jackson and Van Buren.

Blowing Cave. A cave on Poke Bayou near Batesville where air rushed out of the mouth in warm weather and into the mouth in cold weather. Noland describes the cave in "Another Bulletin from Arkansas," *Spirit,* 6 (11 February 1837), 412.

Blue-belly. See McK., Lawyer.

Blue Dick. Foaled in 1837, by Margrave (imported) out of an unnamed dam by Lance. He was owned by John L. White.

Blue Ruin. A fictional horse.

Bob Crittenden. Foaled in 1835, he was by Volcano out of an unnamed dam by Stockholder. He belonged to Thomas T. Tunstall.

Boon. A fictional horse.

Bose. A fictional dog.

Bosting. Boston; the city.

Bosting. See Boston; the horse.

Boston. Foaled in 1833, by Timoleon out of Sister to Tuckahoe. Quite famous during his day, he won 40 out of 45 starts. He was owned jointly by William Ransom Johnson of Virginia and James Long of Washington.

Bowery Theatre, the. Opened in 1826, the Bowery was one of the three leading New York theatres of the age. Others included the Park and the National.

Bradshaw, Sam. Fictional.

Brewerton, Miss Bittry. Fictional.

Broadfute, Mr. [James A. Bradfute] Horse breeder from Franklin, Tennessee, who sold horses sired by Bertrand to several Arkansas horsemen. Pete's comment that the horses "turned out badly" sparked an angry response.

Brown C. [Roberts]. The representative from Izard County in both the Territorial and State legislatures.

Brown, Billy [George William]. (1812-1890) Widely known for his strong stand for orderly government, Brown was involved with Gen. Samuel Smith in attempting to suppress riots attending the failure of the Bank of Maryland in 1836, and during the 1850s opposing the mob rule methods of the Know-Nothing Party in Baltimore.

Brown, Capt. [Jacob]. A captain in the United States Army and the first president of the Arkansas State Bank, serving throughout most of 1837. He was widely criticized for holding the two positions simultaneously.

Brown, Dr. Unknown.

Brown, Jim. Possibly an actual person, though now unidentifiable.

Brown, Tom. Fictional.

Brushy Fork. One of the streams of the Devil's Fork area, now unidentifiable.

Brushy Lake. Unidentifiable.

Bullet-Neck. A fictional horse.

Bullion. A widely-used nickname for Thomas Hart Benton. The name derives from Benton's campaign to reissue coins.

Burns, Paddy. Unknown.

Burns, Squire. Fictional.

Burnt Blanket. A fictional horse.

Bussing Coon. A fictional horse.

Busted-shot-gun. A fictional horse.

Caldwells. James Caldwell, who was one of the early settlers of the Batesville area, and his family.

Calf Killer. Unknown.

Calhoun, John C. (1782-1850) Secretary of War, Vice President, Senator, Secretary of State, and hero of the ante-bellum South.

Camden. The New Jersey city.

Caney Fork. Unidentifiable.

Carnell, Tom. Probably fictional.

Carter, Morg. Fictional.

Carter, Sister. Fictional.

Carter, Thomas. Unknown.

Cass, General [Lewis]. (1782-1866) Strongly nationalistic senator from Michigan. Secretary of War under Jackson (1831-1836). Democratic nominee for president in 1848, Cass served as Secretary of State under Buchanan (1857-1860).

Champion. A horse; unknown.

Chapel Hill Township. Unknown.

Chapman, Dr. [Daniel J.]. A candidate for Congress in 1842, Chapman withdrew from the race just prior to the election. He was from Independence County and was highly influential in state politics.

Charles. Unidentifiable.

Charles Carter. Foaled in 1834, he was by Lance out of Fanny Hill. He was owned by William McCargo.

Charley. A Negro horse trainer who lived in White Sulphur Springs, Virginia. Noland speaks of him in "Races at the Salt Sulphur Springs, Va.," *Spirit*, 9 (7 September 1839), 319.

Charline. A filly by Pacific out of an unnamed dam by Greytail Florizel. She was foaled in 1833 and belonged to Noland.

Charmed Bullet. A fictional horse.

Chiney, Peter. Fictional.

Chiney, Squire. Fictional.

Churubusco. Unknown.

Clinton. The small town which is the county seat of Van Buren County in north central Arkansas.

Coahoma. A horse foaled in 1834 and owned by F. Henderson. He was by Mercury out of an unnamed dam by Oscar.

Cobble, Dick. Fictional.

Coddifiers. The committee, composed of Samuel Calhoun Roane and

William McK. Ball, who were charged with the preparation of a systematic code of Arkansas laws.

Coffee-vault. William G.H. Teevault of Scotia, Pope County, Arkansas.

Cohen, Joe. Fictional.

Cole, Jim. Fictional. Pete's brother-in-law and closest friend.

Cole, Sally. Fictional. Pete's sister who marries Jim Cole. She is the only female character who is sustained throughout the letters.

Col. Wood. An unknown boat.

Contention. An unknown horse.

Cony Fork [also Coney]. Unidentifiable.

Cornwell, Deck. Fictional.

Craig, [William]. One of the leading jockeys of his day, Craig rode for some of the best horsemen in the country. He died during the week of 13 October 1849, at Ogdensburg, New York. See obituary in *Spirit,* 19 (20 October 1849), 414.

Cravat Creek [also Cravat-stuffing Creek]. Unidentifiable.

Cub [formerly named Chlorine]. A filly, foaled in 1836, by Medoc out of an unnamed dam by Sumpter. She was owned by George E. Blackburn of Kentucky.

Culp, Squire. Unidentifiable. The Culp family was prominent in Izard County from the 1830s.

Davie, Maj. Unidentifiable.

Davis, Bill. Fictional.

DeKalb, the. A packet running from New Orleans up the Arkansas. A Captain Lemmon was in charge. See *Arkansas Gazette,* 18 July 1837.

Denton, Maj. William F. (d. 1845) Noland's close friend and business partner. Noland wrote a brief sketch of Denton in "Early Settlers of Arkansas—No. 5," *Spirit,* 19 (26 January 1850), 578.

Devil's Fork of the Little Red River, the. The branch of the Little Red River upon which Pete lives. At the time the letters were composed, the Devil's Fork was in Van Buren County; when Cleburne County was formed, it contained the Devil's Fork area. Much of the area, including the Devil's Fork, is now covered by Greer's Ferry Lake. See map.

Devil's Fork Township. The area along the Devil's Fork.

Dillon, John. A racing enthusiast and horse breeder from Van Buren, Arkansas.

Diomead. A fictional horse. The name is close enough to Diomed, an imported stud, that many would believe him to be actual.

Dish Face. A fictional horse.

Donelson. One of two fictional hounds Dan Looney acquires during his trip to Illinois and Ohio.

Drive. A fictional dog.

Dry-bones. A fictional horse.

Dry Fork of Bear Creek. One of the branches, now unidentifiable, of Bear Creek, a tributary of White River. The Bear Creek area lies directly north of the Devil's Fork. See map.

Duane. A horse, foaled in 1836, by Hedgeford (imported) out of Goodloe W. by Washington. He was owned by William McCargo.

Dutchman, the Little. Martin Van Buren.

Dyer, Jack. Fictional.

Darboy, John. Fictional.

Eagle Fork. No such stream is identified on maps contemporary with the Whetstone era.

Eclipse. A stallion owned by James Swanson of Franklin, Tennessee. He was by Duroc out of Miller's Damsel.

Eklipse. A fictional horse.

Elk-horn. The Elkhorn River, which empties into the Kentucky River about 10 miles below Frankfort, Kentucky.

Ella Wickham. A filly by Volcano foaled in 1835 and belonging to George Caldwell of Batesville.

Emeline. An unidentifiable horse.

Etny. Mount Etna, the Sicilian volcano.

Eudora. A filly, foaled in 1834, by Jefferson out of an unnamed dam by Tennessee Oscar. She was owned by W. L. Alexander.

Evans, Lawyer [Lemuel D.]. A minor Arkansas political figure.

Experiment. A horse, foaled in 1843, by Jack Downing out of an unnamed dam by Rattler. He was owned by David Thompson.

Expedition, Mr. An anonymous Illinois correspondent to the *Spirit,* who complained that Pete wrote too much concerning politics.

Fairfax. The town in Virginia; a suburb of Washington.

Fanny Wyatt. A filly, foaled in 1834, by Sir Charles out of an unnamed dam by Sir Hal. She was owned by John C. Stevens of New York.

Fashion. A mare, foaled in 1835, by Trustee out of Bonnets o' Blue. She was owned by William Gibbons of New Jersey. Fashion was quite famous during her day, setting a number of records. She won 32 out of 36 starts and was second in the other four.

Fayetteville. The county seat of Washington County in northwest Arkansas. The University of Arkansas is located in Fayetteville.

Fillmore. One of two fictional hounds which Dan Looney acquired while on his trip to Illinois and Ohio.

Fire-tail. A fictional horse.

Flanigan, Pat. Fictional.

Flint Island. One of several islands in the Ohio River, 80 miles downstream from Louisville.

Flying Pop Gun. A fictional horse.

Fordham. A horse, owned by John C. Stevens of New York. He was by Eclipse out of Janette.

Forsyth, [John]. (1780-1841) A Georgian, Forsyth was Van Buren's Secretary of State. The two were involved in a number of heated quarrels.

Fort Gibson. The small town on the Arkansas River near Muskogee, Oklahoma.

Fort Smith. The city on the Arkansas River on the western border of the state. One of the oldest cities in Arkansas, it is the county seat of Sebastian County.

Frankfort. The capital city of Kentucky.

Frazier, Mr. Probably E. Frazier, who was surveyor of Independence County from 1835 to 1840.

Fuss and Feathers. Winfield Scott.

Game. A fictional dog.

Garrison, [James S.]. Proprietor of the New Orleans race track.

General Jackson. A fictional dog.

George. An unidentifiable jockey.

Gibbs, Davy. Fictional.

Giddings, [Joshua Reed]. (1795-1864) Giddings was for twenty years (1838-1858) an abolitionist, militant, antislavery congressman from the Western Reserve of Ohio.

Gil. See Patrick, Gilbert.

[Gilfillan], *Janet.* Fictional.

Gilfillan, Squire. Fictional.

Ginel, Jo. Fictional.

Glencoe. An imported stallion owned by James Jackson of Florence, Alabama. He was by Sultan out of Trampoline.

Gobler. See Martin.

Godolphing Arabin. A fictional horse, but near enough in name to several famous studs to have the illusion of reality.

Goodrich and Loomis. A Little Rock clothing store.

Greene, Major. Unknown.

Greene. Possibly Greene County in northeast Arkansas.

Green Tree. The Batesville hotel during the era covered by the letters.

Grey Eagle. A horse, foaled in 1835, by Woodpecker out of Ophelia by Wild Medley. He was owned by Miles W. Dickey and Y.N. Oliver of Kentucky.

Grindstone, Sam. Fictional.

Growler, Capt. Unknown.

Grubbs, Squire. Fictional.

H., Joey. Joseph H. Van Mater.

Hard-times. A fictional horse.

Hard-to-beat, Nicholas. Fictional.

Hare, Otway P. Unknown.

Harris, Stephen. The owner and manager of a "public house" at the mouth of White River.

Haukins, Dick. Unknown.

Hell-fire. Jim Cole's fictional dog.

Hero of Orleans, the. Andrew Jackson.

Hessian Fly. A fictional horse.

Hightower, Bill. Fictional.

Hill, Isaac. (1789-1851) A powerful editor and politician from New Hampshire. He served in the U.S. Senate from 1831 until 1836. Hill was a close friend of President Jackson and a member of the famous "Kitchen Cabinet."

Hinton, Sam. Fictional.

Hiram. A fictional jockey.

Holloway's Ointment. A patent medicine; possibly fictional.

Hombuckle. Fictional, though his name may be drawn from Uncle Tommy Hombuckle who appears as a witness in a trial which Noland describes in "Bulletin from Arkansas," *Spirit,* 7 (8 July 1837), 166. Both characters may be fictional.

Honey, Rube. Fictional.

Huntsville. The county seat of Madison County in northwest Arkansas.

Hyena. A fictional horse.

Independence. A horse by Tom Fletcher (dam unknown) foaled in 1834. He was owned by Thomas T. Tunstall, Noland's close friend.

Independence County. One of the oldest counties in Arkansas. Batesville is its county seat.

Ivings, Christopher. Fictional.

Izard County. The county northwest and bordering Independence County. Melbourne is the county seat.

Jackson County. The bordering county southeast of Independence

County. Newport is the county seat.

Jackson, Poke. Fictional.

Janet [Gilfillan]. Fictional.

Jeff. Jefferson Davis.

Jerry. Fictional.

Jim Townley. James Townley, foaled in 1834, was by Columbus out of an unnamed dam by Winter's Arabian. He belonged to Philo C. Bush.

Jimboden, Ben. Fictional.

Job. A horse, foaled in 1836, he was by Eclipse out of Jemima. He belonged to Walter Livingston.

Joey H. Joseph H. Van Mater.

John Bascomb[e]. A horse by Bertrand out of Grey Goose, owned by Col. John Crowell of Alabama.

Johnny Q. The ex-President, John Quincy Adams.

Johnsin, Kirnel. Fictional, but many *Spirit* readers would associate the name with Colonel William Ransom Johnson.

Johnson, Lawyer [Euclid L.]. A minor Arkansas political figure.

Johnson, Mr. Fictional.

Johnson, Col. [William Ransom]. (1782-1849) The leading turfman in America for generations. Johnson was an important figure in Virginia politics from 1822 until 1837. His main interest was in training and running horses. His obituary is found in the *Spirit,* 19 (24 February 1849), 6.

Jones, Jake. Fictional.

Jones, Judge. Fictional.

Jones, Sally. Fictional. "The prettiest gal on all the forks of Little Red."

Jones, Sam. Fictional.

Jones, Sister. Fictional.

Jones, Squint-eyed. Fictional.

Jones, Squire. Fictional.

Jones, Tom. Fictional.

June. A fictional dog of almost legendary quality.

Juniata Iron. Possibly a brand name; now unidentifiable.

Kalliforny. California.

Kate Longworth. An unknown horse.

Kelarup. An unknown horse.

Kendall, Amos. (1789-1869) A strong supporter of Jackson and Van Buren. His strongest influence was felt during the 1830's when he was a member of Jackson's so-called "kitchen cabinet" and a close advisor to the president. He fought the establishment of the United States Bank and was the principal author of the presidential message of 10 July 1832, vetoing a bill to recharter the national bank. Kendall was also Postmaster General for several years, turning the post office into a fairly efficient operation.

Kendall, James B. The owner of the race track at Baltimore and a well-known horseman of the era.

Kendle. James B. Kendall.

Kindle. Amos Kendall.

Kinderhook. A small community located at the point where the Devil's Fork and Middle Fork of Little Red River joined.

Kinderhook Township. The area around Kinderhook. Now beneath Greer's Ferry Lake.

Know Nothings. The nickname of the American Party which was organized in 1854. Originally the party was a secret organization. It was solidly committed to nativism, its main principle being that immigrants and Catholics should be prohibited from playing an active part in government.

Kraft, Dr. Probably Dr. George B. Croft, a member of the Territorial Council from Greene County.

Lady Cliffden. A filly by Sussex out of Betsey Wilson, she was foaled in 1834. She was owned by James M. Selden of Maryland and was one of the most famous race horses of the day.

Lady Nashville. A filly by Stockholder out of an unnamed dam by Strap.

Lafayette, [Marie Joseph Paul Yves Roch Gilbert du Motier, Marquis de]. (1757-1834) The noted French soldier and statesman who made valuable contributions of influence and intellect to the American Revolution.

Lafford, Jack. Unknown.

Lambert, Daniel. (1770-1809) An Englishman weighing 739 lbs. at his death. The name became a popular synonym for hugeness.

Larry. Fictional.

Lawrence County. The County located to the northeast of Independence County. Walnut Ridge is the county seat.

Levi. See Woodbury, Levi.

Levi Woodbury. Pete's fictional jackass.

Lion. A fictional dog.

Little Red. A horse foaled in 1835. He was owned by Elias Rector and Thomas T. Tunstall. He was by Volcano out of Zephyr.

Little Rock. A steamboat, owned by Captain S. Buckner, which operated for a time as a trader on the Ouachita River in Arkansas. It was commanded by Captain Gordon. See *Arkansas State Gazette,* 2 October 1839.

Little Spot. A fictional dog.

Livingston, Walter. Unknown.

Loco Foco. A radical splinter group of the Democratic Party which held equal rights as its fundamental principle. The name derives from loco-foco matches which members used to light candles at a party meeting in Tammany Hall, New York, 29 October 1835. At this meeting considerable controversy had arisen; the chairman, in an attempt to adjourn, ordered the gas lights extinguished. After radicals, led by George Henry Evans and William Leggett, lit candles with their matches, they formulated their party platform.

Long, [James]. A racing enthusiast from Washington who was part owner of Boston.

Long, Squire. Fictional.

Looney, Dan. Fictional.

Looney, Jim. Fictional.

Looney, Sally. Fictional.

Looney, Squire. Fictional; possibly Dan.

Looser, Squire. Fictional.

Loring, John S. Unknown.

Lower Fork. Not identified on maps, the Lower Fork is the South Fork which flows past the town of Clinton. See map.

Lycurgus. An unknown horse.

McCampbell, Lawyer. Fictional.

McCampbell, Lawyer [the younger]. Fictional.

McCargo, Billy. Unknown.

McCarthy, Col. Unknown.

McCarty, Col. Unknown.

McCormick, Dick. Fictional.

McFudgins, Squire. Fictional.

McK., Lawyer. Probably William McKissick Ball, a Fayetteville attorney and cashier of the short-lived branch of the State Bank. He absconded with the assets of the bank and fled to Texas.

McKonett, Jim. Fictional.

McLloughlin, Lieut. Unknown.

Madison. A small town located on the St. Francis River near Forrest City, Arkansas.

Madrid. Probably New Madrid, Missouri, a town located on the Mississippi River some twenty miles south of Sikeston.

Maffit, [James]. A native of Ireland, Maffit was a Methodist evangelist who attracted huge crowds in the United States during the 1830s and 1840s. He died in 1850.

Manly, Cullen. A free Negro who trained the horses of Thomas T. Tunstall.

Margaretta. An unknown horse.

Marion. The county seat of Crittenden County, Arkansas. Marion is located about fifteen miles northwest of Memphis.

Marion County. The north-central Arkansas county which has Yellville as its county seat.

Marmion. An unknown horse.

Marshall, Sam. Fictional.

Marshall, Tom. Unknown.

Martin. Fictional.

Mary Ellen. A mare foaled in 1831. She was by Sir Charles out of an unnamed dam by Contention. She was owned by W. Mitchell.

Master Henry. A horse foaled in 1834. He was by Henry out of an unnamed dam by Balie Peyton's Eclipse. He belonged to James B. Kendall of Baltimore.

Mealbag, Jim. Fictional.

Mercury. An unknown horse.

Metamora. A filly foaled in 1833. She was by Bott's Lafayette.

Middle Prong. Probably the Middle Fork of the Little Red River. See map.

Middlebury. A post village on Goose Creek in the south-southwest part of Loudon County, Virginia, about 12 miles southwest of Leesburg.

Millerites. Members of the Adventist Church, so called because of their founder, William Miller (1792-1849). Miller predicted the second coming of Christ would occur in 1843.

Mingo. A horse owned by Gen. C. Irvine. He was by Eclipse out of Bay Bett.

Missouri. A mare foaled in 1834. She was by Eclipse out of an unnamed dam by Director. She was owned by William McCargo.

Moat, Old. Fictional.

Mobile. A horse foaled in 1837. He was by Consol (imported) out of Sessions (imported).

Monsieur Tonson. A stallion by Pacolet out of Madame Tonson. Bred by Hardy M. Cryer (one-time manager of Andrew Jackson's stable) and owned in later life by Henry Clay. He lost his debut race, but won all other starts in his long career. He was also the leading American stallion for the 1834 season.

Montgomery, Bill [William]. A well-known figure in territorial Arkansas. Montgomery was a gambler by profession and an extremely wealthy man. He represented Arkansas County in the territorial and state legislatures for years.

Moore, Granny. Fictional.

Murray, Lindley. (1745-1826) A grammarian whose texts virtually monopolized the field prior to 1850. By that time there were supposedly nearly 2 million copies in circulation.

Mussett, Jim. See Old Sense.

Mussett, Tyree. A Fort Smith horse breeder fairly prominent in Arkansas racing circles during the 1840s.

Ned, Uncle. Unidentifiable.

Nedle, Jim. Fictional.

Nelson, Dot-and-carry-one. Fictional; probably peg-legged, hence, the nickname.

New Dublin. Not identified on contemporary maps.

Nicholas. Unidentifiable.

Nick. Czar Nicholas I, of Russia, who reigned 1825-1855.

Nick, Squire. Fictional.

Nick of the Woods. A play (full title: *Nick of the Woods, or The Jibbenainosay, A Tale of Kentucky*) by Robert Montgomery Bird. It was extremely popular during Pete's era.

O'Conner, Dennis. Fictional.

O'Flaherty, Terence. Fictional.

O'Spriggins, Barney. Fictional.

O'Spriggins, Judy. Fictional.

Old Argyle. See Argyle.

Old Bear Meat. See Bear Meat.

Old Bill. Sir William.

Old Boon. A fictional horse.

Old Bose. A fictional dog.

Old Hickory. Andrew Jackson.

Old Missouri. See Missouri.

Old Napoleon. William Ransom Johnson.

Old Reality. See Reality.

Old Sense [Jim Mussett]. Fictional.

Old Shepherdess. See Shepherdess.

Old Shore. A fictional horse.

Old Sledge. A card game also known as Seven Up or All Fours. It was the most popular gambling card game in the United States until poker replaced it in the mid-1800s.

Old Swayback. See Swayback.

Old Tip. William Henry Harrison.

Old Vol. See Volcano.

Old Wagner. See Wagner.

Omega. A filly foaled in 1835. She was by Timoleon out of Daisy Cropper by Ogle's Oscar. She was owned by F. Thompson.

Owens, Bill. Fictional.

Owl Creek Township. Unknown.

Oxford filly, the. An unknown horse.

Ozark. An unknown horse.

Paddy. See Burns, Paddy.

Palafox. An unknown horse.

Pan Handle. Fictional.

Parsons. A Methodist evangelist. See letter 38, fn. 4.

Patrick, Gil[bert]. One of the best known and winningest jockeys of the 1830s and 1840s. At one time or another, he rode virtually every famous race horse in the East. Robertson *(The History of Thoroughbred Racing)* lists his name as "Gilpatrick;" a first name is neither supplied nor mentioned.

Pawnee. An unknown steamboat.

Pendyerit, Capt. [P. Pennywit]. (1793-1868) One of the best known and most popular riverboat captains in Arkansas. He was captain of the *Neosho* and later the *Little Rock.*

Pete Whetstone. A steamboat packet built in 1856 in Jeffersonville, Indiana, and operating out of Louisville.

Peter Simple. An unknown horse.

Peyton, Balie. (1803-1878). A congressman from Tennessee from 1833 to 1836. He then moved to New Orleans where he held a number of military and political positions. He was also a well-known sportsman.

Picton. Foaled in 1834 and owned by William Winn of Virginia. He was by Luzborough (imported) out of Isabella.

Pike, Albert. (1809-1891) A Little Rock attorney and businessman. Pike was a leading figure in Scottish Rite Free-masonry, revising and formulating the ritual of the order. He also published several volumes of poetry and was the author of one of the standard versions of the song *Dixie*.

Pine Hill. Not identified on maps of the Devil's Fork area.

Piney Woods. Possibly the area along the Piney Fork of the Strawberry River north of Batesville.

Pisen Shirt. A fictional horse.

Planter's Bank of Mississippi. A bank established in Natchez by the Mississippi Legislature in 1830. It failed in 1840.

Plumpie, Bill. Probably fictional.

Poinsett, [Joel Roberts]. (1779-1851) A South Carolinian who was Van Buren's Secretary of War.

Poole, Dr. Unknown.

Poolet, Widow. Fictional.

Pope County. The Arkansas county located approximately 70 miles northwest of Little Rock. Russellville is the county seat.

Pope Pius IX. Giovanni Maria Mastai-Ferretti (1792-1878). Pope from 1846 to 1878.

Portsmouth. A horse foaled in 1835. He was owned by C. Halcher. He was by Luzborough (imported) out of Polly Peacham.

Priam. An imported stallion owned by A.T.B. Merritt of Hicksford, Virginia. He was by Emilius out of Cressida. He was one of the more famous sires of the day.

Price, Bill. Fictional.

Price, Uncle Johnny. Fictional.

Price, Uncle Tommy. Fictional.

Profile, Mr. Unknown.

Proof-Sheet. A filly foaled in 1834. She was by Eclipse out of an unnamed dam by Florizel. She was owned by David Thompson.

Pruett, Squire. Fictional.

Pukee. Unidentifiable.

Purty-nax Mac Siccofant. A character in *The Man of the World* (1781) by Charles Macklin (d. 1797).

Q., Johnny. John Quincy Adams.

Raccoon Fork of the War Eagle. The creek directly east of the Devil's Fork. See map.

Raccoon Fork Township. Probably the area through which the Raccoon Fork ran; see map. The area now lies beneath Greer's Ferry Lake.

Ralph. A horse foaled in 1836. He was by Woodpecker out of Brown Mary. He belonged to Walker Thurston.

Randolph County. The county in northeast Arkansas. Pocahontas is the county seat.

Reality. An unknown horse.

Rebecca. An unknown horse.

Rector, Col. [Henry Massey]. (1816-1899) Rector arrived in Arkansas about 1835, having come from St. Louis to attend to extensive land claims held by his late father. He was, throughout the rest of his life, deeply involved in Arkansas politics, serving as Governor from 1860 to 1862.

Red Fork. One of the unidentifiable streams of the Devil's Fork area.

Reel. A filly foaled in 1838. She was by Glencoe (imported) out of Gallopade (imported). She was owned by M. and T. J. Wells.

Reesides, Lord Admiral. Unknown.

Reynolds. Unidentifiable.

Rio Jinery Jim. Although the identity of "Rio Janero Jim" is unknown, he is spoken of in a number of accounts of life in New Orleans during the Whetstone era.

Rival Pages. The full title is *Rival Pages: A Petite Comedy in One Act.* It was written by Charles Shelby (1802-1863).

Rives, William C[abell]. (1793-1868) A strongly Jacksonian political leader from Virginia. Jackson made him minister to France in 1829. He was elected to the U.S. Senate in 1832. He declared his principles to be "anti-bank, anti-tariff, and anti-nullification." In 1835 he expressed dissatisfaction with Jackson's specie circular and opposition to Van Buren's subtreasury system.

Rob Roy. An unknown horse.

Robert Fulton. An unknown steamboat.

Robinson, Amos. Fictional.

Rock, the. Little Rock.

Rocky Fork. Not identified on contemporary maps.

Roman Senator. Unidentifiable.

Ross, John. (1790-1866) The principal chief of the Cherokee Nation from 1828 until his death.

Rossy, Jim. Fictional.

Rozell. Unknown.

St. Anthony's Day. 13 June.

St. Charles. One of the better New Orleans hotels of the age.

Sappington's Pills. A patent medicine for malaria.

Sarah Washington. A filly foaled in 1837. She was by Garrison's Zinganee out of an unnamed dam by Contention. She was owned by William Duvall.

Scott, Winfield. (1786-1866) Distinguishing himself as a general during the Mexican War, Scott was the Whig candidate for the presidency in 1852. He carried electoral votes of only Vermont, Kentucky, Massachusetts, and Tennessee, losing to Franklin Pierce. During the last five years of his life, Scott was the superintendent of the U.S. Military Academy at West Point.

Screviner, Judge. Fictional.

Scroggins, Giles. Fictional.

Seminolys. The Seminoles.

Shakespeare. An imported stallion owned by Robert Hurt of Paris, Tennessee. He was by Smolensko out of Charming Molly.

Sharp-tooth. A fictional dog.

Shepherdess. A mare foaled in 1833. She was by Lance out of Amanda and was owned by Daniel Abbott.

Shippingport. A post village on the Ohio River, 2 miles below the center of Louisville.

Shoulderstrap. Fictional.

Sims, Aunt Peggy. Fictional.

Sims, Billy. Fictional.

Sims, Johnny. Fictional.

Sims, Mr. Fictional; possibly one of the above.

Sims, Squire. Fictional; possibly one of the above.

Singleton, Col. Unidentifiable.

Sir Archibald. Fictional, but easily associated with Sir Archy, a horse quite famous in the early 1800s.

Sir Charles. A stallion owned by James J. Harrison of Virginia. He was by Sir Archy out of an unnamed dam.

Sir William. A horse foaled in 1834. He was owned by Joseph D. Thompson and was by Clay's Sir William out of Polly Fox.

Sister Sal. Pete's sister who marries Jim Cole.

Sister to Lady Nashville. A mare belonging to a Major Dillard. She raced in Batesville in 1841. She was by Stockholder out of an unnamed dam by Strap.

Slippery Elm. A figure of speech used to suggest deviousness in a person.

Smidt, Dick. Fictional.

Smith, Bill. Fictional.

Smith, Bob. Fictional.

Smith, Deaf. Fictional.

Smith, Jim. Fictional.

Smith, Piney-woods. Fictional.

Smith, Sister. Fictional.

Smith, Squire. Fictional; possibly one of the above.

Smithland. A small Kentucky town on the Ohio River at the mouth of the Cumberland River.

Snakebite Prong. Not identified on contemporary maps.

Sneeves, Squire. Fictional.

Snodgrass, Mr. Probably fictional.

Snowden's. Evidently a fine hotel in Trenton, New Jersey.

South Fork. The branch of Little Red River flowing near Clinton in Van Buren County.

Southern Belle. An unknown horse.

Speckel Back. A fictional horse.

Spence, Bill. Fictional.

Spence, Jim. Fictional.

Spence, Tom. Fictional.

Spencer, Bill. Fictional.

Spinel, Sally. Fictional.

Sporting Magazine. The London *New Sporting Magazine*.

Spring River. A small river in Lawrence County, approximately fifty miles northeast of Batesville. The Spring joins the Black River which in turn joins the White.

Springs. Probably the site of Sulphur Rock in Independence County. Sulphur springs are a principal feature of the town.

Stackpole, Captain Ralph. One of the principal characters in Robert Montgomery Bird's play, *Nick of the Woods.* He was a very popular stage version of the "ringtail roarer."

Stanhope. A horse foaled in 1835. He was by Eclipse out of Helen Mar, by Rattler.

State's Feliciter, the. The State's Solicitor.

Steele [Steel]. A horse foaled in 1836. He belonged to William McCargo. He was by Fylde (imported) out of Dimont.

Stevens, John C[ox]. The founder of the New York Yacht Club and head of the group which sent the *America* to England to compete for the international cup. He also was prominent in horse racing circles.

Stevens, Robert L[ivingston]. (1787-1856) A leader in naval architecture, he designed and had built upwards of twenty steamboats and ferries, incorporating in them his successive inventions. He was also a pioneer in locomotive design, bringing the first railway service to New Jersey.

Stones, Bill. Fictional.

Stones, Zacky. Fictional.

Stout, Bill. Fictional.

Swayback. A fictional horse.

Swob-tail. Probably a fictional horse.

Sydney. Unidentifiable.

Tague Orengan. A fictional fighting cock. Possibly named for Teague O'Regan, a character in Hugh Henry Brackenridge's *Modern Chivalry.*

Talleyrand. A widely used name for Chester Ashley.

Taturs Mare. Fictional.

Taylor, Arthur. One of the better known jockeys of the 1830s.

Telamon. A horse foaled in 1834. He belonged to James K. Duke of Kentucky. He was by Medoc out of Cherry Elliott by Sumpter.

Temptation Societies. Temperance Societies.

Thompson, Mr. Fictional.

Thompson, Asa. One of the more colorful figures in early Arkansas history. Originally Thompson was from North Carolina, but he migrated to Arkansas prior to 1820. Severely hunchbacked, he was said to be taller sitting than standing. He spent several terms in the state legislature where he was said to have great influence. He made his living by dealing faro and fits Pete's description of a faro dealer. Noland gives a thumbnail biography in "Early Settlers of Arkansas—No. 4," *Spirit*, 19 (12 January 1850), 559.

Thompson, Davy. A horse breeder and trainer from Van Buren, Arkansas.

Thompson, Dick. A U. S. Representative from Indiana during the era of the Whetstone letters.

Thompson, Moll. Fictional.

Thorp, Old. Fictional.

Thurston, Walker. Unknown.

Tigertail, Mrs. The wife of Thlocks-Tustenuggee, a Tallahassee Indian.

Tippecanoe. William Henry Harrison.

Tolbert's Settlement. No place by this name appears on contemporary maps; however, a settlement named Talbot was located on the White River in Searcy County, approximately seventy-five miles northwest of Batesville.

Tom. Fictional.

Tom Fletcher. A stallion owned by Thomas T. Tunstall of Batesville. He was by Stockholder out of an unnamed dam.

Tomson. See Thompson, Davy.

To-nail. Fictional.

Tonson. See Monsieur Tonson.

Trebla. Albert C. Ainsworth, of New Orleans.

Trenton. The New Jersey city.

Triplett, Hedge[man]. (1792-1840) A member of the Arkansas House of Representatives from Chicot County. Triplett apparently came to Arkansas in 1825; his former home is unknown. His obituary appears in the *Arkansas State Gazette,* 23 December 1840.

Tunstall, Capt. [Thomas Todd]. (1787-1862) A wealthy and influential planter who lived near Batesville. He pioneered navigation of the White River and owned several packets. He also bred and raced horses. Tunstall was one of Noland's closest friends. The best biography is Duane Huddleston, *Of Race Horses and Steamboats: The Pride of Captain Thomas Todd Tunstall* (Batesville: Independence County Historical Society, 1973).

Tyree. Fictional.

Tyrse. Fictional.

Upper Fork. Not identified on contemporary maps.

Upshire, Judge. Undoubtedly Abel Parker Upshur of Virginia, who was Secretary of State under Tyler from 8 May 1843 until his death 28 February 1844.

Up-to-snuff, Esquire. Fictional.

Van Buren. The county seat of Crawford County, on the western border of Arkansas.

Van Buren County. The county joining Independence on the west. At the time the Whetstone letters were written, the Devil's Fork area lay in Van Buren County. Cleburne County is now located between Van Buren and Independence. Clinton is Van Buren's county seat.

Van Mater, Joseph H. Unknown.

Vashti. A filly foaled in 1835. She was by Leviathan (imported) out of Slazy by Bullock's Mucklejohn. She was owned by David McDaniel.

Vermillion County, Indiana. A county in west-central Indiana, bordered on the east by the Wabash River and on the west by Illinois.

Virginius. A flamboyant blank verse, highly theatrical tragedy in 5 acts by James Sheridan Knowles (1784-1862).

Volcano. An unknown horse.

Wagner. One of the most famous horses of his day, Wagner was foaled in 1835. He was by Sir Charles out of Maria West by Marion and was owned by James S. Garrison of New Orleans.

Walker, Sam. Fictional.

Wapponocca. Probably William D. Ferguson, a state senator from Crittenden County. Wapponoca is a small lake in that county.

War Eagle. No stream by this name appears on maps of the area.

Warping Bars. A fictional horse.

Washington City. Washington, D.C.

Washington County. The county in northwest Arkansas. Fayetteville is the county seat.

Waters, Sam. The manager of the first theatre company in Little Rock, which opened in 1838. Waters was also a locally well-known comic singer.

Waxy. An unknown horse.

Weeping Willow. A fictional horse.

Wells, Jef. Unidentifiable.

Whaley, Billy. Little is known about Whaley. Noland mentions him several times in connection with stagecoach travel. Later he is said to be proprietor of a stage line. See " 'N. of Arkansas' in Virginia," *Spirit,* 19 (4 August 1849), 283.

Whetstone, Jim. Fictional; Pete's father.

Whetstone, Sal. [Sister Sal, Sally Cole]. Fictional; Pete's sister.

White Oak. A figure of speech used to suggest a person's high integrity.

White River. The river rising in northwest Arkansas and flowing through the north-central part of the state to join the Mississippi near the junction of the Arkansas and Mississippi Rivers. It flows past Batesville. See map.

White Sulpher. Now located in West Virginia, White Sulphur Springs is about 50 miles northwest of Roanoke, Virginia. The town has long been a popular spa.

Whitney, Reuben [M.]. An adviser to Jackson. At one time he was a director of the U.S. Bank; later he was a lobbyist for state banks.

Widow Cheerly. A filly foaled in 1834. She was by Stockholder out of Polly Baker. She was owned by John Dillard.

Wiley, a-perfect-case. Fictional.

William French. An unknown steamboat.

Willis. A horse foaled in 1834. He was by Bertrand out of an unnamed dam by Southern Eclipse and was owned by John Short.

Wilson, Dick. Fictional.

Wiseman, Tommy. Unknown.

Wonder. An unknown horse.

Woodbury, Levi. (1789-1851) A native of New Hampshire, Woodbury was appointed Secretary of the Navy in 1831. While in Jackson's cabinet, he sided with Blair and Kendall in approving the removal of deposits from the Bank of the United States. In 1834 Jackson appointed him as Secretary of the Treasury.

Woodruff, Buck [William Edward]. (1795-1885) Founder of the *Arkansas Gazette* and powerful political figure in Arkansas.

Woods, Squire. Fictional.

Worm-Eater. A fictional horse.

Worth, General [William Jenkins] (d. 1849) Worth had a long, distinguished military career. He was made Brigadier General in 1842 for gallantry and highly distinguished service as commander of forces in the war against the Florida Indians.

Yell, Governor [Archibald]. Arkansas' second governor (1840-1844).

Yellville. The small town which is the county seat of Marion County in north-central Arkansas.

York City. New York.

York's Tall Son. William T. Porter, the editor of the *Spirit.*

Young America. Probably George Nicholas Sanders.

Young Gourd Vine. Fictional.

Z. Probably Mark W. Izard, state senator from St. Francis and Greene Counties.

Zephyr. An unknown horse.

APPENDIX 3
Glossary of Words and Phrases

A-B, AB to Crucifix. The exact meaning is unclear; however, usage suggests the term means "completely or totally;" perhaps "from A to X."

Ager. Ague, or malaria.

Ager-coke. "Ague cake," a swelling resulting from the disease.

Arter. After.

Ax. Ask.

Bald Face. Whiskey which was home-made and unaged; moonshine or "white lightning."

Bar. Bear.

Bark Mill. A mill used for grinding bark from trees, especially oak and hemlock, in preparation for securing tannin for use in tanning leather.

Bars-Ile. Bear oil.

Bekase. Because.

Benton's Mint Drops. Gold coins which returned to circulation during President Jackson's administration as a result of Thomas Hart Benton's championing "hard money" and revising the gold-silver value ratio to 16 to 1.

Bime-By. By and by.

Bite. The clear advantage in a wager; a bet which one feels is a certainty.

Black Jack. A small variety of oak tree of the eastern United States having nearly black bark and wood of little value except as fuel.

Black Tans. Black-and-tan hounds; a variety of hound which is black with tan markings above the eyes and on the muzzle, chest, legs, feet, and breech.

Blather. Probably bladder.

Blowing Horn. The horn blown to signal the start of a horse race.

Blue Back. Paper money printed with blue ink. Usually of little value.

Bolt. (verb) Drink.

Bone Razor. The first.

Boot. Money or goods added to one side of a trade, purchase, or wager to equalize the two. Probably the origin of the usage comes from the idea of money or goods added to "kick" or "boot" up the offer.

Bottynist. Botanist.

Bouters. Banters.

Briled. Broiled.

Broad Horn. A flat-boat.

Bulger. An unusually big person.

Buster. A very large, strong man.

Camp Meeting. A religious gathering, usually lasting for several days.

Cat Hop. Probably the four of clubs in a deck of cards, so called because of its resemblance to the footprint of a cat.

Cavort. To frisk, frolic, or caper about. It frequently connotes noisiness and boisterousness. Terrific boasts were a frequent aspect of cavorting.

Cherow. An onomatopoeic coinage describing the sound of a blow from a fist.

Chucks (quantity). Not a specific number; merely a group.

Cogenial. Congenial.

Cohoot. A secret partnership.

Coleu Nine. The black nine in roulette.

Confab. A talk, conversation, or conference.

Corn Dodger. Hard bread made of fried or baked corn meal.

Corn Stealer. The right hand.

Cotting. Cotton.

Coulter. A sharp blade or wheel attached to the beam of a plow; used to cut the ground in advance of the plowshare.

Crowder. An excellent specimen.

Crumpification. A coined word signifying a jumbled mixture.

Curry Comb. A comb, usually with rows of metal teeth, for cleaning horses.

Curus. Curious.

Dandy. Effeminate.

Darlint. Darling.

Darsent. A contraction of "dares not."

Doggery. A general store which also sold whiskey, thus serving as the local tavern.

Dung-Hill Mare. A mare which is in an extremely poor or worthless condition.

Faro. Originally "Pharoah." The principal gambling game in America before the twentieth century.

Faro Bank. The house and its equipment in the faro game.

Fed him so high he lost his toenails. Figuratively, fed him so well he developed gout.

Feliciter. Solicitor.

Fight the Tiger. To play against the bank at faro.

Fizzyognomy. Physiognomy.

Flesh Marks. Identifying features.

Fork. (verb) Shake hands.

Forninst. Against.

Fotch. Fetch.

Fourth July. Possibly the results of gouging the eyes, as "seeing stars," or cuts upon the surface of the eyelids and above the eyes.

Fout. Fought.

Freshet. A flood due to unusually heavy rains.

Frolic. A party, dance, or other lively social gathering.

Fuireigner. Foreigner.

Fust. First.

Gallowses. Suspenders.

Gemman. Gentleman.

Giddy-Giddy-Gout. [Giddy Goat] A fool, a happy-go-lucky person.

Gilflint. Gilflirt or jill flirt, a female in which the perineal orifices are exceptionally close together.

Gin. Given.

Ginivine. Genuine.

Gobler. A complimentary term; a person physically or mentally above his peers. Literally, this is a male turkey, the leader of the flock.

Gos Seven—Mulberry Eight, and Spanker Nine. The term "gos seven" is unclear; however "mulberry eight" is probably the eight of clubs, and "spanker nine" the nine of spades, suggested by the shape associated with the suits.

Grease. Butter, or its substitute.

Grist. A quantity; quite a large number.

Hearn. Heard.

Heifer. A cow that has not produced a calf and is under three years of age.

Hiptoptaimus. Hippopotamus.

Holp. Helped.

Horn. A drink of whiskey.

Hurrah's Nest. A confusion, a jumble.

Ile. Oil.

Illigant. Elegant.

Infar. An infare, a housewarming, particularly an entertainment given by a newly married couple.

Ingen. Indian.

Inshow. Insure.

Insinivate. Insinuate.

Jack-Screw. A lifting-jack with a screw.

Jine. Join.

Kalkilation. Calculation.

Kerrecter. Character.

Kertillion. Cotillion; a complex, formalized dance for a large number of people in which a head couple leads the other dancers through elaborate and stately figures.

Ketch. Possibly "keltch"—a Negro who is light-skinned enough to pass as a white person.

Kiff. Cuff.

Killdevil. A term frequently applied to a hunting rifle; refers to no specific type of gun.

Kiver. Cover.

Kivering horse. Probably "covering" horse, a plow horse.

Knock [the] possum out of. Probably reference to "playing possum" or pretending sleep. Thus the drink wakes one and makes him talkative.

Koppras Dye. Possibly "Copperas" dye—green.

Kune. Coon, raccoon.

Larver. Lava.

'Lasses. Molasses.

Leg. (verb) Trip.

Lift out of boots. To hit really hard. In this case, Pierce had knocked Pete out of office, or removed him from his position.

Limmon. Lemon.

Long Fire. Probably the result of improper mixture of gunpowder; the gun produced much noise and fire but little power behind the shot.

Long-tailed blue. Probably a set of tails, a formal jacket.

Looker into a week. One with the ability to see into the future.

Martingale. The strap on a horse's harness for holding its head down.

Mast. Acorns, nuts, berries, small animals, worms, bugs, and other contributions to the diet of bears.

Morphradite. Hermaphrodite.

Nager. A pejorative form of "Negro."

Nor. Than.

On Kore. Encore.

Orfing. Orphan.

Os-Frontis. Possibly a coined term meaning "forehead." "Os" from Latin words referring to bone, and "frontis" the Latinized "front," thus, "front-bone."

Osifer. Officer.

Painter. Panther.

Path. The course over which horse races were run.

Pe-anny. Piano.

Pecoonietily. Pecuniarily.

Physic. Strong drink and the accompanying effects.

Pie-doings. Parties where food is served.

Play. A singing, action game played by adults. In many smaller communities of the old Southwest, religious custom prohibited dancing. The answer was a play-party. The action of the song-game in Pete's letter 12 is fairly typical of play-party games.

Plaze. Please.

Plum from taw. "Plum" means completely; "taw" comes from the children's game of marbles and means (in Pete's usage) to be in office. The taw is the marble one uses to play the game, knocking the others out of the ring. Thus, to be knocked plum from taw means to be removed completely out of office.

Plunder. Gain or profit; hence, goods secured by betting or trading.

Poke. The small green heron.

Pole Cat. Skunk.

Putty. Pretty.

Quarter Race. A horse race which was a quarter of a mile (1760 yards) in length.

Rake down the corn. Corn or other produce was frequently used to secure gambling bets in the earliest days of the frontier. Thus to "rake down the corn" later meant to win everything that had been wagered.

Rale. Real.

Rantenkerous. Cantankerous.

Rattlesnake gals. Girls from the "Rattlesnake Fork" of the Little Red River.

Rite. Write.

Riz. Frequently the past tense of "rise;" in some cases the word is used to mean "high."

Roll the Bones. A crap game.

Rooster. Cock or hammer.

Rousenest. Most rousing.

Saddle Riders. Saddle bags.

Sarn me to the sarneds. An expletive similar to "I'll be darned."

Sassinges. Sausages.

Scase. Scarce.

Segar. Cigar.

Sesin. Season.

Seven Up. The card game popularly known as All Fours or Old Sledge. The name "Seven Up" simply meant that seven points were required to win. It was the favorite gambling card game in the United States until poker replaced it in the mid-1800s.

Sham Pain. Champagne.

Shiner. A silver dollar; occasionally applied to any metallic money.

Shin Plaster. Greatly depreciated paper money.

Sign. Excrement, remains of food, broken twigs and limbs, claw marks, tracks, and other evidence of the presence of bears.

Sing Ingen. Whoop and holler.

Six Bits. The equivalent of seventy-five cents.

Sledge. Another name for Seven Up or All Fours.

Sloo. Slough or swamp.

Slope. Leave or depart.

Sovereigns. Citizens.

Spun Truck. Truck which was described only; which was not actually present to be seen. As one might "spin" a yarn or tale, he might also "spin" truck.

Squz. Squeezed.

Stifle. The joint at the junction of the hind leg and the body (between the femur and the tibia) in a horse or other quadraped; corresponding anatomically to the knee in man.

Stilyard. [Stillyard; Stillion] A stand or gantry.

Stump Speech. Originally, a political speech made at a logrolling, house raising, or similar occasion. The speaker stood on a stump in order that the crowd could see and hear him. The term was later used to apply to any political speech made outdoors at informal gatherings.

Subject to the cramp. A pun meaning to feel the pinch in the wallet due to gambling losses.

Swate. Sweet.

To take the corn. To win; same meaning as "rake down the corn."

Tanyard. A poorhouse.

Tarnal. An expletive, probably a corruption of "eternal."

Temptation Societies. Temperance societies.

Thaving. Thieving.

Three Bits. The equivalent of 37½ cents. A bit was a one-eighth section of a Spanish dollar; the equivalent of 12½ cents. Bits were widely circulated in the Southwest where specie was scarce.

Tick-Doly-rue. Tic doloreux [douloureux]. Facial neuralgia.

Tighting and Tighting. Close; neck and neck.

Timber poured on . . . with perfect looseness. Horse allowed to run as fast as possible; expression comes from steamboating where, in races especially, boilers were fed as much timber as possible without regard to the danger of overheating.

Truck. Goods used in place of money.

Tumble Bug. A beetle which rolls balls of dung in which it deposits its eggs and in which the young develop.

Varmints. Vermin; frequently small game animals, e.g., squirrels, rabbits, raccoons.

Venter. Venture.

Wabbles. Welts; swollen inflamations of the skin which are the result of insect bites or stings.

Wagging. Wagon.

Walk chalk. To be very careful in one's actions. This is still in current usage: "To walk the chalk line" or "To toe the mark."

Wallet. A knapsack.

Wice Wersa. Vice versa.

Wring In. Probably similar to "twist-in." To manipulate an unscheduled entry into a race. Usually carries the connotation of sure victory.

Yoke. To engage in a fight.

Yot. Yacht.

APPENDIX 4
Textual Apparatus

To date no manuscripts of the Pete Whetstone letters have been discovered. Probably they were either destroyed as the type was set or else were lost with the manuscript files of the newspapers and magazines in which they appeared. Therefore, the copy-text for each story is the first available printing. Subsequent reprintings were taken from these versions and only increased the possibility of textual errors. None of the existing derivative texts shows evidence of revision or correction by Noland; thus, they offer no aid in establishing a definitive text, if one was intended. Collation of all printings has, therefore, been neither necessary nor useful. Microfilmed copies of the *Spirit of the Times* files owned by the New York Society (supplied by University Microfilms) have served as copy-text for the fifty-eight pieces first appearing there. Photocopies of *Porter's Spirit of the Times* housed in Yale University Library have served as copy-text for the two stories first published in that journal. The microfilm copy of the *Arkansas State Gazette and Democrat* owned by the Arkansas History Commission has supplied copy-text for the one Whetstone piece carried there. Photocopies of texts appearing in the *New Sporting Magazine* housed in the New York Public Library have been used as copy-text for the two stories Noland composed for that journal.

Four of the *Spirit* texts (letters 1, 2, 4, and 6) have been collated against originals from the Meine Collection housed in the Rare Book Collection of the University of Illinois Library. Five texts (letters 2, 12, 34, 41, and 47) have been collated against photocopies of *Spirit* originals housed in Hillman Library of the University of Pittsburgh. The two texts from the *New Sporting Magazine* have been collated against originals in the University of Illinois Library. No variant readings have been discovered.

The Whetstone letters are filled with intentional misspellings, dialect spellings, inconsistent punctuation, and peculiar sentence structure. Unless comprehension is impeded, these have been retained, for one purpose of such idiosyncratic language is to formulate the personality of Pete Whetstone. The text of the first printing has been reproduced exactly except for the following changes: All apparent typographical errors have been corrected; spellings of most proper names (such as Dan Looney) have been adjusted to make them consistent throughout; in several letters, quotation marks have been inserted to improve readability; salutations and closings have been made consistent. Otherwise, the punctuation has not been altered, and peculiarities of nineteenth-century typography, such as frequent italics and capitalization, have been preserved. All emendations are, within the text, silent; however, all are listed below under "Emendations to the Copy-Text." The only exception is that headlines throughout have been silently adjusted to capital letters.

Furthermore, in an effort to prevent interruption and preserve readability, the use of "sic" has been avoided. What editorial interpolation is necessary has been kept to a minimum and is in brackets. Excerpts have been labeled as such. For ease and clarity of reference, each letter is assigned a number which appears in brackets.

Following the list of "Emendations to the Copy-Text" is a second list, headed "Word Division," containing possible compound words which are hyphenated at the ends of lines in the copy-text. While many of the words appearing here may seem unnecessary, Pete's frequent hyphenation of "to-day" and his splitting of "any thing" make their inclusion desirable.

Two objectives have governed the editing of this text: (1) the desirability of producing a scholarly yet readable volume, and (2) the preservation of the individuality and spontaneity of Pete Whetstone's language. Thus, emendation of the copy-text has been kept to a minimum; the majority of editorial changes involves the addition of quotation marks. The extremely topical nature of so many of the letters is difficult for the modern reader; therefore, many of the historical, cultural, and literary allusions are explained in annotations. In order to reduce their quantity and length, two glossaries have been included: (1) proper names, which appears as Appendix 2; (2) unfamiliar words and phrases (such as "arter" and "bald face"), which appears as Appendix 3. In both the annotations and the glossaries, explanations are qualified whenever the editor has indulged in speculation.

Emendations to the Copy-Text

The emended reading as it appears in the text is given first, followed by a square bracket and the rejected copy-text reading. All emendations originate with the editor, although certain ones agree with emendations made by the *Spirit* in letters reprinted from the *New Sporting Magazine*. Emendations coinciding with those in the Worley and Nolte edition are purely accidental. Line references include headlines and datelines.

59.11	Fork] Fort	92.27	Whetstone,"]
61.18	burr] butt		"Whetstone,"
66.21	Woods] Wood	93.4	do,"] do."
67.3	fork] park	94.5	"Who] Who
67.24	priusque] prinsque	94.5	wins?"] wins?
69.6	*coon."*] *coon.'*	94.5	"Devil's] Devil's
69.9	dodgers"] dodgers	94.5	fork,"] fork
71.14	woods,] woods.	94.5	"for,"] for
78.9	Harris,] Harris.	94.6	"that] that
82.6-7	don't know/what]	94.6	corn;"] corn;
	don't what	94.21	Wiley] Viley
82.9	on her.] on. her	94.28	Buck's] Buck?
82.10	oats] cats	94.31	"Buck] Buck
82.19	mare.] mare	94.31	Times"] Times
83.21	*"Three*] *Three*	94.31	"take] take
88.14	means."] means.	94.33	list;"] list;
92.6	*"Calhoun*] *Calhoun*	94.33	I felt] I I felt
92.7	*Benton;"*] *Benton*	94.34	"Lawyer] Lawyer
92.9	"Come] Come	95.1	McCampbell,"]
92.9-10	gen/tlemen,"]		McCampbell,
	gentlemen,	95.1	"we] we
92.10	"don't] don't	95.2	think,"] think,
92.10	fight."] fight.	95.3	"a] a
92.15	"Come,] Come,	95.3-4	busi/ness?"]
92.15	friends,"] friends,		business?
92.15	"make] make	95.4	"may] may
92.16	up."] up.	95.4	so,"] so,
92.25	Culp] Culf	95.5	"lawyer] lawyer

95.6	principles?"] principles?	108.1	"Col.] "Col,
		108.10	live."] live"
95.6	*"that*] *that*	108.23	1838] 1837
95.6	up;"] up;	109.5	Stones'] Stone's
95.8	"are] are	109.9	*Rube*] Ruby
95.8	McCampbell?"] McCambell?	111.3	fellow.] fellow."
		111.12	feet."] feet
95.8	"if] if	111.17	"The] The
95.9	*am."*] *am.*	111.17	up,"] up,
95.9	"You] You	118.19	Rube] Ruby
95.9	traitor,"] traitor,	123.5	"Butter] 'Butter
95.9	"softly"] softly	123.8	*"On What,"*] *On*
95.10	"don't] don't		*What,*
95.11	*once:"*] *once:*	125.9	she] he
95.12	"Lawyer] Lawyer	125.28	he] het
95.14	party."] party.	127.13	and bad-quality]
95.14	"Buck] Buck		and-bad/quality
95.17	you."] you.	129.2	old and had] old had
95.19	"Mr.] Mr.	129.26	"Mister] Mister
95.20	triumphant:"] triumphant:	129.26-27	bar-keeper;"] bar-keeper;
95.22	*"I'm*] *"I m*	129.27	"sir;"] sir;
95.22	"Excuse] Excuse	129.27	"can] can
95.22-23	mo/ments,"] moments,	129.27-28	"gov/ernment;"] government;
97.16	Sal?"] Sall?"	129.28	"certingly,"] certingly,
97.33	scared] scoved		
97.34	"Mr.] Mr.	129.28	"whereabouts"] whereabouts
97.34	*kertillions;"*] *kertillions;*		
97.35	"ladies] ladies	129.28	"No. 127"] No. 127
97.36	life;"] life;	130.1	"Mr.] Mr.
98.20	Devil's Fork] Devil's-fork	130.2	Snodgrass."] Snodgrass.
99.8	you] y u	130.3	"Col.] Col.
99.22	way."] way	130.4	Whetstone."] Whetstone.
101.19	fur] fun		
104.5	oats] cats	130.4	"What,] What,
104.11	1838] 1837	130.5	Fork?"] Fork?
106.34	"Jerry,"] "Jerry,	130.5	"adzactly;"] adzactly;
106.35	'Fly] "Fly	130.5	"well] well
106.35	brand';"] brand;"	130.6	arrive,"] arrive,

130.6	"last] last	130.27	"well"] well
130.6	night"] night	130.27	"if] if
130.7	"I] I	130.29	way;"] way;
130.9	business."] business.	130.29	"oh] oh
130.9	"Griefs,"] Griefs,	130.29	but,"] but
130.9	"well] well	130.29	"this] this
130.11	stomach;"] stomach;	130.30	grief;"] grief;
130.11	"but,"] but,	130.30	"yes] yes
130.11	"let] let	130.30	take,"] take,
130.12	government;"] government;	132.6	there.] there
		132.15	Looney] Loony
130.13	"they] they	132.27	go."] go.
130.14	about."] about.	133.8	1839.] 1838.
130.18	"Well"] Well	135.24	sprinkling] spinkling
130.19	"I'll] I'll	136.23	'if] if
130.19	sloping;"] sloping;	136.23	d___d,'] d___d,
130.19	"Mr.] Mr.	136.25	'I'm] I'm
130.20	bye;"] bye;	136.26	d___d,'] d___d,
130.20	"I] I	144.36	do," says he.] do, says he."
130.20	Whetstone,"] Whetstone	146.10	thing is jist] thing jist
130.20	"and] and	146.18	caution.] caution
130.21	Washington;"] Washington;	147.18	how] ow
		148.26	couldent] ouldent
130.21	"well] well	149.3	moon.] moon
130.22	it,"] it,	155.13	McCampbell] Mac Campell
130.23	"oh,"] oh,		
130.24	"why] why	155.17	Woods'] Wood's
130.24	know;"] know;	156.8-9	"Hur/rah] Hurrah
130.24	"I] I	156.9	Dan!"] Dan?
130.24	don't,"] don't,	159.10	Sal] Sall
130.24	"or] or	160.4	eye.] eye
130.25	you;"] you;	160.18	kivered] kiveed
130.25	"It] It	161.1	got] go
130.25	Smith,"] Smith,	162.4	rattlesnake] rattle-nake
130.25	"one] one		
130.26	citizens;"] citizens;	162.6	hell,"] well,"
130.26	"when] when	162.7	Meat."] Meat."
130.26	die,"] die,	163.6	"Saturday,"] "Saturday,
130.26	"yesterday,"] yesterday,	163.6	"and] and

164.4	"I] I	196.18	"Hurrah] Hurrah
164.5	tail,"] tail,	196.18	Pete,"] Pete
164.5	the] he	198.8	Bill were always] Bill
164.5	feller.-] feller-		always
164.5	"Yes] Yes	200.21	"Mr.] Mr.
164.5-6	'Bear/Meat'] "Bear	200.23	country."] country.
	Meat"	200.23	"With] With
164.6	'Weeping Willow,']	200.23	heart,"] heart
	"Weeping Willow,"	200.25	"My] My
164.6	truck,"] truck,	201.7	'good] good
164.17	sinful.] sinful	201.7	Terence,'] Terence,
167.16	IN] IM	201.7	'the] the
170.10	N.B.] N.P.	201.8	man?'] man?
172.17	it.] it,	201.8	'It] It
173.5	he] be	201.9	landing,'] landing,
178.3	JIM] JEM	201.10	'Well] Well
181.13	*Face!"] Face!*	201.10	boy,'] boy,
181.26	is] *is*	201.10	'is] is
182.14	amusing.] amusing	201.11	behind'] behind
182.22	gun?"] gun!"	201.14	children,] children.
184.8	afloat.] afloat	201.14	'It] It
184.32	CHINEY's.] CHINEY's	201.14	comfort,] comfort.
185.13	politician] pol tician	201.15	Terence,'] Terence,
186.16	"be] 'be	201.15	'The] The
186.28	everything]	201.16	priest,'] priest
	everyting	201.16	'and] and
187.16	she] he	201.22	horse?'] horse?
190.21	"Boys,"] 'Boys,'	201.25	'may] may
190.21	"it] 'it	201.26	Terence,'] Terence
190.23	it!"] it!'	201.26	'you] you
190.24	"Boys,] 'Boys,	201.27	Ireland.'] Irelaud.
190.26	live.] live	201.32	tune myself] tune
190.28	nigh] nig h		tune myself
190.30	way,"] way,'	201.33	'Good] Good
190.31	"I] 'I	201.33	honor,'] honor,
191.2	Brown."] Brown.'	201.34	'the] the
193.15	everything]	201.34	you,'] you
	everythiug	201.34	'If] If
194.7	Pete's] Peter's	201.34	plazes,'] plazes
196.18	Congress."]	201.34	'its] its
	Congress.	201.36	ones,] ones.

201.36	bill.'] bill.	202.25	'if] if
201.36	'What] What	202.26	animals?'] animals?
201.37	numbers,'] numbers	202.27	'Mr.] Mr.
201.37	'Bad] Bad	202.31	mouth.'] mouth.
201.38	honor.'] honor.	202.31	'It] It
202.1	'It] It	202.31	honor,'] honor,
202.2	am'—] am—	202.31	'and] and
202.2	'you] you	202.32	you'—] you—
202.2	welcome,'] welcome	202.34	am."] am.
202.2	'but] but	203.19	"boys,] boys,
202.3	Nothings.'] Nothings.	203.20	fizzyognomies."] fizzyognomies.
202.3	'The] The	203.20	"Fizzy] Fizzy
202.4	Nothings,'] Nothings,	203.20	what?"] what?
202.4	'why] why	204.1	"Hush] Hush
202.6	country.'] country.	204.4	to."] to.
202.6	'It] It	204.4	Looney] Loony
202.6	mean.'] mean.	204.6	"boys,] boys,
202.6	'A] A	204.8	Spirit."] Spirit.
202.9	monster.'] monster.	204.16	"well] well
202.9	'Well] Well	204.16	daddy,"] daddy,
202.10	then,'] then,	204.16	"I] I
202.10	'they] they	204.17	gun."] gun.
202.10	office.'] office.	204.31	*Major] Major*
202.11	'Forninst] Forninst	204.31	Looney] Loony
202.12	alive,'] alive,	205.1	looks."] looks.
202.12	'Against] Against	205.1	"Well,] Well,
202.12	office,'] office,	205.1	Capting,"] Capting,
202.13	'May] May	205.1	"for] for
202.14	purgatory,'] purgatory,	205.2	before."] before.
202.14	'They] They	205.2	"Well,] Well,
202.15	American,'] American,	205.3	Looney] Loony
202.15	'The] The	205.5	price."] price.
202.16	them,'] them,	205.5	"Cap.] Cap.
202.22	he, 'Mr.] he Mr.	205.6	scholar;"] scholar;
202.25	scrape.'] scrape.	205.8	"What] What
202.25	'Squire] Squire	205.8	pray?"] pray?
202.25	Sneeves,'] Sneeves,	205.8	"Not] Not
		205.9	Capting,"] Capting,
		205.9	"whatever] whatever
		205.10	me."] me.

205.10	"Well,"] Well,	205.13	squz?"] squz?
205.10	"I] I	205.13	"Squz,"] Squz,
205.10	punch;"] punch;	205.20	mast,] ma'sh
205.10	"the] the	206.17	you] yon
205.11	me,"] me,	207.21	man.] man."
205.12	"Major] Major	208.1	himself.] h mself.
205.13	Looney] Loony	209.21	coat."] coat.

Word Division: 1

The following compounds or possible combinations are hyphenated at the ends of lines in the copy-text. The form in which they appear in this text is that in keeping with other occurrences within the Whetstone letters. The reading as it appears in this text is given first, followed by a square bracket and the hyphenated copy-text reading.

66.16	half-pint] half-pint		snorting-routing-
71.24	sweethearts]		/roaring-studhorsical
	sweet-hearts	119.20	*tune*-maker]
71.29	Irishman] Irish-man		*tune*-maker
77.6	*rattlesnake*] *rattle-snake*	120.17	today] to-day
77.12	seven-and-seventy]	124.14	steamboat]
	seven-and-/seventy		steam-boat
83.24	double-/fisted]	134.9	water-pot] water-pot
	double-fisted	134.16	Bussing-coon]
91.13	Maybe] May-be		Bussing-coon
102.25	nothing] no-thing	144.15	nothing] no-thing
106.6	flat-footed]	144.26	outside] out-side
	flat-footed	144.36	landlord] land-lord
106.16	sometimes]	146.16	Piney-wood]
	some-times		Piney-wood
110.19	*Worm-Eater*]	160.34	something]
	Worm-Eater		some-thing
111.18	Piney-woods]	162.4	rattlesnake]
	Piney-woods		rattle-[s]nake
114.14	ripping-/snorting-	163.31	anything] any-thing
	routing-roaring-	165.5	schoolmaster]
	studhorsical] ripping-		school-master

165.21	Piney-wood] Piney-wood	192.2	*Sharptooth*] *Sharp-tooth*
166.26	bear-fight] bear-fight	194.12	twenty-three] twenty-three
168.26	nothing] no-thing	201.19	something]
177.30	*Gourd-vine*] *Gourd-vine*	202.4	some-thing Nothings] No-things
179.8	Old-Bullet-neck] Old-/Bullet-neck	205.15	barefooted] bare-footed
184.3	forever] for-ever	206.24	small-size] small-size
185.2	aforethought] afore-thought	208.31	out-and-out] out-/and-out
187.25	giddy-/giddy-gout] giddy-/giddy-gout	209.4 209.37	anything] any-thing back-lock] back-lock
187.35	barefooted] bare-footed	210.9	Piney-woods] Piney-woods

Word Division: 2

The following compounds or possible combinations are hyphenated at the ends of lines in this edition. The reading as it appears in this text is given first, followed by a square bracket and the copy-text reading.

68.12	bear-hunter] bear-hunter	107.22	pocket-book] pocket-book
68.23	three-fourths] three-fourths	109.2	*Cravat-Stuffing*] *Cravat-Stuffing*
72.6	some-thing] something	109.5 110.1	*Apple-Sas*] *Apple-Sas* with-out] without
77.12	camp-meetings] camp-meetings	111.13	Piney-woods] Piney-woods
82.10	steam-boat] steamboat	112.22	Piney-woods] Piney-woods
83.24	double-fisted] double-/fisted	114.14	ripping-/snorting- routing-roaring-
90.2	up-hand] up-hand		studhorsical] ripping-
97.17	ghost-looking] ghost-looking		snorting-routing- /roaring-studhorsical

117.4	over-heard] overheard	173.18	sure-enough-fun eye-teeth] eye-teeth
117.19	some-body] somebody	181.24	double-trouble] double-trouble
118.26	thirty-seven] thirty-seven	187.25	giddy-/giddy-gout] giddy-/giddy-gout
120.14	your-self] yourself	193.22	home-stead]
123.16	App-ious] App-ious		homestead
125.12	pe-anny] pe-anny	194.14	sugar-houses]
128.21	new-comer] new-comer	194.19	sugar-houses horse-back]
129.26	bar-keeper] bar-keeper	196.23	horse-back him-self] himself
131.19	gentle-man] gentleman	201.20	gintle-man] gintleman
145.8	nut-crackers] nut-crackers	202.7	cloven-footed] clo-/ven-footed
148.2	Curry-/kill-dare] Curry-kill-dare	204.26	steam-boat] steamboat
154.9	Post-master] Postmaster	207.18 209.2	pe-anny] pe-anny nigger-driver]
158.17	buck-skins] buck-skins	210.18	nigger-driver Piney-woods]
173.7	sure-/enough-fun]		Piney-woods

APPENDIX 5
The Pete Whetstone Letters:
A Checklist of Appearances

This checklist includes all the letters, tales, and sketches C.F.M Noland published under his pseudonym of Pete Whetstone. Also included are the letters appearing over Noland's own name which contain significant reference to Whetstone. All known reprintings of these pieces are also given, though undoubtedly dozens of unknown reprints exist. In Noland's day, newspapers freely lifted material from each other; usually no record of these reprints is available. In many cases, files of the various newspapers known to have contained reprints are quite incomplete. It is unlikely that a complete accounting of such reprints of the Whetstone letters can ever be made.

Items within the checklist are arranged chronologically, and each item bears a number. Since reprint appearances are considered within the numbering, these numbers, which facilitate cross-reference, are not synonymous with the numbers assigned the letters within the text. The checklist is a separate matter. Unless stated, the place of publication is always the *Spirit of the Times;* this eliminates the undesirable and needless repetition of that title. The entry is otherwise complete, i.e., volume number, date, and pagination.

1837

01. "Scenes and Characters in Arkansas," 7 (18 March), 36.
    Reprinted:
    03 *Arkansas Times and Advocate,* [p. 1].
    78 Hudson, pp. 542-544.
    79 Masterson, pp. 41-43.
    82 Worley and Nolte, pp. 1-3.

02. "Pete Whetstone's Bear Hunt," 7 (25 March), 46.

Reprinted:
82 Worley and Nolte, pp. 4-5.
83. *The* [Independence County, Arkansas, Historical Society] *Chronicle,* pp. 2-3 [Under title: "Bear Hunting in 1837"].
84 Cohen and Dillingham, pp. 109-110.

03. "Scenes and Characters in Arkansas," *Arkansas Times and Advocate,* 1 May, [p. 1].
Reprint of 01.

04. "Bulletin from Arkansas," 7 (27 May), 117.
Reprinted:
79 Masterson, p. 161 [excerpt].

05. "Pete Whetstone Alive and Kicking," 7 (3 June), 121.
Reprinted:
79 Masterson, p. 43 [excerpt].
82 Worley and Nolte, pp. 5-8.

06. "Pete's Very Last," 7 (3 June), 121.
Reprinted:
79 Masterson, pp. 160-161, 162 [excerpt].
82 Worley and Nolte, pp. 8-10.

07. "Match, Sir William vs. Independence," 7 (3 June), 125.

08. "Pete Whetstone Again," 7 (10 June), 132.
Reprinted:
82 Worley and Nolte, pp. 10-13.

09. "Letter from Pete Whetstone," 7 (8 July), 166.
Reprinted:
13 *New Sporting Magazine,* pp. 185-186.
82 Worley and Nolte, pp. 13-15.

10. "Bulletin from Arkansas," 7 (15 July), 171.

11. "Matters and Things in Arkansas," 7 (29 July), 188.

12. "Pete Whetstone's Very Last," 7 (19 August), 212.
Reprinted:

82 Worley and Nolte, pp. 15-17.

13. "Letter from Pete Whetstone," *New Sporting Magazine*, 13 (September), 185-186.
Reprint of 09.

14. "Letter from Pete Whetstone," 7 (7 October), 265.
Reprinted:
79 Masterson, pp. 136-137 [excerpt].
82 Worley and Nolte, pp. 17-23.
87 Williams, pp. 39-42 [excerpt].

15. "Letter from Pete Whetstone," 7 (11 November), 305.
Reprinted:
82 Worley and Nolte, pp. 23-26.

16. [Untitled], 7 (11 November), 305.
Reprinted:
82 Worley and Nolte, pp. 26-27.

17. "Letter from Pete Whetstone," 7 (18 November), 316.
Reprinted:
82 Worley and Nolte, pp. 27-29.

18. "Letter from Pete Whetstone," 7 (2 December), 333.
Reprinted:
82 Worley and Nolte, pp. 29-32.

19. "Letter from Pete Whetstone," 7 (16 December), 348.
Reprinted:
79 Masterson, pp. 43-44 [excerpt].
82 Worley and Nolte, pp. 32-34.

20. "Letter from Pete Whetstone," 7 (30 December), 368.
Reprinted:
79 Masterson, p. 45 [excerpt].
82 Worley and Nolte, pp. 35-36.

1838

21. "Letter from Pete Whetstone," 7 (27 January), 397.
Reprinted:

82 Worley and Nolte, pp. 36-38.

22. "Letter from Pete Whetstone," 7 (3 February), 405.
    Reprinted:
    82 Worley and Nolte, pp. 38-40.

23. "Pete Whetstone at a Faro Bank," 8 (17 February), 6.
    Reprinted:
    79 Masterson, pp. 44-45 [excerpt].
    82 Worley and Nolte, pp. 40-44.

24. "Pete Whetstone's Last: Race Between 'Worm-Eater' and 'Apple-Sas,'" 8 (10 March), 29.
    Reprinted:
    82 Worley and Nolte, pp. 44-50.
    84 Cohen and Dillingham, pp. 110-114.

25. "Pete Whetstone Alive and Kicking," 8 (24 March), 44.
    Reprinted:
    82 Worley and Nolte, pp. 50-51.

26. [Untitled], 8 (14 April), 69.
    Reprinted:
    86 Williams, p. 54.

27. "A Word from Pete Whetstone," 8 (25 August), 220.
    Reprinted:
    82 Worley and Nolte, pp. 51-52.

28. "Pete Whetstone Again in the Field!" 8 (15 December), 348.
    Reprinted:
    79 Masterson, p. 160 [excerpt].
    82 Worley and Nolte, pp. 52-54.

29. "'Monsieur Tonson Come Agin!'" 8 (29 December), 364.

1839

30. "Pete Whetstone's Last," 8 (2 February), 406.
    Reprinted:
    79 Masterson, pp. 45-46, 169 [excerpts].

82 Worley and Nolte, pp. 54-56.

31. "Pete Whetstone's Last Frolic," 9 (16 March), 20.
Reprinted:
34 *The Batesville News,* [p. 1].
79 Masterson, pp. 46-47 [excerpt].
82 Worley and Nolte, pp. 56-59.
84 Cohen and Dillingham, pp. 114-116.

32. "Pete Whetstone on His Travels," 9 (4 May), 102.
Reprinted:
79 Masterson, pp. 47-48 [excerpt].
82 Worley and Nolte, pp. 59-61.

33. "Pete Whetstone in the Old Dominion," 9 (11 May), 115.
Reprinted:
82 Worley and Nolte, pp. 61-63.

34. "Pete Whetstone's Last Frolic," *The Batesville News,* 16 May, [p. 1].
Reprint of 31.

35. "A Letter from Pete Whetstone," 9 (18 May), 123.
Reprinted:
82 Worley and Nolte, pp. 64-66.

36. "Pete's Last," 9 (18 May), 123.
Reprinted:
79 Masterson, pp. 48-49 [excerpt].
82 Worley and Nolte, pp. 63-64.

37. "Pete Whetstone in New York," 9 (25 May), 138.
Reprinted:
39 *The Batesville News,* 20 June, [p. 3].
82 Worley and Nolte, pp. 66-68.

38. "The Mile Race at Trenton," 9 (8 June), 163.

39. "Pete Whetstone in New York," *The Batesville News,* 20 June.
Reprint of 37.

40. "Reminiscences of His Visit to the East, by Kurnel Whetstone," 9 (13 July), 223.
    Reprinted:
    82 Worley and Nolte, pp. 69-73.

41. "Intercepted Letter from Pete Whetstone," 9 (27 July), 247.
    Reprinted:
    44 *New Sporting Magazine,* pp. 65-66.
    82 Worley and Nolte, pp. 73-76.

42. "Intercepted Letter from Pete Whetstone," 9 (26 October), 397.
    Reprinted:
    82 Worley and Nolte, pp. 76-79.

43. "Pete's Return to the Old 'Diggings,'" 9 (21 December), 498.
    Reprinted:
    82 Worley and Nolte, pp. 79-82.

1840

44. "Intercepted Letter from Pete Whetstone," *New Sporting Magazine,* 18 (January), 65-66.
    Reprint of 41.

1841

45. "Doings on the Devil's Fork," *New Sporting Magazine, NS 1* (January), 8-9.
    Reprinted:
    47 *Spirit,* p. 558 [excerpt].
    79 Masterson, pp. 49-50 [excerpt].
    82 Worley and Nolte, pp. 83-86.

46. "A Letter from Jim Cole to Pete Whetstone," 10 (2 January), 523.
    Reprinted:
    82 Worley and Nolte, pp. 82-83.

47. "Doings on the Devil's Fork," 10 (23 January), 558.
    Reprint of 45 [excerpt].

48. "Letter from Pete Whetstone," 11 (27 March), 42.
    Reprinted:

82 Worley and Nolte, pp. 86-87.

49. "A Bounce Among the Bears and Quarter Racing on the Barren Fork," *New Sporting Magazine*, NS 1 (June), 401-404.
Reprinted:
50 *Spirit*, p. 211.
82 Worley and Nolte, pp. 89-93.

50. "A Bounce Among the Bears and Quarter Racing on the Barren Fork," 11 (3 July), 211.
Reprint of 49.

51. "Letter from Pete Whetstone," 11 (9 October), 378.
Reprinted:
53. *The Batesville News*, 11 November, [pp. 2-3].
82 Worley and Nolte, pp. 87-88.

52. "Letter from Pete Whetstone," 11 (6 November), 426.
Reprinted:
79 Masterson, pp. 113-114 [excerpt].
82 Worley and Nolte, pp. 93-95.

53. "Letter from Pete Whetstone," *The Batesville News*, 11 November, [pp. 2-3].
Reprint of 51.

1842

54. "Pete Whetstone Again in the Field!" 11 (26 February), 615.
Reprinted:
82 Worley and Nolte, pp. 95-98.

55. "Pete Whetstone's Trip to New Orleans," 12 (23 April), 85.
Reprinted:
79 Masterson, pp. 50-51 [excerpt].
82 Worley and Nolte, pp. 98-101.

56. "Kurnel Pete Whetstone on His Travels!" 12 (23 July), 241.
Reprinted:
79 Masterson, p. 37 [excerpt].
82 Worley and Nolte, pp. 101-103.

57. "Letter from Col. Pete Whetstone," 12 (10 September), 325.
Reprinted:
82 Worley and Nolte, pp. 104-105.

58. "Sporting Epistle from the Devil's Fork; Letter from Jim Cole to
Pete Whetstone," 12 (24 September), 349.
Reprinted:
82 Worley and Nolte, pp. 106-107.

1843

59. "Sporting Epistle from Pete Whetstone," 13 (4 March), 7.
Reprinted:
79 Masterson, pp. 169-170 [excerpt].
82 Worley and Nolte, pp. 108-110.

60. "Sporting Epistle from 'N. of Arkansas,'" 13 (13 May), 127.
Reprinted:
64 Porter, *The Big Bear of Arkansas,* pp. 143-145 [excerpt].
74 Porter, *Big Bear's Adventures,* pp. 143-145 [excerpt].
76 Meine, pp. 133-135 [excerpt].
77 Allsopp, II, 198-199 [excerpt].
79 Masterson, p. 171 [excerpt].
80 Botkin, pp. 435-436 [excerpt].

1844

61. "A New Arkansas Correspondent: 'Sam Grindstone,' an Acquaintance of 'Pete Whetstone,'" 13 (20 January), 553.
Reprinted:
64 Porter, *The Big Bear of Arkansas,* pp. 145-146 [excerpt].
74 Porter, *Big Bear's Adventures,* pp. 145-146 [excerpt].
76 Meine, p. 135 [excerpt].
82 Worley and Nolte, pp. 110-112.

62. "Letter from Col. Pete Whetstone," 14 (28 December), 522.
Reprinted:
82 Worley and Nolte, pp. 112-114.

1845

63. "Old Sense of Arkansas," *The Big Bear of Arkansas, and Other
Sketches, Illustrative of Characters and Incidents in the South and*

Southwest, ed. William T. Porter. Philadelphia: Carey and Hart, 1845, pp. 143-145.

64. Porter, William T., ed. *The Big Bear of Arkansas, and Other Sketches, Illustrative of Characters and Incidents in the South and Southwest.* Philadelphia: Carey and Hart, 1845, pp. 143-146.
Reprints of 60 [excerpt] and 61 [excerpt].

1846

65. [Untitled], 16 (18 April), 85.

1850

66. "'Col. Pete Whetstone' Again 'About,'" 19 (19 January), 570.
Reprinted:
79 Masterson, pp. 51-52 [excerpt].
82 Worley and Nolte, pp. 115-117.

1853

67. "Col. Pete Whetstone Turned Up Again," 22 (12 February), 615.
Reprinted:
79 Masterson, p. 38 [excerpt].
82 Worley and Nolte, pp. 117-120.

68. "Pete Whetstone and the Mail Boy," 23 (26 February), 17.
Reprinted:
75 Pope, pp. 119-120.
81 Fletcher, p. 96.
85 Anderson, pp. 60-61 [under title: "One Man and Two Beds"].

69. "Col. Pete Whetstone 'About,'" 23 (4 June), 182.
Reprinted:
82 Worley and Nolte, pp. 120-121.

70. "Still Later," 23 (4 June), 182.
Reprinted:
82 Worley and Nolte, pp. 122-123.

1855

71. [Untitled], *Arkansas State Gazette and Democrat,* January 12, [p. 3].

1856

72. "Peter Whetstone's Reception of the Spirit," *Porter's Spirit of the Times,* 1 (1 November), 140.
    Reprinted:
    79 Masterson, p. 39 [excerpt].
    82 Worley and Nolte, pp. 123-126.

73. "Dan Looney's Big Fight in Illinois," *Porter's Spirit of the Times,* 1 (8 November), 159.
    Reprinted:
    82 Worley and Nolte, pp. 126-131.
    84 Cohen and Dillingham, pp. 116-120.

1858

74. Porter, William T., ed. *Big Bear's Adventures and Travels.* Philadelphia: T. B. Peterson, 1858, pp. 143-146.
    Reprints of 60 [excerpt] and 61 [excerpt].

1895

75. Pope, William F. *Early Days in Arkansas : Being for the Most Part the Personal Recollections of an Old Settler.* Little Rock: Frederick W. Allsopp, 1895, pp. 119-120.
    Reprint of 60 [slightly modified].

1930

76. Meine, Franklin J., ed. *Tall Tales of the Southwest: An Anthology of Southern and Southwestern Humor, 1830-1860.* New York: Alfred A. Knopf, 1930.
    Reprints of 60 [excerpt] and 61 [excerpt].

1931

77. Allsopp, Frederick W. *Folklore of Romantic Arkansas.* [New York]: The Grolier Club, 1931, II, 198-199.
    Reprint of 60 [excerpt].

1936

78. Hudson, Arthur Palmer, ed. *Humor of the Old Deep South.* New York: Macmillan, 1936, p. 542.
    Reprint of 01.

1942

79. Masterson, James R. *Tall Tales of Arkansaw.* Boston: Chapman and Grimes, 1942.
    Reprints of 01 and excerpts of 04, 05, 06, 09, 14, 19, 20, 23, 28, 30, 31, 32, 36, 45, 52, 55, 56, 60, 66, 68, and 73.

1944

80. Botkin, Benjamin A., ed. *Treasury of American Folklore.* New York: Crown, 1944, pp. 435-436.
    Reprint of 60 [excerpt].

1947

81. Fletcher, John Gould. *Arkansas.* Chapel Hill: Univ. of North Carolina Press, 1947, p. 96.
    Reprint of 68 [slightly modified].

1957

82. Worley, Ted R., and Eugene A. Nolte, eds. *Pete Whetstone of Devil's Fork: Letters to the Editor of the Spirit of the Times by Charles F. M. Noland.* Van Buren, Arkansas: The Press-Argus, 1957.
    Reprints of 01, 02, 05, 06, 08, 09, 12, 14, 15, 16, 17, 18, 19, 20, 21, 22, 23, 24, 25, 27, 30, 31, 32, 33, 35, 36, 37, 40, 41, 42, 43, 45, 46, 48, 49, 51, 52, 54, 55, 56, 57, 58, 59, 61, 62, 66, 67, 69, 70, 72, and 73.

1961

83. "Bear Hunting in 1837," *The* [Independence County, Arkansas, Historical Society] *Chronicle,* 2 (January), 2-3.
    Reprint of 02.

1964

84. Cohen, Hennig, and William B. Dillingham, eds. *Humor of the Old Southwest.* Boston: Houghton Mifflin, 1964.
    Reprints of 02, 24, 31, and 73.

1967

85. Anderson, John Q., ed. *With the Bark on: Popular Humor of the Old South.* Nashville: Vanderbilt Univ. Press, p. 60-61.
    Reprint of 68 [under title: "One Man and Two Beds"].

1969

86. Williams, Leonard. "Charles F.M. Noland: One Aspect of His
Career," *The* [Independence County, Arkansas, Historical
Society] *Chronicle,* 10 (April), 52-58.
Reprint of 26.

1974

87. Williams, Leonard. "An Early Arkansas 'Frolic': A Contemporary
Account," *Mid-South Folklore,* 2 (Summer), 39-42.
Reprint of 14 [excerpt].

88. Masterson, James R. *Arkansas Folklore: The Arkansas Traveler, Davey
Crockett, and Other Legends.* Little Rock: Rose.
Facsimile reprint of 79.

A NOTE ON SOURCES

The sources which treat such hitherto unknown subjects as C.F.M. Noland or, even more obscure, sixty-three fictional letters he composed under the pseudonym of Pete Whetstone should be few and highly specialized. Such, however, is anything but the case, for almost any study dealing with early Arkansas history, nineteenth-century American humor, politics of the Jackson–Van Buren era, or the American frontier has some bearing upon Noland's career, if only indirectly. Any discussion of sources, then, must be highly selective in order to avoid undue length; thus, only the most important works are mentioned here. For a complete list of works consulted in writing annotations and developing glossaries as well as in preparing the introduction, the reader is directed to my dissertation, "Cavorting on the Devil's Fork: The Pete Whetstone Letters of C.F.M. Noland," University of Louisville, 1976.

Manuscript material offering usable information on Noland's career is almost nonexistent; virtually every available shred has been employed here and is cited in the notes. No manuscript copies of any Whetstone letters or of any of Noland's other published writing are known to exist. Twenty-six of Noland's personal letters are contained in the Berkeley Papers, Alderman Library, the University of Virginia (files 38-113-32 through 38-113-34). One of these is Noland's letter to his father, dated 4 March 1841, in which he briefly mentions his published writing. Also included in the Berkeley Papers are a letter from Sam Houston to Noland and the report of the inquiry into circumstances leading up to Noland's resignation from the Army. Numerous other papers offering valuable background information are also contained in this enormous quantity of materials. The Noland Papers, also housed in Alderman Library at the University of Virginia, contain only one letter by Fenton; however a letter from Noland's father to a brother, dated 30 July 1839, speaks of Fenton's publishing career. Twelve letters from Noland to

Jesse Turner are included with the Turner Manuscripts in Perkins Library at Duke University. The Noland family Bible, owned by Mrs. William C. Noland of Richmond, Virginia, affords important material concerning Fenton's ancestry and establishes the date of his birth. Noland's deposition to Jesse Searcy, which confirms the year of his migration to Arkansas, is housed with the Independence County Clerk Records in the County Court House at Batesville, Arkansas. Photocopies of most of this material as well as a few scattered and uninformative manuscripts (mostly legislative and legal papers) are housed in the Arkansas State Archives in Little Rock.

The main source for texts and for much of the information concerning Noland's life and the Whetstone letters is, of course, the *Spirit of the Times: A Chronicle of the Turf, Agriculture, Field Sports, Literature and the Stage,* volumes 1-31, 1 December 1831–2 November 1861. Other extremely useful printed materials include the Little Rock *Arkansas Gazette,* 20 November 1819 to date [title varies], for the years Noland resided in Arkansas; the Little Rock *Arkansas Advocate,* 31 March 1830–20 April 1837; *Porter's Spirit of the Times: A Chronicle of the Turf, Field Sports, Literature and the Stage,* volumes 1-11, 6 September 1856–2 November 1861, for 1856–1858, the final two years of Noland's life; and the London *New Sporting Magazine,* volumes 1-19, May 1831–December 1840 and NS 1, 1841–1870, for the years 1838–1841.

Treatments of Noland's life, other than Alfred Arrington's amazing account in *The Lives and Adventures of the Desperadoes of the South-West: Containing an Account of the Duelists and Dueling; Together with the Lives of Several of the Most Notorious Regulators and Moderators* (New York: William H. Graham, 1849), include James R. Masterson, *Tall Tales of Arkansaw* (Boston: Chapman and Grimes, 1942), which has been reprinted in facsimile as *Arkansas Folklore: The Arkansas Traveler, Davey Crockett, and Other Legends* (Little Rock: Rose, 1974); Ted R. Worley and Eugene A. Nolte, eds. *Pete Whetstone of Devil's Fork: Letters to the Editor of the Spirit of the Times by C.F.M. Noland* (Van Buren, Arkansas: Press-Argus, 1957); Josiah H. Shinn, "The Life and Public Services of Charles Fenton Mercer Noland," *Publications of the Arkansas Historical Association,* 1 (1906), 330-343; Lonnie J. White, "The Pope-Noland Duel of 1831; An Original Letter of C.F.M. Noland to His Father," *Arkansas Historical Quarterly,* 22 (1963), 117-123; Ted R. Worley, "An Early Arkansas Sportsman: C.F.M. Noland," *Arkansas Historical Quarterly,* 11 (1952), 25-39. My own contributions include "Charles F.M. Noland: One Aspect of His Career," *The* [Independence County Historical Society]

Chronicle, 10 (1969), 52-58; "An Early Arkansas 'Frolic': A Contemporary Account," *Mid-South Folklore,* 2 (Summer, 1974), 39-42; and "Lingering in Louisville: Impressions of an Early Visitor," *The Filson Club History Quarterly,* 52 (1978), 191-205.

Of the numerous treatments of Southwestern humor, almost none examines Noland's career. Richard Boyd Hauck, "The Literary Content of the New York *Spirit of the Times,* 1831-1856," unpublished dissertation, University of Illinois, 1965, writes knowingly of Noland's contributions to the *Spirit.* Norris W. Yates, *William T. Porter and the Spirit of the Times: A Study of the Big Bear School of Humor* (Baton Rouge: Louisiana State University Press, 1957), affords a good, though incomplete, analysis of Noland's association with the *Spirit* and influence on contemporary writers. Yates's volume, the first full-length treatment of the *Spirit* and the only study of Southwestern humor to make more than brief mention of Noland, provides insight into the development of Southwestern humor from mere awkward episodes into carefully written short stories. The result is that Yates offers a fresh, original, and extremely valuable approach from which all later studies have substantially benefitted.

The pioneer treatment in Southwestern humor scholarship, however, was Franklin J. Meine's *Tall Tales of the Southwest: An Anthology of Southern and Southwestern Humor, 1830-1860* (New York: Alfred A. Knopf, 1930). In the opening sentence of his introduction, Meine accurately summarizes contemporary prejudices: "Before Mark Twain and Artemus Ward it is popularly supposed that there was little or no American humor" (p. xv). He proceeds to refute such attitudes by printing forty-nine tales, forty-eight of which were published before Twain began his career with "The Dandy Frightening the Squatter." This exhumation of forgotten but skillful tales is an achievement in itself. But the real value of *Tall Tales* is that Meine's introduction is the first study given exclusively to Southwestern humor, and it has served as a springboard for subsequent examinations.

The next important study was Constance Rourke's *American Humor: A Study of the National Character* (New York: Harcourt, Brace, 1931; rpt. Garden City, New York: Doubleday, 1953). Although this book, like Meine's study, has served as a point of departure for latter-day students, it suffers from Rourke's efforts to treat the whole of American humor. Consequently, it is quite superficial in spots and often fails to follow conclusions to their logical ends. Furthermore, Rourke seeks to prove the thesis that all of American humor is interrelated; such a thesis occasionally necessitates forcing features of regional humor (Southwestern humor was, after all, regional) into molds which do not conveniently fit them. Rourke wants very badly to see a close parallel between the backwoodsman of frontier humor and the Yankee of Down East humor. Unfortunately, they are not simply different comic portraits of the same classic type. *American Humor* is not without value, however. Quite the contrary. Its appearance aided in attracting serious attention to the backwoods. Rourke also succeeded in raising questions concerning popular regional literature; in searching for the answers, numerous students have shed light upon the role of the frontier in American literary tradition.

Another important treatment of Southwestern humor was Bernard DeVoto's *Mark Twain's America* (New York: Little, Brown, 1932; rpt. Boston: Houghton Mifflin, 1967). In defining the context in which Twain wrote and his relationship to that context, DeVoto focused attention upon the importance of the Southwestern humorists as forerunners of Twain, a subject Meine had not fully explored. In many ways DeVoto took up where Meine left off. DeVoto's treatment of Southwestern humor, climaxing in his brilliant analysis of Twain as the culmination of a tradition rather than the origin of another, later impulse, prompted the application of several fresh approaches and has helped to bring about a reexamination of Twain and his relationship to Southwestern humor.

Only a few years elapsed before the appearance of Walter Blair's *Native American Humor* (New York: American Book Company, 1937; rpt., *Native American Humor, (1800-1900)*, [San Francisco: Chandler, 1960]), probably the most influential of all studies of the subject. Like Meine's *Tall Tales*, Blair's book is largely an anthology; like Rourke's *American Humor*, it treats the whole of American humorous writing. Its splendid introduction, at once brief and thorough, and its valuable bibliography constitute an impressive volume.

Quite unlike these earlier examinations, but owing much to them, is Hennig Cohen and William B. Dillingham's *Humor of the Old Southwest* (Boston: Houghton Mifflin, 1964). Essentially an anthology, it presents a number of selections by lesser-known humorists, including four Pete Whetstone letters, anthologized for the first time. Perhaps the book's chief contribution, however, is its introduction which, possibly excepting Meine's essay, remains the most thorough and valuable examination of Southwestern humor.

Other important studies include John Q. Anderson, *With the Bark On:*

Popular Humor of the Old South (Nashville: Vanderbilt University Press, 1967); James M. Cox, "Humor of the Old Southwest" in *The Comic Imagination in American Literature,* ed. Louis D. Rubin, Jr. (New Brunswick, New Jersey: Rutgers University Press, 1973), pp. 101-112; Walter Blair, "Traditions in Southern Humor," *American Quarterly,* 5 (Summer 1953), 132-142; M. Thomas Inge, "Literary Humor of the Old Southwest: A Brief Overview," *Louisiana Studies,* 7 (1968), 132-143; and Inge, ed., *High Times and Hard Times: Sketches and Tales by George Washington Harris* (Nashville: Vanderbilt University Press, 1967), a truly fine edition. One other study must be mentioned: J.A. Leo Lemay, "The Text, Tradition, and Themes of 'The Big Bear of Arkansas,' " *American Literature,* 47 (1975), 321-342, is a splendid example of the new trends in the scholarly study of Southwestern humor and should point the way for future work.

INDEX

This index is highly selective; it includes only the most significant of the hundreds of fictional characters found in the Pete Whetstone letters. To identify entries as fictional, their names are enclosed in brackets.

The inclusion of historical figures and events is also selective. Literally hundreds of race horses are mentioned in the letters; they are indexed only if significant information is given. Otherwise, any item which might be of interest to a researcher is indexed, however slight the mention.

273